QE2 Deck Plan

Deck Signal

Signal Deck, Sports Deck, Boat Deck
Upper Deck and Quarter Deck are not in scale.

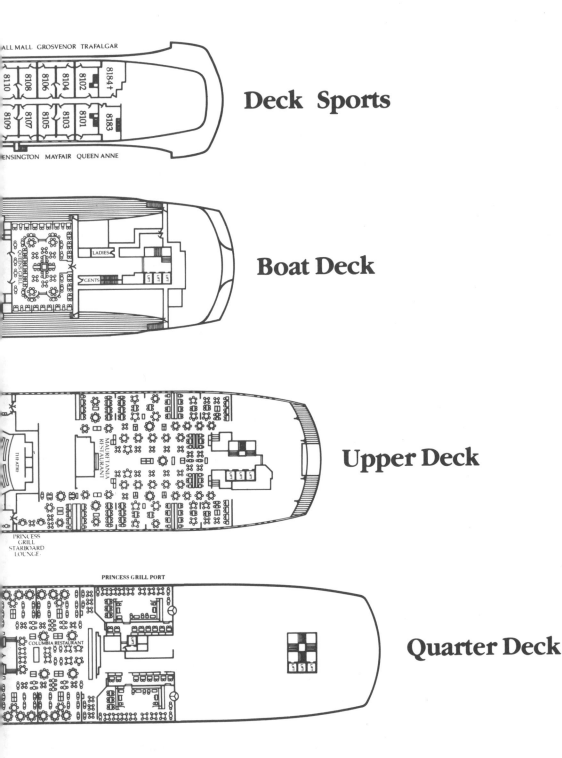

ALL MALL GROSVENOR TRAFALGAR

8110 8108 8106 8104 8102 8184†

8109 8107 8105 8103 8101 8183

KENSINGTON MAYFAIR QUEEN ANNE

Deck Sports

Boat Deck

QUEEN'S GRILL   LADIES   GENTS   LIFT LIFT

Upper Deck

THEATRE   MAURITANIA RESTAURANT

PRINCESS GRILL STARBOARD LOUNGE

Quarter Deck

PRINCESS GRILL PORT

COLUMBIA RESTAURANT

(Continued on back)

To Barbara
with best wishes

Roddarweek

W·W· Norton & Company   New York • London

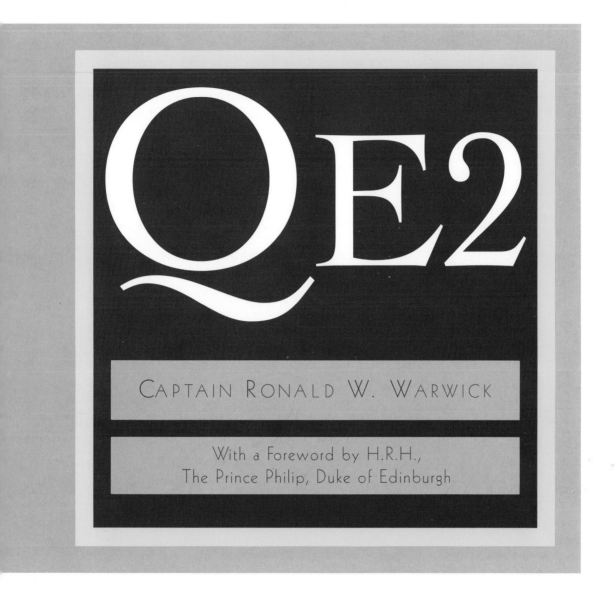

QE2

CAPTAIN RONALD W. WARWICK

With a Foreword by H.R.H.,
The Prince Philip, Duke of Edinburgh

Copyright © 1993 by Ronald W. Warwick
Copyright © 1985 by W.W. Norton & Company
Second Edition

The text of this book is composed in Cochin
with the display set in Kabel
Composition by Trufont
Book design by Guenet Abraham

Library of Congress Cataloging-in-Publication Data
Warwick, Ronald W. QE2
The Cunard Line flagship, Queen Elizabeth 2 / Ronald W. Warwick.
p.   cm.
Includes bibliographical references.
1. Queen Elizabeth 2 (Ship)   I. Title.
VM383.Q32W38   1993
387.2'432—dc20   93-20186

ISBN 0-393-03547-6
Printed in Hong Kong by South China Printing Co. (1988) Ltd.
W.W. Norton & Company, Inc., 500 Fifth Avenue,
New York, N.Y. 10110

W. W. Norton & Company, Ltd., 10 Coptic Street,
London WC1A 1PU

1 2 3 4 5 6 7 8 9 0

The Cunard liner *Queen Elizabeth 2* was laid down just as the world entered a period of rapid technological development, and suffered some of the penalties of innovation. She was completed just as the era of the great North Atlantic passenger liners was coming to an end, beaten by the faster and cheaper liners of the air. Fortunately for her, she found a new career in cruising, although, at least in one respect, she followed the tradition of her predecessors by acting as a troopship. Among much other detailed information, this book describes her crucial part in the successful Falkland Islands campaign, which is likely to remain the most dramatic episode in an already very full career.

H.R.H., the Prince Philip
Duke of Edinburgh

Acknowledgments

In preparing this new edition, I received a great deal of help; and I would particularly like to extend my gratitude to the late Susan Alpert, Ian Denton, Robin Ebers, Eric Flounders, Glyn Genin, Simon Gillan, Janice Hall, Steve Hare, Martin Harrison, Pricilla Hoye, Judge Paul Huot, Cecil Lyon, Elaine Mackay, James Mairs, Leslie McNair, and Captain Robin Woodall.

Dr. William H. Flayhart, III, and I received a considerable amount of assistance from a broad selection of friends, colleagues, and associates for the first edition of this book for which I extend my thanks once again.

I am also grateful to the many officers and crew members of the *Queen Elizabeth 2* who made small but very important contributions.

A very special thanks is due to my wife, Kim, for her never-ending support, encouragement, and editorial assistance throughout the preparation of this book.

Ronald W. Warwick
Somerset, 1993

This book is dedicated to my father,
Captain W. E. Warwick, C.B.E., R.D., R.N.R.,
Commodore of the Cunard Line and
First Master of the *Queen Elizabeth 2*

CONTENTS

A note on the Second Edition

Queen Elizabeth 2 epitomizes the ultimate in world class travel. Uniquely she has continued to offer the very best in service while providing tha most up-to-date facilities available at sea.

It is with great pride that we at Cunard share in the editorial triumph that Captain Warwick has achieved in the publication of the Second Edition of his book *QE2*.

All of us at Cunard congratulate Captain Warwick for his fine rendering of what life is like aboard the *Queen Elizabeth 2*.

With best wishes,
John Olsen
Chief Executive

CHAPTER ONE

THE BRITISH AND NORTH AMERICAN ROYAL MAIL STEAM PACKET COMPANY (1840)

The maritime heritage that gave birth to the *Queen Elizabeth 2* stretches back over a period of nearly a century and a half and involves a transatlantic experience from its inception. The men who conceived the spanning of the western ocean with a line of steamships came together from North America and Great Britain and began 150 years of international cooperation and strong commercial ties sustained by the Cunard Line and the other great North Atlantic lines.

The Industrial Revolution had progressed far enough by the 1830s to make the idea of transatlantic communication by means of a fleet of steamships plausible. The desire for dependable delivery of the mails on which imperial communication and commerce depended prompted the government of Her Majesty Queen Victoria to invite interested parties to bid for a contract. Samuel Cunard of Halifax, Nova Scotia, was the successful contender. His contract to deliver the mails across the Atlantic from Great Britain to North America was signed on May 4, 1839.

Samuel Cunard was a highly successful and enterprising Canadian businessman of German ancestry and one of a group of twelve individuals who substantially directed the affairs of Nova Scotia. Cunard was largely unknown in Britain, although he was the agent of the East India Company in Halifax and was instrumental in establishing a thriving mail service between Halifax, Boston, and Bermuda. He also was one of the founders of the Quebec and Halifax Steam Navigation Company. Their steamer *Royal William* had enjoyed one of the earliest successful crossings of the Atlantic in 1833. Cunard had the reputation for being not only a very astute businessman but also an individual endowed with exceptional diplomatic ability. He would need all the ability and charm he possessed to succeed!

In Halifax Cunard's breadth of vision in wanting to bid for the Admiralty con-

Samuel Cunard (1787–1865), of Halifax, Nova Scotia, was the guiding force in 1840 behind the creation of the British and North American Royal Mail Steam Packet Company, which from the very beginning was known as the Cunard Line.

tract went unappreciated. The reputation of the North Atlantic was too awesome and the steamship too novel for enough of his worthy associates to back him. Accordingly, in January 1839, Cunard sailed for Britain to pursue matters on his own. His willingness to cross the North Atlantic in a sailing ship in midwinter demonstrated the intensity of his ambitions. He carried with him a letter of introduction from the governor general of Nova Scotia, which may have helped him gain an interview with Charles Wood, the secretary to the Admiralty. Wood encouraged the Canadian entrepreneur to submit a formal bid.

The Cunard bid for the privilege of carrying the mails was handed to the Admiralty on February 11, 1839, and involved a commitment to provide three steamships of 800 tons and 300 horsepower each. A feeder service from Halifax to Quebec using a smaller vessel was envisaged, as well as one from Halifax to Boston, with the Canadian port being the western terminus of the North Atlantic service. Cunard felt that the contract should run for ten years at a compensation of £55,000 per year. The commitment on the part of Cunard was daring, because at the time of submitting the bid he had neither financial backers for the line nor a builder for the ships.

James C. Melvill, the secretary of the East India Company in London, advised Cunard about who would be the best builder of the new ships. He recommended Robert Napier of the Scottish firm of Wood & Napier, who had built a number of steamships, including the very successful *Berenice* for the East India Company. John Wood built the hulls, while Robert Napier was the engineering genius responsible for creating the engines. Napier and Cunard became business associates and close friends; their relationship lasted for the rest of their lives. After Cunard's death in 1865, Napier commissioned a portrait of his friend to be given to Cunard's daughter Elizabeth. In acknowledging receipt of the painting, Elizabeth Cunard thanked

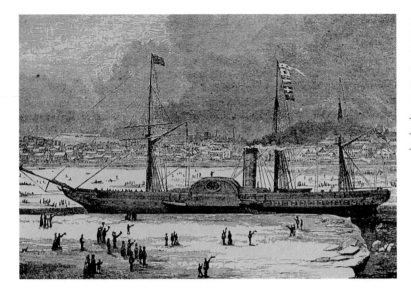

The first Cunarder built for the North Atlantic was the wooden paddle steamer Britannia, *which took the first regular sailing of the line from Liverpool to Boston via Halifax on July 4, 1840. Later, during the severe winter of 1840–1841, Boston Harbor froze over, and the local merchants raised a fund to cut a path through the ice to the sea for the* Britannia.

Napier "for a gift that must be valuable to me for its own sake, as well as for the sake of the donor, whose name has been familiar to me from early childhood in connection with much I have heard of science and natural energy and talent."[*]

Cunard wrote to Napier for prices on the ships, and Napier quoted a price of £40 a ton. When Cunard met Napier in Glasgow, he admitted that the quotation was fair but, because he was ordering three identical vessels, he was willing to pay £30,000 per ship for the multiple contract. Napier agreed and Cunard got his ships for £37 a ton—a good Scottish bargain. What Samuel Cunard may not have known was that Napier had also contemplated transatlantic service as early as 1833 and had drawn plans for vessels of approximately the same size and power as the future Cunarders, but he had not been able to interest anyone in his proposals. At that time the idea of establishing a transatlantic steamship line had seemed as unreasonable as a flight to the moon. Less than a decade later the ships were being ordered.

Robert Napier fully realized that the success of the Cunard ships would be vested in their dependability. If they could depart and arrive on schedule time after time, then the public would patronize the vessels and they would earn their keep. Nothing else really mattered. Napier believed that the finest area of the world in which to observe steamship traffic was the Clyde and the highly competitive short sea route from Glasgow to Belfast. Accordingly, Napier became a familiar figure crossing back and forth on existing steamships, recording their characteristics and evaluating their performances. Out of these observations Napier concluded that

[*]Cunard Line, *The Cunarders 1840–1969, A Transatlantic Story Spanning 129 Years* (London: Cunard Line, 1969), 31.

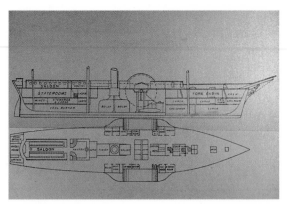

The deck plans of the Britannia *show the basic arrangement of a paddle steamer, with the machinery and paddle boxes occupying the center of the ship and the passenger areas fore and aft. The 1,135-ton ship, with a length of 207 feet and a breadth of 34 feet, could steam at 9 knots and transport 115 passengers and 225 tons of cargo.*

the ships Samuel Cunard had ordered were too small and underpowered for dependable service on the North Atlantic. He took the figures to Cunard, and the decision was reached to increase the size of the first ships from 800 to 960 tons, and their engines from 300 to 375 horsepower. Unfortunately the increase in size and horsepower added £2,000 per ship to the cost. In addition, Napier convinced Cunard that at least four ships were needed if year-round operations were to be maintained. The new expense was a hard blow to Cunard's plans, but Napier introduced him to three other Scots, James Donaldson, George Burns, and David MacIver, all of whom had important maritime interests on the Clyde and in Liverpool and were willing to follow where Napier led. The result was the creation of the British and North American Royal Mail Steam Packet Company, which was founded with a capital of £270,000 acquired in a matter of days from thirty-two businessmen. George Burns's business acumen and good sense were so well known that he became the critical fund-raiser, but Samuel Cunard put up the largest amount (£55,000), and the new line was familiarly known as the Cunard Line from its inception. The contract for the new ships was signed on March 18, 1839, and the creation of the enterprise was guaranteed.

One of the strengths of the company from its founding was sufficient capital to establish itself and to weather adversity. Its solid foundation permitted Napier to enlarge the size of the ships once again to 1,100 tons and 420 horsepower. At the same time Cunard returned to the Admiralty with the information on the ships and suggested that it would be an excellent postal and economic proposition if the vessels continued on to Boston from Halifax. A new contract was signed on July 4, 1839, with an increased subsidy of £60,000 for the enhanced service. The Admiralty agreed to Cunard's having a biweekly service between March and October and only a monthly service in the winter months of November to February, when the cost in men and ships with little cargo or passengers would be too high. Napier's company was feverishly at work on the engines, but he had elected to subcontract for the hulls, and the first of these was launched by Robert Duncan of Greenock on February 5, 1840, as *Britannia*.

The mail contract was supposed to take effect on June 4, 1840, but the fitting out and trials of the *Britannia* took a little longer than expected and she was not ready to sail until July 4, 1840. A special Admiralty dispensation was allowed, fortunately, because the penalty for missing a sailing was £15,000, one fourth the annual subsidy. Under normal circumstances an unexcused delay of more than twelve hours resulted in a £500 forfeiture, although the Admiralty usually looked with a generous eye upon any mechanical failure or natural catastrophe.

The maiden sailing of the *Britannia* captured the imagination of the Liverpool public, and she was given a rousing send-off, as commemorated by the famous painting of the occasion. At the time of her commissioning the *Britannia* was 1,135 tons, 207 feet in length, and 34 feet in breadth, with a service speed of 9 knots and accommodations for 115 individuals, as well as 225 tons of cargo. The *Britannia* sailed with 63 brave passengers, including Samuel Cunard, and made the 2,534-mile crossing to Halifax in twelve days, ten hours. She remained there a brief eight hours before continuing on to Boston, which she reached in forty-six hours, with a net steaming time of fourteen days, eight hours. Each morning at 0600 while she was at sea, her engineers were instructed to "weigh up" twenty-three baskets of coal, with fifty pounds of the precious fuel per basket, and to watch the consumption carefully during the day in order to ensure that there would be enough left to reach Halifax or Boston. Coal was like gold to the new steamship line, costing 8 shillings ($10.00) a ton in Liverpool and 20 shillings ($25.00)* a ton in Boston. The projections were that the furnaces of the line's ships would consume 9,960 tons of coal a year.

The citizens of Boston gave the ship and her owner a hero's welcome. Contemporary accounts credit Samuel Cunard with receiving 1,873 invitations to dinner from delighted Bostonians. He was also presented with a large ornate silver vase suitably engraved with a commemorative inscription and a picture of the *Britannia* that now graces the main entrance to the Columbia Restaurant on the *Queen Elizabeth 2*.

The *Unicorn*, a 640-ton paddle steamer hitherto of the Burns Line between Glasgow and Liverpool, made her maiden voyage on May 16, 1840—three months before the *Britannia*. The *Unicorn* established the feeder service between Pictou and Quebec, although on this voyage she continued from Halifax to Boston with Cunard Line supplies. The *Britannia*'s own return crossing to Liverpool from Boston took only ten days, with the Gulf Steam and favorable winds to help (and, as a rule, most eastbound crossings were faster than westbound ones). The *Britannia* was followed by the *Acadia* (a poetic name for Nova Scotia), the *Caledonia* (Scotland), and the *Columbia* (the United States), with the last of the four being in operation by January 5, 1841.

*Throughout the text the monetary exchange rate is of that of the year concerned.

Cunard Line sailings were normally on the fourth and nineteenth days of each month (March through October), and on the fourth day during the winter (November through February). If the date fell on a Sunday, a Monday sailing was substituted. One-class fares were quoted at 34 guineas (£35.7, or $882.40) to Halifax and 38 guineas to Boston, initially with all food and wine included. After about nine months it was stated in the company literature that all wines and liquor would be extra. Costs soon outran all estimates, and the situation became quite serious. The partners put together a forthright explanation of their position for the Admiralty and, after due consideration, the subsidy was raised to £81,000 per year, but with the understanding that a fifth steamer would be built to ensure the continuity of service in the case of disaster. The *Hibernia* (named for Ireland) entered service on April 18, 1843, and proved herself a record breaker, crossing from Halifax to Liverpool in nine days, ten hours at 11.21 knots. The wisdom of the Admiralty's insistence on a fifth vessel was soon made dramatically clear when the *Columbia* was wrecked in dense fog on Seal Island near Cape Sable. All passengers and crew miraculously were rescued and were transported to Halifax and Liverpool by the *Margaret*, a paddle steamer that normally alternated with the *Unicorn* in the Canadian feeder service. The company did not even have to charter a replacement vessel and thus lose the fares of those who were saved by virtue of this stroke of luck. The Cunard line began to establish a reputation for safety that eventually gave it the proud record of not having lost, through the fault of the company, a single passenger at sea during peacetime in nearly 150 years. When news of the disaster of the *Columbia* reached Liverpool, a replacement was promptly ordered and named *Cambria* (for Wales).

Without the Admiralty subsidy, all the other British-flag North Atlantic passenger lines ceased to exist by 1846. Cunard was willing to extend operations to New York if an appropriate contract could be negotiated. This was achieved in 1847, when the subsidy for carrying the mails was increased to £156,000 in return for Cunard's commitment to maintain a weekly service during the period March through October and a biweekly sailing during the winter months. The feeder service from Pictou to Quebec never lived up to Cunard's expectations and was withdrawn.

The *Hibernia* sailed from New York on January 1, 1848, thereby beginning Cunard's long association with that American port. Four new paddle steamers were ordered to maintain the new schedule, and they were substantially larger than the original ships of the fleet, with dimensions of 251 by 38 feet and a passenger capacity of 140. Napier again won the contract for the ships and built the engines while subcontracting the hulls. The first of the new steamers was the 1,826-ton *America*. Her sister ships were the *Niagara*, *Europa*, and *Canada*, all completed in 1848. This brought the Cunard Line up to nine ships, six of which were sufficient to maintain the weekly service. Hence the first two ships, the *Britannia* and the *Acadia*, were sold to the German Confederation Navy. The *Britannia* continued in service until she was sunk as a target vessel in 1880. Among the new vessels, the *Canada* distinguished herself by an eastward passage of eight days, twelve hours, forty-four min-

The great American competitor of Samuel Cunard in the 1850s was Edward Knight Collins (1802–1878), who founded the New York and Liverpool United States' Mail Steam-Ship Company in 1850, which was universally known as the Collins Line.

utes from Halifax to Liverpool at an average speed of 12.41 knots.* The evolution of communication on land by virtue of the invention and introduction of telegraph facilities meant that during the late 1840s and 1850s messages landed at Halifax were telegraphed ahead to Boston and reached major American metropolitan areas far ahead of the Cunarders themselves.

The guiding philosophy of the British and North American Royal Mail Steam Packet Company was conservatism. Under no circumstances would the Cunard Line tackle innovations or major advances in marine architecture or propulsion until the results were well established by other steamship lines. Upon occasion this placed the Cunard Line at a disadvantage when superior ships were brought into service by enterprising competitors; but the Cunard fleet also contained very few unsatisfactory ships during the nineteenth century, and their safety record was unsurpassed by any competitor.

In the 1850s the great opponent of the Cunard Line was an American-flag concern, the New York & Liverpool United States' Mail Steam-Ship Company, universally known as the Collins Line after its principal founder, Edward Knight Collins. This American venture was established with the goal of providing direct service from New York to Liverpool with larger, faster, and more luxurious vessels than Cunard. The first Collins steamers were named for the great bodies of water of the world and the 2,845-ton *Atlantic* (284 feet by 50 feet and 12 knots) followed by the *Pacific*, *Arctic*, and *Baltic* (1850) were substantially larger than even the newest Cunarders (*America* class, 1,826 tons), surpassing them by over 1,000 tons!

*N.R.P. Bonsor, *North Atlantic Seaway*, 2d. ed., 5 vols. (Jersey, Channel Islands: Brookside Publications, 1975), 5: 1876.

The Atlantic *was the first Collins steamer. At 2,845 tons, 284 feet by 50 feet, and 12 knots, she was substantially larger and faster than the Cunard competition. The Collins steamers proved to be record breakers, but also prone to accident, since they were driven hard. The disastrous losses of the* Arctic *in 1854 and the* Pacific *in 1856, when combined with a reduction in the American subsidy, brought the end of the line in 1858.*

Collins also was the proud possessor of a U.S. Post Office mail subsidy of $385,000. When the *Atlantic* made her maiden departure from New York, on April 27, 1850, the American newspapers were generous in their praise, but they had good reason to be. The new liner boasted luxurious private cabins with paneling and damask drapes, a generous-sized dining saloon, steam heat throughout—representing a radical improvement in comfort—and a means by which each occupant of a major cabin could communicate with the steward in order to obtain service. The result of such luxury was that the Collins Line soon was garnering for itself the cream of the traffic. Jenny Lind, the Swedish Nightingale, crossed on the *Atlantic* during the summer of 1850, and every cabin was booked for that crossing. In Liverpool one of the local newspapers printed a little ditty to the effect that Cunard should charter the Collins ships to pull the Cunarders over. Unfortunately for E. K. Collins, his ships cost substantially more to build than had been expected and much more to maintain in service that had been projected. Furthermore, a series of incidents occurred involving broken paddle blades and broken main shafts. The United States Congress took notice of these factors when it agreed to increase the Collins Line subsidy from $385,000 to $858,000 in return for a biweekly service all year around. An additional stipulation was that the U.S. government could cancel the subsidy at any time on six months notice. On May 10, 1851, the luxurious *Pacific* sailed from New York and thrashed her way across the North Atlantic in the record-breaking time of nine days, twenty hours, fourteen minutes, with 240 passengers—a record-breaking number. Collins ships were carrying an average of 50 percent more passengers than Cunard. Yet Samuel Cunard was a crafty old fox and had the perspicacity to protect his company's revenues by reaching a working agreement with the Americans. The result was that from May 25, 1850, through March 31, 1855, the vast majority of the income of the two lines was shared on the basis of one third to Collins and two thirds to Cunard, an arrangement that supplied Collins with a guaranteed income and share of the trade. The two great rivals were certainly among the most friendly of competitors for the better part of five years until Collins became overwhelmed by adversity.[*]

It is a fact that the Collins Line ships were driven terribly hard and gangs of workers reportedly swarmed over them whenever they were in New York. Disaster struck on September 27, 1854, when the *Arctic*, nearing Cape Race in dense fog, suddenly collided with the French steamer *Vesta*. Extending superhuman effort to reach land, the *Arctic* went down nearly five hours later, taking with her somewhere between 285 and 351 individuals out of the 383 on board. Included among those who lost their lives were E. K. Collins's wife, son, and daughter, combining a business catastrophe with a shattering personal loss.

Cunard was not in a position to realize the maximum advantage from this situation, because many of their ships had been chartered by the British government as troop transports during the Crimean War (1853–1856)—the first time such assistance was rendered by Cunard. Collins, therefore, was able to continue his business in spite of the disaster. The final blow came when the *Pacific* sailed from Liverpool on January 23, 1856, and was never heard of again. The presumption has always been that the vessel hit an iceberg and went under without a survivor or trace. To his credit E. K. Collins chartered a ship, loaded her with supplies, and sent her out to crisscross the North Atlantic, searching steamer lanes without success. Congress gave notice of reducing the subsidy in August 1857, and the ill-fated Collins Line terminated operations in 1858.

The Cunard Line had elected to meet the threat of the Collins Line ships by building the iron paddle steamer *Persia* (1856). The new liner of 3,300 tons, 376 by 45 feet, and 13½ knots was built from the keel up to be a record breaker. She was three times the size of the *Britannia*, with engines five times as large that burned twice as much coal. She also could carry more than twice as many passengers in luxury equaling that of the Collins Line vessels. The *Persia* soon captured the transatlantic record with a crossing of nine days, ten hours, twenty-two minutes from New York to Liverpool at 13.47 knots, nearly half a knot faster than the best speed of the Collins paddlers, and regularly improved upon her records. She was the first iron-hulled Cunard mail steamer and marks another major advance in marine technology for the line, although other lines, such as Royal Mail, had pioneered the use of iron.[†] Wood had become increasingly unacceptable for oceangoing steam vessels, and for the next forty years British yards were far ahead of all others in iron and steel shipbuilding. In fact, not until the four-funnel *Kaiser*

[*]Francis E. Hyde, *Cunard and the North Atlantic, 1840–1973* (London: Macmillan, 1975), 39–45.

[†]N.R.P. Bonsor, *South Atlantic Seaway* (Jersey, Channel Islands: Brookside Publications, 1935), 5.

The paddle steamer Persia of 1856 was part of the Cunard response to the Collins Line. She was the first iron-hulled mail steamer in the Cunard fleet and marks the critical transition from wood to iron as a building material. This technological advance would make British shipbuilding yards dominant in the world for the next forty years.

The Persia captured the transatlantic record with a crossing of 9 days, 10 hours, 22 minutes from New York to Liverpool at an average speed of 13.47 knots. Last of the Cunard paddle steamers built for the North Atlantic, she was a substantial improvement at 3,300 tons, 376 feet by 45 feet, and 13.5 knots.

Wilhelm Der Grosse (1897) was constructed in a German yard for the North German Lloyd Line was there a non-British-built record breaker.*

The Cunard Line broadened out into other fields of commercial activity besides the North Atlantic. In 1853 ships started to run from Liverpool to the Mediterranean, calling at Gibraltar, Malta, and Istanbul. Initially the arrangement was somewhat informal, but as trade developed the British & Foreign Steam Navigation Company was created, with ownership shared by Samuel Cunard, George Burns, and Charles MacIver, who was rapidly becoming the dominant force on the Liverpool maritime scene. In time the Mediterranean trade represented a substantial percentage of the total income Cunard vessels earned, particularly as the immigrant trade from Southern Europe increased after the American Civil War (1861–1865). Between 1858 and 1861 eight sister ships of around 1,800 tons were constructed for the Mediterranean trade (Palestine, Olympus, Marathon, Atlas, Hecla, Kedar, Sidon, and Morocco), while five more vessels of 2,000 tons followed in their wake between 1861 and 1863 (Tarifa, Tripoli, Aleppo, Malta, and Palmyra). Periodically all these ships, except the Morocco, took North Atlantic sailings when trading conditions or need warranted. They all carried a relatively small number of "cabin class" passengers (40–70) but had generous steerage accommodations for 500 or more. The Sidon carried in excess of 300 steerage class passengers to New York from Liverpool and Queenstown (Cóbh) in May 1863, and subsequently much greater numbers were common.

*John H. Shaum, Jr., and William H. Flayhart III, Majesty at Sea, The Four Stackers (New York: W. W. Norton, 1981) 9.

Cunard commissioned two outstanding ships in 1862. One, the 3,871-ton paddle steamer *Scotia*, represented the end of an era because she was the last major ship in the fleet to employ paddles for propulsion; and the other, the 2,638-ton *China*, was the first Cunard-built mail steamer to be driven by propellers. Cunard had been a little slow in recognizing the superiority of propellers over paddles for first-class tonnage, but by the mid-1860s there remained little doubt about the matter. The huge machinery of the paddlers occupied the prime commercial area of the ship amidships, and they required enormous quantities of coal. A propeller-driven vessel was much more economical to run and permitted the positioning of the very best and most expensive cabins in the center section of the ship, an advantage put to use with the advent of the White Star Line in 1870. Furthermore, there was little room left for steerage in a paddle-driven mail steamer, and the immigrant trade could not be ignored. The *China*, at 326 by 40 feet and 2,638 tons, consumed 80 tons of coal a day at 12 knots; whereas the *Scotia*, at 389 by 48 feet, burned 387 tons to produce 14 knots. As a return on investment the *China* could carry 268 cabin and 771 steerage, as well as an additional 1,400 tons of cargo; while the *Scotia* had accommodations for 573 cabin, no steerage passengers, and only 1,050 tons of cargo. The great thrashing paddles of the *Scotia* may have inspired confidence and been impressive, but the slim, screw-propelled hull of the *China* spelled profits in the Cunard ledgers.

The financial success of the *China* inspired the Cunard Line to order additional vessels, including the *Russia* (1867), which was the first screw Cunarder to equal the size and speed of the first-class paddlers (2,960 tons, 358 feet by 43 feet). The new *Russia* joined the paddlers *Scotia* and the *Persia* in the biweekly service between

George Burns (1795–1890) was a Scotsman with shipping interests on both the Clyde and Mersey. When Samuel Cunard needed additional capital to finance the first ships, Robert Napier introduced him to George Burns, who was able to persuade a substantial number of investors to follow his lead.

Charles MacIver (1811–1885) was a very astute and unrelenting Liverpool shipowner who became a major force in the Cunard Line. In 1878 MacIver was the senior godfather at the birth of the Cunard Steam-Ship Company Limited when the existing partners turned the firm public in order to raise money for new tonnage.

Liverpool and New York. This combination provided travelers with an interesting opportunity to evaluate paddles versus propellers in relatively equal vessels as part of the premier service of a great North Atlantic line.

The official Cunard mail connection with Boston came to an end in 1867, when the new mail contract, now drawn up by the postmaster general instead of the Admiralty, assigned to Cunard the responsibility of a weekly service from Liverpool via Queenstown to New York in return for a subsidy of £80,000. The Inman Line, a Cunard rival, secured the mail contract for the Liverpool–Boston route, but Cunard did not abandon the port that had treated the line so generously. A biweekly service was initiated with secondary steamers in 1867 and was revised upward to a weekly service the following year.

Sir Samuel Cunard had been honored by Queen Victoria with a baronetcy in 1858 for his contributions to trade and commerce and for the service of his line to the military in the Crimean War (1853–1856) and the Sepoy (Indian) Mutiny (1857), when many ships were used as troop transports and supply vessels. The twenty-fifth anniversary year of the Cunard Line in 1865 brought cause for celebration and cause for sadness. In the same newspaper edition carrying the news of the assassination of President Abraham Lincoln was the obituary of Samuel Cunard, who died on April 28, 1865, at the age of seventy-eight. David MacIver, another founder, died in 1845, to be succeeded by his energetic brother Charles. George Burns retired in 1860, although he lived to the advanced age of ninety-five, while Robert Napier reached eighty-six. The two decades between the 1850s and the 1870s saw the creation of a number of formidable rivals to the Cunard Line. In Britain were founded the Inman Line (1850), Anchor Line (1856), Guion Line (1863), and White Star Line (1871). On the continent the Hamburg-American Line started a steamship service in 1856, followed by North German Lloyd (1858),

Compagnie Générale Transatlantique (French Line, 1864), Red Star Line, and Holland-America (1873), in the United States the American Line (1873), and in Italy the Navigazione Generale Italiana (1881). None of these companies affected the future of the Cunard Line as much as the founding of the White Star Line. Cunard had lost the Blue Riband to the Inman Line in 1869 after holding it for thirteen years; however, the White Star Line inaugurated a service between Liverpool and New York in 1871 with a fleet of ships having compound engines and passenger accommodations so far ahead of existing standards that they outdated the entire Cunard fleet overnight. Cunard did all they reasonably could in the way of modernizing their existing ships. The *Hecla*, *Olympus*, *Marathon*, and *Atlas* were lengthened by 60 feet, thereby increasing their tonnage to 2,400, and the other ships were fitted with compound engines. Much more important was the commissioning of the 4,550-ton *Bothnia* in 1874 and *Scythia* in 1875. They were larger but slower than the White Star *Oceanic* (1871).[*]

In due course the Cunard owners met and decided that, in the face of the White Star competition, there was no alternative but to establish a public company. Therefore in 1878 the assets of the founders, or their heirs, in the British and North American Royal Mail Steam Packet Company and in the British & Foreign Steam Navigation Company were transferred to the new Cunard Steam-Ship Company Limited. The partners received stock worth a total of £1,200,000 out of the £2,000,000, and two years later a general offering was made to the British public of the remaining £800,000, which were subscribed immediately. The Cunard prospectus simply stated: "The growing wants of the Company's transatlantic trade demand the acquisition of additional steam ships of great size and power, involving a cost for construction which may best be met by a large public company."[†]

The new influx of capital made it possible in 1881 to order the first steel Cunarder, the 7,392-ton *Servia* (515 feet by 52 feet, 16 knots). The *Servia* attracted considerable attention when she entered service on November 26 and received many favorable comments about the luxury of her first-class accommodations. She could carry 480 in first class and as many as 750 in steerage, which was critical to any steamship line's success. The *Servia* was an outstanding Cunard ship, but she actually only followed existing trends. Other liners before her had been built of steel (*Buenos Ayrean*, and *Parisian* of the Allan Line) or were larger (*City of Rome*, 8,415 tons, of the Inman Line) or were faster (*Arizona*, Guion Line). In the luxury of her accommodations the *Servia* approached some of the ships of the White Star Line, Cunard's closest competitor, and began to lure back some of the customers Cunard had lost in previous years.

[*]Bonsor, *North Atlantic Seaway*, 1:92.
[†]Cunard Line, *The Cunarders 1840–1969*, p. 38.

The completion of the *Aurania* (1883) reinforced the first-class fleet, but this ship certainly experienced some teething troubles. En route to New York on her maiden voyage, the *Aurania's* engines blew up in mid-Atlantic. Once again, with phenomenal good luck, there was no loss of life. She completed her crossing under sail, ultimately making her maiden arrival in New York Harbor eleven days out from Liverpool with the assistance of three tugs. The damage to her engines was so severe that she was dispatched to Glasgow using only a low-pressure cylinder and did not return to service for nearly a year. After repairs were made, however, she proved herself a worthy addition to the fleet and provided dependable sailings for the next fifteen years.

Cunard occasionally acquired a vessel through luck; this was the case in 1884 when the Guion Line was in severe financial difficulties as a result of the trade depression and could not make the payments to the builders for the new *Oregon*. Cunard bought the vessel, and she took her maiden sailing for the line on June 8, 1884. The 7,375-ton *Oregon* was constructed of iron and proved herself a record breaker as she raced outward bound to New York in six days, nine hours, forty-two minutes (18.16 knots) on her third Cunard crossing, and home to Liverpool in six days, eleven hours, nine minutes (18.39 knots). The result for Cunard was a record-breaking passenger liner for the first time in fifteen years.

War scares in the mid-1880s occurred all around the British Empire—from the Balkans, to the Middle East, Africa, Northern India, and the Far East. Although no major conflict occurred until World War I, the fact that war clouds often looked so ominous was reason for the Admiralty to charter Cunard vessels, even if on a temporary basis. The *Oregon* was required for Admiralty service in 1885 as an armed merchant cruiser. When she returned to Cunard, the decision was made that she would open a new express service to Boston once again. The *Oregon* sailed from Liverpool with nearly 900 passengers on her last scheduled voyage to New York. Approaching Long Island on March 14, 1886, she collided with an unknown sailing ship. The two vessels parted in the fog and the *Oregon* rapidly began to sink. Fortunately the North German Lloyd steamer *Fulda* was nearby and she rescued all the

Cunard's safety record over its entire history is little short of phenomenal, because not a single passenger's life has been lost through the company's fault at sea during peacetime. Upon occasions they have been very lucky. The Malta *(1866, 2,152 tons) of the Mediterranean service was lost in a spectacular wreck near Lands End on October 10, 1889, without loss of life.*

The Oregon *(7,374 tons, 501 by 54.2 feet, 18 knots) was acquired in 1884. The* Oregon *obtained the Blue Riband of the Atlantic for Cunard in August 1884. On March 14, 1886, the liner was in a collision with an unknown sailing vessel eighteen miles east of Long Island, N.Y. and sank. All passengers and crew were rescued by the North German Lloyd liner* Fulda.

passengers and crew of the *Oregon*, thus preserving the distinguished reputation of the Cunard Line through phenomenal good fortune.

The loss of the *Oregon* was deeply regretted, but Cunard still had adequate tonnage available. The delivery of the 7,718-ton *Umbria* and *Etruria* in November 1884 and April 1885, respectively, gave them a well-balanced first-class fleet again. Both ships were record breakers, and they were the last large greyhounds to have compound engines and only a single propeller. An interesting feature of both ships was that their performances improved with the passage of time. The premier Cunard service from Liverpool to New York was maintained by the excellent quartet of the *Servia, Aurania, Umbria,* and *Etruria* after 1885. This would have been adequate for the next ten years under normal conditions of ship renewal; however, this was not to be the case. Competition on the North Atlantic went wild with the building of new ocean greyhounds, and patrons of the various steamship lines plying these sea-lanes sometimes referred to it as the "frantic Atlantic."

In the mid-1880s the severe economic depression that drove the Guion Line into bankruptcy also threatened the financial stability of the Inman Line, whose founder, William Inman, had died in 1881. Shortly thereafter the Inman Line had taken delivery of the new *City of Rome*, arguably one of the most beautiful ships ever to cross the Atlantic. Unfortunately the *City of Rome*, which had been contracted for as a steel-hulled vessel, had been built of iron because of a shortage of the other metal. As a result, she was slower and had a reduced carrying capacity compared with the contract specifications. The Inman Line, in the uncertainty following William Inman's death, returned the ship to the builders and refused to accept her. The fortunes of the line deteriorated substantially in the economic depression of the next four years, and their ships fell far behind those of Cunard and White Star, the other Liverpool shipping giants. Some discussion took place between T. H. Ismay of White Star and other Liverpool shipowners about saving the Inman Line. Ismay reportedly was ready to loan as much as £1,000,000 to the bankrupt company, but

The publications of steamship lines provide a valuable description of their services. In 1897 Cunard was operating a fleet of twenty-four vessels in addition to other tonnage chartered when needed.

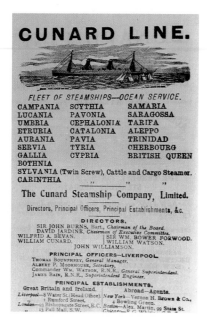

Cunard and others were unwilling.* The idea behind Ismay's charity was "never to let a weak man out of your trade, thus letting a strong one in." This doctrine was verified when Clement Acion Griscom, the Philadelphia shipping magnate, succeeded in gaining control of the Inman Line and the company was reborn as the Inman & International Steamship Company Ltd. (1886). The rejuvenated steamship line went to its builders for two greatly improved vessels, the *City of New York* (1888), and the *City of Paris* (1889), which in turn forced Cunard and White Star to build when neither really wanted to have the expense. In the long run it probably would have been far less of a financial strain to have kept the Inman Line in operation.

Cunard immediately retaliated against the new American owners of the Inman Line by insisting that they would have nothing to do with any postal contract that involved that line. Critical discussions followed during which Cunard was warned it might be sued for failing to carry the mails, but the line held firm and was supported by White Star. The subsequent mail contract called for a reduction of the official sailings from Liverpool from three a week to twice weekly, with the Tuesday Inman sailing eliminated, the White Star Thursday sailing switched to Wednesday, and the Cunard Saturday departure remaining fixed. The refusal to share the postal revenues in some ways backfired on the British Lines, because it led to the creation of the rejuvenated American Line of 1893, and ultimately to J. P. Morgan's huge American shipping trust, the International Mercantile Marine, in 1902.

*Roy Anderson, *White Star* (Prescot, Lancashire: T. Stephenson & Sons, Ltd., 1964), 87.

The new ships ordered by the American Line forced Cunard as well as the other major shipping lines back to their builders for new tonnage. The result for Cunard was the commissioning of the 12,950-ton twin-screw *Campania* and *Lucania* in 1893. These famous ships were propelled by twin sets of five-cylinder, triple-extension engines that were so large that their engine rooms were virtual cathedrals of the Industrial Revolution. They were the first Cunarders to dispense with sails as a safety measure. The *Campania* and *Lucania* were designed to take all the luxury of a wealthy Victorian home to sea: solid paneling, heavy brocade, rich wood carvings, stained-glass windows, and palm trees. These two impressive ships were very popular with the elite traveling public. Cunard Line brochures of the 1890s stressed the fact that the *Campania* and *Lucania* could provide the ultimate luxury of "privacy" for the single person in that they were fitted with a number of single-berth cabins. In earlier ships, even in first class, a single passenger frequently had to share a cabin with another traveler and be faced with the "luck of the draw." Most

The Carmania *(1905, 19,524 tons), a large intermediate liner built for the Cunard Line, was outfitted with the "new" steam turbines as a working experiment. Her sister ship,* Caronia *(1905, 19,687 tons), was given quadruple-expansion engines. The end result was that the* Carmania *was 3/4 knot faster, or slightly cheaper to operate at the same speed. Accordingly, the decision was made to equip the two new giant Cunarders with turbines.*

The Ivernia *and* Saxonia *(1900, 14,058 and 14,281 tons, respectively) were two large intermediate liners created for the Liverpool–Boston service. Liverpool was the Cunard European terminus, but the tide conditions in the Mersey made it difficult for larger ships to come alongside the pier on many occasions.*

travelers still expected to share facilities, but at least the option (at an appropriate surcharge) of complete privacy was available. Another first for Cunard was the provision of suites consisting of a single or double cabin with an adjoining sitting room. The popularity of the "Suites" among the wealthiest clientele made them a planned part of future tonnage.

The *Campania* and *Lucania* proved themselves fast and solid performers. The *Campania* was responsible for the fastest maiden voyage on record in April 1893, and for regaining the eastbound Blue Riband for the Cunard Line by sailing home in five days, seventeen hours, and twenty-seven minutes at an average speed of 21.30 knots, followed by a record 21.12 knots westbound. The two ships were very well balanced and frequently averaged over 21 knots both westbound and eastbound over many successive voyages. Of the two ships, the *Lucania* was slightly

The Carpathia *(1903, 13,555 tons) carried cargo, 204 second-class, and 1,500 third-class passengers. She was employed extensively in the immigrant trade between Trieste on the Adriatic and New York. On the night of April 12, 1912, the* Carpathia *was outward bound from New York to the Mediterranean when she heard the distress signal of the giant White Star liner* Titanic *and went to her aid. All of the 700 survivors were rescued by her.*

faster. Such dependability earned the respect of the public and brought dividends, although the competition between Cunard and White Star in Liverpool and the American Line ships sailing from Southampton frequently was cutthroat. Furthermore, the challenge of the continental lines such as HAPAG, North German Lloyd, and the Compagnie Générale Transatlantique was becoming increasingly acute. Cunard was impressed by the competition, but the firm's first priority was to make a profit, not record breakers. The latter were exceedingly costly to build, maintain, and operate, rarely making money unless they were integrated into a carefully developed fleet program.

The premier new ships of the Cunard fleet at the turn of the century were the 14,000-ton *Ivernia* and *Saxonia* specifically designed for the Liverpool–Boston trade, where they proved themselves to be among the most popular ships of any fleet on the North Atlantic. At 15 knots no speed record was threatened, but the *Ivernia* and *Saxonia*, sporting the tallest single funnels ever given a North Atlantic steamer (106 feet), had accommodations in three classes for 1,964 passengers. On April 23, 1901, when a large number of small children and infants were being carried, the *Saxonia* sailed from Liverpool with the astonishing number of 2,260 souls on the passenger list! She and the *Ivernia* were among the most profitable single ships in the Cunard fleet.

The creation of John Pierpont Morgan's International Mercantile Marine Corporation in the period 1901–1903 placed a premium on the Cunard Line as the White Star Line and numerous other British concerns either were bought by the IMM or signed agreements with the shipping trust. Even Albert Ballin of the gigantic German HAPAG agreed to reduce competition with J. P. Morgan. Cunard felt the pressure acutely and approached the British government with the proposition that the line would build two new contestants for the Atlantic record and remain both a British-flag and British-owned company if the government would extend assistance in financing the needed tonnage. The alternative was the selling out of the last major British steamship line on the North Atlantic, to foreigners. After a considerable period of hard negotiating the British government agreed to assist the Cunard Line with the necessary financing of the proposed superships, provided that they remained British in every way and would be available to the Admiralty whenever needed.

Having arranged financing, Cunard's next major problem was the character of the propulsion system for new ships. Should they involve the traditional reciprocating engines or the still-novel Parsons turbines? The decision was made to experiment in two similar ships with the different propulsion systems. Two large intermediate steamers were ordered for delivery in 1905, the *Carmania* and the *Caronia* (20,000 tons, 650 by 72 feet, 18 knots). The *Carmania* was constructed with the new steam turbines and proved herself to be appreciably faster and somewhat less expensive to run, depending on the demands placed upon her. As a result, Cunard became daring in the conception of its fleet for the first time since Samuel Cunard ordered the initial quartet and decided to build two giant liners powered with the largest turbines then available. Technology was stretched to the limits in the creation of these ships. The contract for one of the liners was won by John Brown on the Clyde, and the other went to Swan, Hunter & Wigham Richardson on the Tyne.

June 7, 1906, marked a milestone not only in the history of the Cunard Line, but also in the entire development of the transatlantic ferry. On that day John Brown launched the *Lusitania*, and instantly all the first-class tonnage on the North Atlantic became obsolete. The *Lusitania* was the largest ship in the world at 31,550 tons with a length of 762 feet and a breadth of 88 feet. She had accommodations for 563 in first, 464 in second, and 1,138 in third class and sailed at capacity on her maiden voyage September 7, 1907. Superlatives greeted her wherever she went, and she fulfilled the expectations of her owners and builders by making the fastest crossing of the Atlantic in both directions during October 1907 at speeds of 23.99 knots westbound and 23.61 knots eastbound. The "*Lucy*" thus became the first ship to make the Atlantic crossing in less than five days, even if only by fractions and from Queenstown. The *Mauretania* followed after some adjustments for vibration and soon proved herself a worthy consort to her sister. The two ships exchanged the Blue Riband back and forth for nearly two years until the installation of new propellers on the *Mauretania* gave her an advantage over the *Lucy*. With a record passage of four days, ten hours, and fifty-one minutes at an average speed of 26.06 knots over a distance of 2,784 miles from Queenstown to New York, the *Mauretania* created a record that would stand for twenty years. If the *Lusitania* was "the" ship as the first of the new class of superliners, the "*Maury*" became one of the most popular and beloved ships ever to grace the North Atlantic and enjoyed a very full career, from 1907 to 1935.

The loss of the aging *Lucania* through a fire while in the Huskisson Dock, Liverpool, in August 1909 underlined the need for a third vessel to partner the big two. Accordingly, Cunard ordered a slightly larger but slower version of their two speed

The Lusitania *(1907, 31,550 tons) remains one of the most famous of all Cunarders. She was the first of the giant trio built by the line between 1907 and 1914 to maintain the first-class service. A highly successful vessel, she captured the Blue Riband in October 1907 with an average speed of 23.99 knots. After eight years of commercial service she was torpedoed on May 7, 1915, off the Irish coast and went down with 1,198 souls in twenty minutes.*

The Mauretania *(1907, 31,938 tons) was the second of the Cunard big three before World War I. Entering service two months after the* Lusitania, *she proved herself slightly faster and held the Blue Riband from 1907 to 1929. A consistent performer between 1909 and 1911, she averaged well over 25 knots for forty-four round-trip voyages.*

queens, thus creating the "Ship Beautiful" *Aquitania.* She was one of the largest ships in the world, at 45,647 tons, when delivered in 1914. Basically, she was a *Lusitania* with an extra deck but had a standard of appointments that made her one of the most distinguished ships of her era. Her speed of 23 knots made it possible to deliver her passengers (597 in first, 614 in second, and 2,052 in third—over 1,000 more than her swifter consorts) to New York in a balanced three-ship schedule with the *Lusitania* and *Mauretania.* The basic idea was to have one ship ready to sail from Liverpool, one ready to sail from New York, and one in mid-Atlantic, thereby maintaining the weekly sailing schedule from both sides of the Atlantic.

The *Aquitania* barely had time to complete three voyages in 1914 before the beginning of World War I plunged Britain into the first general European war in ninety-nine years. She was requisitioned for duty as an armed merchant cruiser,

The Aquitania *(1914, 45,647 tons) was the third of the giant Cunarders before World War I. Basically a* Lusitania *with an additional deck, the* Aquitania *was the epitome of luxury, even if slightly slower, at 23 knots, than her consorts. She fitted into the three-ship service beautifully and survived to serve in both world wars, being scrapped only in 1950.*

but this service was short-lived because her size made her too vulnerable. Furthermore, on August 25, 1914, the *Aquitania* returned to Liverpool with heavy damage to her bow as the result of a collision with the Leyland liner *Canadian* off the Old Head of Kinsale, Ireland. The *Lusitania* had sailed from New York in pitch darkness at 0100 hours on August 5 and made a fast crossing to England. There were thousands of Americans caught in Europe as a result of the declaration of war, and the decision was made to use the *Lusitania* and the *Mauretania* to carry tourists and others back to the United States during the fall of 1914. Then the *Mauretania* joined the *Aquitania* in lay-up until a satisfactory employment for these valuable ships could be found.

The *Lusitania* maintained a reduced Cunard sailing schedule by herself for the first few months of 1915. Her last sailing from New York started on May 1, 1915, with 1,959 passengers and crew on board. Five days later, as the big Cunarder approached the Irish Coast near the Old Head of Kinsale, she was torpedoed by the German submarine U-20 and went down with 1,198 of those who had sailed with her. The subsequent international furor over unrestricted submarine warfare contributed to the American decision to enter World War I on the side of the Allies in April 1917 after Germany resumed such activity.

In May 1915 the *Mauretania* and the *Aquitania* were converted into troopships for use in the Mediterranean in support of the ill-fated Dardanelles campaign. Following their trooping duties both ships also served for a period as hospital ships, painted white with great red crosses emblazoned on their sides and sporting buff funnels. Subsequently both ships served as troopships for the Canadian forces bound to Europe and then, after April 1917, for the American Expeditionary Force as it crossed to France. Immediately following the armistice the steamship lines were desperate for tonnage, and as quickly as possible the *Mauretania* and *Aquitania* were returned to Cunard to handle the flood of travelers trying to cross the Atlantic. It was decided that they would partially replace the prewar German lines in the Southampton–Cherbourg–New York trade, the first such sailing being made by the *Aquitania* on June 14, 1919. Both ships required extensive renovation of all passenger accommodations and a total overhaul of their machinery after the rigors of wartime service. The decision was made to convert both ships from coal to oil, which eliminated the horrendous labor of coaling the giant liners in port and of maintaining the coal-fired boilers at sea. In fact, the crews of the ships were reduced from 350 to 50 in the "stokers" category.

The loss of the *Lusitania* might have made Cunard short of first-class tonnage for the three-ship service if it had not been possible to acquire the ex-HAPAG liner *Imperator* (1913, 52,226 tons, 883 by 98 feet), which was renamed the *Berengaria*. The *Imperator* and her sister ship, *Bismarck*, were both assigned as war reparations to Britain after World War I and were jointly bought by Cunard and White Star in order to avoid outbidding each other. This cooperative effort remained in force for approximately ten years, although each line assumed complete control of its own vessel. White Star renamed their ship the *Majestic*, but she only had one suitable running mate, the *Olympic*. Cunard, therefore, had the best-balanced trio of giant ships on the Atlantic from 1919 to 1935 with the *Mauretania*, *Aquitania*, and *Berengaria*.

The 1920s saw Cunard rebuilding its fleet, but with great caution, because the revision of the American immigration laws all but eliminated the need for steerage. In the place of the immigrant trade, which was drastically reduced, came an ever-increasing group of American tourists. Parts of the third-class quarters were modified and upgraded as tourist third cabin (later called tourist class) in recognition of this increase. The 1920s were not a boom time everywhere, and competition on the North Atlantic for travelers was fierce. As a result, much wider use of vessels for cruising came into vogue, particularly during the winter months. By the late 1920s the introduction of new first-class tonnage by German and Italian lines emphasized the need for Cunard to complete plans for the next generation of superliners. When White Star ordered a 60,000-ton ship and the French Line signed a contract for an 80,000 ton vessel, time became critical. Insofar as Cunard was concerned, the ultimate North Atlantic service appeared obtainable.

In 1840 Samuel Cunard had built a fleet of four ships in order to ensure regular service across the Atlantic. Initially biweekly, the service soon was established on a weekly basis, with ships sailing from either side of the Atlantic on a given day each week. Throughout the intervening ninety years every major advance in marine technology had resulted in larger, faster, and *fewer* ships to maintain the first-class service. By 1893 the *Umbria*, *Etruria*, *Campania*, and *Lucania* were capable of maintaining Cunard's weekly sailings. By 1907 it was possible for Cunard to think in terms of three ships for the first-class service from Britain to the United States, and the *Lusitania*, *Mauretania*, and later the *Aquitania* had been born. Now in the late 1920s the ultimate service appeared to be within the grasp of Cunard. The possibility existed because of advances in marine technology of building two giant super-

The Berengaria *(1920, 52,226 tons, 22 knots) was launched as the* Hapag Imperator *in 1912. After the war she became the Cunard* Beregaria, *named for the wife of Richard I, the "lion hearted." As such she was the largest Cunarder and replaced the lost* Lusitania *in the weekly express service.*

liners that would be both large enough and fast enough to maintain the weekly sailings by themselves: two great liners sailing from Europe and America each week, passing each other in a majestic and thrilling mid-Atlantic meeting (weather and course permitting), and racing on to their destinations at nearly 30 knots. The vision was heroic; the realization in the face of the Great Depression would be extremely difficult.

The keel of an 80,000-ton Cunard liner was laid at John Brown's Shipyard on the Clyde, on December 12, 1930, and given the yard number 534. Work proceeded on the enormous hull until December 10, 1931, when construction was suspended as a direct result of the economic devastation of the depression. Cunard could not build the ship without passenger and freight revenue, and trade on the North Atlantic had virtually dried up. The colossal hull of 534 rusting away on the Scottish slip was a gaunt reminder of how bad economic conditions were. Under the pressure of the depression, steamship lines collapsed in many trades. White Star had become British owned again after World War I, but was undercapitalized and began to go bankrupt as the depression deepened. When Cunard approached the British government for aid in completing No. 534 and an appropriate sister ship, the terms offered involved a merger of the two foremost British-flag North

The Queen Mary *(1936; 80,774 tons, 29 knots) was built at John Brown & Co., Ltd., on the Clyde and launched by Her Majesty Queen Mary on September 26, 1934. The merger of the Cunard and White Star lines as a result of the depression had produced some excitement about the name of the new liner. The name* Queen Mary *was highly appropriate.*

Atlantic lines. In February 1934 the Cunard-White Star Line was created, and work resumed on No. 534 in April, with the proposed launching date scheduled for September 26, 1934. Considerable excitement above and beyond the usual surrounded the launching. The merger of Cunard and White Star created a potential problem in naming the new ship, because all Cunard vessels ended in *ia* and all White Star ships ended in *ic*. Few guessed the solution that had been devised until Her Majesty Queen Mary ascended to the launching platform and at the appointed time in the rain-soaked ceremony christened the giant hull *Queen Mary*. A gracious monarch had consented to give the new superliner her own name in recognition of the fact that the ship had become a symbol of national unity and determination in the face of the dark clouds of the depression.

The merger of Cunard and White Star required drastic rationalization of the combined fleet. In the depths of the depression it was difficult enough to maintain a single first-class fleet, let alone twice the tonnage. The *Mauretania* was withdrawn from service in the fall of 1934, the *Olympic* in the spring of 1935, and the *Majestic* and *Homeric* early in 1936, while the *Berengaria, Aquitania,* and *Queen Mary* maintained the service from 1936 to 1938.

The *Queen Mary*'s maiden voyage from Southampton to New York began on May 27, 1936, with an intermediate stop at Cherbourg. Wherever she went, the new liner was greeted by crowds and unprecedented enthusiasm. Her entry into New York was a publicity triumph, with the superliner accepting the thunderous salutes of all the vessels in the harbor and a flotilla of escorts seeing her to her North River pier. The *Queen Mary* overwhelmingly was the largest British-flag ship at 80,774 tons and with a length of 1,019 feet, 5 inches and a breadth of 118 feet, 6 inches. These statistics also compared very favorably with her greatest competitor, the giant *Normandie* of the French Line, which emerged from the builder's yard at 79,280 tons, 1,029 feet, 4 inches by

The Queen Elizabeth *(1940, 83,673 tons) was the largest passenger liner ever built. She was due to enter service in 1940, when World War II intervened and her first crossing of the Atlantic was a secret dash from Scotland to New York. Subsequently she and the* Queen Mary *carried as many as 16,000 per voyage and were credited by Eisenhower with shortening the war in Europe by a full year.*

117 feet, 9 inches but whose tonnage subsequently was increased by various modifications to 83,423. The *Normandie* had taken her maiden sailing from Le Havre on May 29, 1935, nearly a year ahead of the *Queen Mary*; construction of the liner had not been interrupted thanks to the French government's assistance. The *Normandie* took the Blue Riband of the North Atlantic in 1935 with crossing of four days, three hours, and two minutes westbound (29.98 knots) and four days, three hours, and twenty-five minutes eastbound (30.31 knots). The French liner thus became the first vessel to push the speed over 30 knots for an entire Atlantic crossing, and the *Queen Mary* faced a real challenge.

When pressed about the record, Cunard found it necessary to state that their new liner would not compete for the Blue Riband, but simply would seek to perform up to the highest standards consistent with a regular service. On the crossings of August 20–24, 1936 (westbound), and August 26–30 (eastbound), the *Queen Mary* steamed across from Bishop's Rock to Ambrose in four days and twenty-seven minutes (30.14 knots) and returned in three days, twenty-three hours, and 57 minutes (30.63 knots), becoming the first ship ever to complete back-to-back 30-knot crossings and the first vessel to lower the time below four days for a crossing. Thereafter the *Queen Mary* and the *Normandie* exchanged the Blue Riband between them before the Cunarder proved herself the faster in 1938 by a fraction of a knot. The French line announced the building of a slightly larger and faster consort for the *Normandie*, with construction to begin in 1940, but by then World War II was under way.

Cunard had received sufficient funds to underwrite the building of the sister ship to the *Queen Mary*, and the keel of this vessel was laid on December 4,

1936, at John Brown's. The launching of the new liner occurred after the accession of King George VI and Queen Elizabeth (the queen mother), and the new queen was asked by Cunard to launch the second liner. Accordingly, on September 27, 1938, Queen Elizabeth came to Clydebank and gave her name to the new ship as *Queen Elizabeth*.

In September 1939 a world war interrupted regular Cunard services for the second time in the century. The *Queen Mary* was immediately taken over as a fast troopship and the *Queen Elizabeth* was still being fitted out on the Clyde in Scotland. She was too valuable to remain in that vulnerable position, and at the earliest possible opportunity she sailed for "trials" on March 2, 1940, which resulted in her safe arrival in New York five days later. The *Normandie* of the French Line, the giant rival of the *Queens*, had been requisitioned by the U.S. government and renamed the U.S.S. *Lafayette*. She caught fire at her pier in New York in January 1942 and never returned to service. Between them, the two *Queens* ferried 320,000 of the 865,000 U.S. troops landed in Britain before the invasion of Europe. General Dwight D. Eisenhower credited the two giant Cunarders with shortening the war in Europe by a full year through their unique ability to transport 15,000 troops at a time. The loan of the two largest ships in the world by Britain to the United States constituted a significant reverse "lend-lease" factor during World War II and a major contribution on the part of Britain to the American war effort. Together the two *Queens* carried the astonishing number of 1,622,054 passengers during the war years and steamed 1,150,406 miles.

Although all the Cunard fleet was involved in the war, two ships rendered major service: the new intermediate liner *Mauretania*, 35,738 tons, which had entered service in 1939 and been given the name of her famous predecessor, and the aging *Aquitania*, which would have been retired when the *Queen Elizabeth* entered service had the war not intervened. The old *Aquitania* became the only major ship of the Cunard fleet to serve in both World Wars I and II, continuing her service until 1950.

As soon as possible after the war, Cunard refurbished the *Queens*, and in 1946 the two-ship transatlantic service became a reality with the *Queen Mary* and the *Queen Elizabeth*. Sir Percy Bates, the chairman of Cunard-White Star whose vision had seen the creation of the two *Queens*, collapsed and died at Southampton shortly after the maiden sailing of the *Queen Elizabeth* from her home port on October 16, 1946. When entering the regular North Atlantic service of the Cunard Line in 1946, the *Queen Elizabeth*, at 83,673 tons, 1,031 feet by 118 feet, 6 inches held the distinction of being the largest passenger liner ever built. The *Queen Mary* and the *Queen Elizabeth* maintained Cunard's first-class service for the next twenty-one years and established an enviable record of popularity. The total number of passengers carried by the *Queen Elizabeth* during her first full year in service was 102,292 during the course of twenty-three round trips–an average of 2,224 per trip! The healthy financial

The Caronia *(34,183 tons, 715 by 91 feet, 22 knots) was Cunard's "Green Goddess," built especially as a luxurious long cruise liner and only occasionally serving on the North Atlantic. The* Caronia *took Cunard's World Cruise, or long cruise, every year from her commissioning in 1949 through 1967 and was the largest unit of postwar fleet prior to the* QE2.

picture of the Cunard Line in 1949 permitted them to buy out the remaining White Star interest and change the name back to the Cunard Steam-Ship Company, Limited. The *Britannic* (1930), (26,943 tons, 712 feet overall by 83 feet), last of the White Star ships, retained the buff funnels with the black crown of White Star until she was retired in 1960, but little else remained of what once had been one of the world's foremost steamship lines.

The *Mauretania* was reconditioned and rejoined the fleet in April 1947, while new tonnage included the 13,345-ton *Media*, the first new postwar passenger vessel; a sister ship, the *Parthia*; and the spectacular 34,183-ton *Caronia*, in 1949. Other prewar ships that slowly returned to commercial activity were the *Ascania* (14,013 tons), *Britannic* (revised tonnage 27,650), *Samaria* (19,602 tons), *Scythia* (19,730 tons), and *Franconia* (20,158 tons). The French terminal at Cherbourg was repaired after war damage by May of 1952, and continental passengers could now embark directly onto the biggest Cunarders without the use of tenders to ferry them out to the ships. A new train, the Cunarder, was created to run between Waterloo Station, London, and the Southampton docks in order to expedite the movement of thousands of passengers to the ships. It began service for the July 2, 1952, sailing. The departure of the Cunarder from the cavernous Waterloo Station always was a dramatic moment as the distinguished bass voice of the train announcer indicated that the boat train for R.M.S. *Queen Mary*, sailing from Southampton to New York was about to leave. The excitement was incalculably enhanced if other liners also were sailing and a long series of boat trains for other ships was being called. The train ride through the rolling English countryside to the Southampton docks provided a brief interlude and a means of catching one's breath for the thrill of embarkation on a ship that had come to be so much more than a living bit of history and tradition.

In the early 1950s Cunard also ordered a quartet of 22,000-ton liners, *Saxonia* (1954), *Ivernia* (1955), *Carinthia* (1956), and *Sylvania* (1957), all of which were intended for use in a service between Britain, Quebec, and Montreal, although they took some New York sailings during the winter months. The interior fittings of the quartet were luxurious for the 110 to 154 first-class passengers, but out of step for the times in connection with the 800 tourist-class cabins, most of which lacked private facilities. Cunard realized this, and during 1963 the *Saxonia* and *Ivernia* were refurbished as cruising liners with greatly refined accommodations. They were renamed *Carmania* and *Franconia* and were painted in the light green cruising colors made popular by the *Caronia*. The *Carinthia* and the *Sylvania* were laid up in 1967 and then sold to the Sitmar Line in 1968 to become the *Fairsea* and the *Fairwind*. The *Carmania* and the *Franconia* proved to be popular Bermuda and Caribbean cruise liners, but a combination of labor problems and the rising cost of fuel forced their retirement in 1971. Ultimately they were sold to the Soviet Union in 1973 and renamed the *Leonid Sobinov* and *Fedor Shalyapin*. The earning capacity of the Canadian quartet was severely affected by the advent of jet aircraft after 1958, as were the revenues from the *Queens*.

The year 1958 was the last time that more passengers crossed the North Atlantic by sea than by air. The Industrial Revolution as applied to transportation made another great leap forward as 3½-day Blue Riband passages, even by the superliner *United States*, which in 1952 took the record from the *Queen Mary*, became inconsequential in the face of air flights reckoned in hours. At the same time the policies of the British government toward taxation of business profits and the reserves necessary to finance new construction continuously wore down the resources of an old, established firm like Cunard. The Cunard Steam-Ship Company began to lose money on its passenger operations at an ever-increasing rate. Drastic action had to be taken in many areas, but the most critical problem facing the line in the early 1960s was what action to take with the first-class North Atlantic service. The *Queen Mary* and *Queen Elizabeth* remained remarkable vessels, but they were aging and their fuel consumption at nearly 1,000 tons a day represented an enormous expense.

One set of plans for a new liner had been created in the late 1950s, and

The Queen Mary *inspired many artists, but this painting by John Nicholson of Leeds is one of the best. She is shown on the North Atlantic, steaming along at 29 knots on a normal crossing. She would maintain the weekly service in peacetime from 1936 to 1967, when she was retired and sold to the city of Long Beach, California, for use as a maritime museum and hotel.*

the ship had been dubbed *Q3*. If built, that liner would have been around 75,000 tons and basically a modernized version of the *Queens*. The times had changed radically, however, and the *Q3* design was scrapped in favor of a slightly smaller and more versatile vessel capable of alternating at will between the North Atlantic and cruising—the *Q4*. John Brown and Company won the contract, which was signed on December 30, 1964, and the ship was laid down on July 5, 1965—almost exactly 125 years after the maiden sailing of the *Britannia*. Plans were made to rationalize the fleet to recognize the financial facts of the maritime world. In line with this, the *Mauretania* was scrapped in the fall of 1965. Matters worsened before the new construction could be completed, and Sir Basil Smallpeice, who had strong business experience, was brought in as chairman of Cunard in November 1965. In order to raise additional funds, the Cunard headquarters was transferred from Liverpool to London, and the Cunard buildings in Liverpool, London, and New York were sold, while Cunard ticket offices were replaced by agencies in many cities. The 1965 figures revealed that Cunard had lost £2,700,000 on passenger ship operations and made only £900,000 on freight operations, for a net loss of £1,800,000. No company could stand that strain, finance a new ship, and still survive. Accordingly, the difficult decision was made to withdraw the *Queen Mary* at the end of the 1967 summer season and the *Queen Elizabeth* late in 1968 just prior to delivery of the new ship.

The *Queen Mary* brought the astonishing sum of £1,230,000 when sold to the city of Long Beach, California. She sailed from Southampton for the last time on September 16, 1967, with 1,040 passengers on board for a cruise to California around Cape Horn (she could not transit the Panama Canal). The Cunard "Green Goddess" *Caronia* also was retired in November 1967 and led a checkered life until sold for scrap in 1974, only to be wrecked and sunk at Guam during a storm while under tow to a Chinese yard. The *Queen Elizabeth* maintained the North Atlantic service by herself during 1968, alternating sailings with the *France* of the French Line in a gentlemen's agreement not to have both big ships on the same side of the Atlantic. She was withdrawn from service on November 4, 1968, and sold to a group who intended to use her as a floating attraction in Port Everglades, Florida. This ultimately collapsed, as did a subsequent venture, and finally the ship was offered for auction. It looked as though she would be scrapped when C. Y. Tung, the Hong Kong shipping magnate, bought her. Tung intended to renovate and refurbish her as a floating university and rename her Seawise University. The reconstruction was nearly complete when a mysterious fire broke out on January 9, 1972, and the giant liner turned on her side and burned for days in Hong Kong Harbor, becoming a total loss. She has since been completely scrapped—an unfortunate end for the largest passenger liner ever built.

The drastic fleet rationalization on the part of Cunard was the only option open to the line if it was going to survive. Time, money, and changing tastes were telling arguments against the older units, as well as the enormous rise in fuel costs, which would be even more critical in the decade to come. By late 1968 the fortunes, future, and survival of the Cunard Steam-Ship Company lay with the spectacular new *Queen Elizabeth 2*.

CHAPTER TWO

THE ORDERING AND BUILDING OF THE QE2

The decision to invest $70,000,000 in a project certainly never would be an easy one to make. When an industry is under acute stress as the result of changes beyond its control and a revolutionary new approach to design and technology is required, the strain of such a move would be tremendous. This was the situation when the Cunard management faced the issue of what type of vessel should replace the *Queen Mary* and the *Queen Elizabeth* in the late 1950s and early 1960s.

Official public notice of plans to replace the *Queens* occurred on April 8, 1959, when Harold Watkinson, of the ministry of transport, announced to the House of Commons that negotiations were under way with Cunard to try to maintain the first-class North Atlantic service. The previous month Colonel Denis H. Bates told the annual meeting of Cunard that the entire future of the North Atlantic service had been placed before the government. Particular notice was taken of the fact that the U.S. government built the liner *United States* at a cost in excess of $75,000,000 and then made the vessel available to the U.S. Lines, Cunard's competition, for less than $34,000,000. "Faced with the overwhelming odds of ever-increasing governmental subsidies to our competitors on the score of national prestige," Bates commented, "your board have decided it is impossible to continue under such unequal and unfair competition to free enterprise." The *Queens* were described as "full of life," but they could not be run forever, and the *Queen Mary* probably would be well over thirty before her replacement would take to sea. Competitively that was not advantageous to the Cunard Line.

The official government group given the responsibility for evaluating the situation was the Chandos committee, which began with the assumption that two liners ultimately would be built to replace the *Queens* and maintain the existing service. The recommendation of the Chandos committee on June 1, 1960, was in favor of support for the construction of a 75,000-ton liner with a length of 990 feet and a service speed of 29½ knots capable of carrying 2,270 passengers. The estimated cost in 1959 was £25 million to £30 million, with up to £18 million being provided by a low-interest government loan. On October 10, 1960, some five months later, Ernest Marples, then minister of transport, announced the government's acceptance of the recommendations of the Chandos committee. Vociferous opposition occurred almost immediately from some members of Parliament who regarded the loan as an unprecedented subsidy, and from a vocal group of Cunard stockholders who regarded the building of another giant Atlantic liner in the face of competition from the jet airplane as insane. The critics contended that to build another traditional liner in the face of the changing nature of the transportation and travel industries was to fly in the face of common sense and reality. Certainly the *Q3*, as the new liner was dubbed, would enjoy only limited cruising flexibility during the winter months. The winter payloads on the older *Queens* already were reduced virtually to nothing, and every time such a unit left port, she was destined to cast off into a sea of red ink. On one occasion the giant *Queen Elizabeth* made a winter crossing with only sixty-three passengers.

The whole complexion of the North Atlantic was undergoing radical change. In 1957 the division of passengers between ships and airlines was roughly 50 percent to 50 percent. By 1965 the ratio had changed to an astonishing 14 percent to 86 percent, and the number of individuals crossing by sea had dropped from over 1 million to around 650,000. In the same period the airlines saw their figures soar to over 4 million as the jets reduced the Atlantic crossing to a matter of hours. Even the British government investment concessions after 1957 which allowed a company to take investment tax credits meant little, because the Cunard Line had to earn substantial profits in order to make additional investments and thus take advantage of the new arrangement. Those days of high profits were gone forever with the existing fleet.

Cunard endeavored to place itself in a more favorable position by acquiring British Eagle Airways in 1959, but that concern ran afoul of the government policy to restrict competition with BOAC in 1961. Subsequently Cunard and BOAC reached a trading agreement that created BOAC-CUNARD to operate the principal British-flag air service on the North Atlantic. Cunard owned 30% of the new concern and enjoyed an increasing profit in the period between 1962 and 1965. By 1965 it was clear that a substantial new investment was going to be necessary to maintain a competitive edge in air travel. Cunard could not build a new liner and order new airplanes at the same time. An agreement was reached in 1966 for BOAC to purchase Cunard's share of their joint operations at a price of £11½ million in cash that freed Cunard's assets

The 125th anniversary of the Cunard Line was commemorated with a special menu that surveyed the history and status of the fleet on July 4, 1965. Preparations were simultaneously being made for the laying of the keel plate of a giant new superliner at John Brown's on the Clyde.

and saved the company from an additional cash drain. Unfortunately between 1960 and 1965 the passenger ships of the line had lost £14.1 million, which was only partially offset by tax refunds. A total rethinking of the future of the maritime industry and Cunard's role in it was imperative. The debate over the nature of the new vessel must be considered against this background of financial crisis.

The introduction of the magnificent *France* of the French Line in 1962 and the pairing of that vessel with the *United States* of the U.S. Lines provided additional competition for the *Queens*. Cunard countered by having the *Queens* skip their annual summer refitting, which prior to this had cost them a round trip at the height of the season. This added appreciably to their high-season revenues and helped the line. Cunard also took a hard look at their competition, particularly the highly successful *Rotterdam* (1959) of Holland-America, which had been designed both as a North Atlantic liner when the trade warranted and as a cruise ship in warmer waters when winter made the Atlantic inhospitable.

Sir John Brocklebank, chairman of Cunard, reluctantly announced on October 19, 1961, that the Cunard Line could not see its way clear to ordering the *Q3*. The plans for the 75,000-ton vessel were shelved forever because trading conditions could not justify replacing the *Queens* by similar tonnage, and it was back to the drawing boards. For over a year things looked grim, until it was announced in December 1962 that Cunard was deeply involved in plans for a smaller and more versatile liner. Details of the new design were provided by Sir John Brocklebank early in 1963. It was announced that the new ship would be around 55,000 tons and capable of transiting most of the major waterways of the world, such as the Panama and Suez Canals. It was to have a width of less than 110 feet and a length of less than 990 feet. In April 1963 it was announced that a decision was near on a new liner that would be totally revolutionary in design, rather than evolutionary as the *Queens* had been. By early summer 1963 plans for the ship were submitted to Marples at the ministry of transport once again. This time the government refused Cunard a special loan for the vessel but did not completely close the door to aid. Instead, it was suggested that Cunard reapply for assistance to the new loan fund under the direction of Lord Piercy that had been established to aid shipowners willing to place contracts with British yards. Cunard promptly did so and received assurances of a loan of £17,600,000 toward the cost of the new liner.

Plans were sent to British yards interested in tendering for the ship on September 9, 1964. The earlier contract for the *Q3* almost assuredly would have gone to a consortium led by Vickers-Swan Hunter of Tyneside, but this was not to be the case now. Strict attention to cost and delivery times was imperative for Cunard when the bids were received on November 30, 1964. The winner was announced within one month, and the contract for the new liner was signed on December 30, 1964, with John Brown (Clydebank), Ltd., which had quoted both the lowest price and the earliest delivery date (May 1968). The ship was described in glowing terms as capable of holding her own on the North Atlantic and also as being one of the most fabulous resorts in the world. She could cruise anywhere and provide her passengers with a level of luxury unsurpassed by any competition.

The new ship was to cost £25,427,000, with an escalation clause to cover inflationary factors: £17,600,000 of the price was to be met by a government loan upon delivery of the vessel. However, Cunard had to find the money to pay the builders in order to receive substantial advance payment credits of some £4,000,000. There was no alternative but to mortgage the fleet. Accordingly, five liners and six cargo ships were mortgaged to a consortium of British banks to raise the money for the new ship. It was a difficult and dangerous time for the line, further complicated by the serious illness and subsequent retirement in November 1965 of Sir John Brocklebank as chairman. His successor was Sir Basil Smallpeice, an energetic and respected former general manager of BOAC.

The goal for the new ship was to create a vessel capable of presenting and selling to the public a whole new way of travel. There was no question anymore of her being just a means of getting from point A to point B. Conditions in the travel industry had changed so drastically that to be successful the new liner had to be viewed as a floating luxury resort, a five-star hotel with the ad-

ditional advantage of being able to go anywhere in the world. Happily for Cunard, the tremendous innovations in design, materials, and construction techniques in the 1950s and 1960s made possible the creation of a daring ship that
could capture the attention of the space-age traveling public.

July 2, 1965, was established as the day on which the first section of the
keel would be laid at John Brown's on the Clyde for Yard No. 736. The berth
to be used was the same from which the two earlier *Queen* liners had been
launched. The welded steel section was in one gigantic piece weighing 180
tons, 117 feet long, 23 feet wide, and 6 feet 3 inches high. In actuality, the initial unit involved three pieces welded together. When the first attempt was
made to slide the 180-ton unit onto the greased oak blocks of the slipway, it
had a mind of its own. The keel section refused to budge, but the cement anchor blocks began to lift out of the ground as the cranes took up the strain.
Dry weather in western Scotland had played a trick on the Clydeside builders,
and the keel-laying ceremony went ahead without the formal act itself. Subsequently the lifting and anchor equipment was reinforced and the 180-ton first
section of the keel was moved into position on July 5, 1965, while the 125th
anniversary celebration of the Cunard Line was still under way. Special menus
graced the tables of diners the previous evening on the vessels of the fleet as
the Cunard Line extolled the past and heralded the future with the keel laying
of the new ship, No. 736.

Already publicists were eager for details of the giant new Cunarder. Certainly her machinery was going to be revolutionary, as she was to be the
largest twin-screw ship in the world. Her three boilers were to produce super-
heated steam at 950 degrees Fahrenheit for turbines that would generate
110,000 shaft horsepower. All this was to be done on half of the fuel consumption of the old *Queens*. The electrical generators in the new liner were to create
enough power to serve the needs of a city of over 20,000. The list of superlatives seemed to go on forever.

Extensive design work on the hull was carried out by the Cunard designers and by the National Physical Laboratory. Then the staff at John Brown's also put the hull form of the ship through test after test in the yard's restructured experimental tank and fed the results into a new IBM computer. The computer analyzed the statistics and fed back evaluations within an hour—a process that used to take weeks. Time was of the essence and a tight organization was crucial to the financial success of the project, from the standpoint of the builders and of the steamship line. John Rannie, managing director of John Brown, was a key individual in the process of overseeing the entire shipyard, but George Parker, shipyard director, was the individual who kept a tight watch on the actual building and ensured that materials were in place as required. Organization was greatly assisted by the ability of computers to keep track of the whereabouts and status of such things as the 100,000 different pieces of pipe that the ship would need.

Cunard wanted to have their personal representative on the scene at John Brown's at the earliest possible opportunity. Accordingly, on December 7, 1966, at a management conference held in Winchester, where the head officers of the company and seventeen of the twenty-seven captains were present, it was announced that Captain William Eldon Warwick, relief captain of the

By September 29, 1966, fifteen months after the keel laying, 1,400 men were at work on the ship. The large stern frame weighing 62 tons was ready for positioning, and special sheer legs had to be positioned to lift the large casting that had been brought to the site by barge. The stern frame provides a secure housing for the rudder. (Photo courtesy of the John Maxtone-Graham Collection.)

Queen Mary and *Queen Elizabeth*, was being appointed as master-designate of the new ship, effective immediately. Captain Warwick, a native of Birkenhead, was fifty-four at the time. He was the youngest captain ever to be appointed master of a *Queen* liner. He had been with the line for thirty years, having joined Cunard as third officer of the *Lancastria* in 1937.

Among the revolutionary aspects of the new Cunarder was the use of 1,100 tons of welded aluminum in the superstructure of the ship. So much of the light metal had never been used before in marine construction, but the advantages in stability and weight were enormous. This was also the first time that aluminum was to be an integral part of the stress-bearing hull of a ship. The development of complex and sophisticated alloys had brought the metal "of age," and the invention of the "inert-gas shielded metal arc (MIG) welding process" made possible both semiautomatic assembly and fast construction. The "state of the art" techniques developed and refined for the installation of the aluminum components on the new ship by Alcan Industries, Limited, were so advanced that representatives of the builders, the line, and Lloyds were invited to a series of seminars at Alcan's Banbury facilities in order to learn about the processes. The work target for the superstructure once erection began was 30 to 35 tons a week, and this allowed little room for delay. Because steel and aluminum will interreact if they come into contact with each other, great care had to be taken to maintain the purity of the aluminum operations. To this end the cement floors of the erection sheds were sealed with a special compound to eliminate any steel fragments or dust from previous construction, and heavy-duty industrial vacuum cleaners were constantly in use.

A 12-ton section of the aluminum super-structure of the ship is lifted into place. Approximately 130 sections like this one would make up the superstructure of the liner, and the weight saved would make it possible for her to have a draft 7 feet less than the old Queens.

Looking at the construction of the new ship from a fabricating point of view, one can consider an all-welded superstructure, like an all-welded hull, as a single piece made up of a large number of subpieces. The sections were prewelded in the shipyard's shops and subsequently moved to the building berth for assembly in the ship. The lightness of aluminum allowed great freedom in the size of the prefabrications; the only limitation was due to the size of the doors through which they would have to pass to reach the building berth.

By November 1966, when this picture was taken, 2,500 men were at work on the new Cunarder. The steelwork was up to the prom-enade deck, some 80 feet high. The John Brown Yard and Clydebank, Scotland, spread out in a panorama before the photographer working from one of the giant cranes. (Photo courtesy of the John Maxtone-Graham Collection.)

By April 1967 the huge hull of No. 736 soared 95 feet into the Clyde sky-line. The assembly schedule called for the installation of 30 to 35 tons of steel and aluminum a week into the ship. (Photo courtesy of the John Maxtone-Graham Collection.)

These doors were 36 by 22 feet and could accommodate aluminum assemblies up to 12 tons. The result was that approximately 130 separate multi-ton pieces were welded together to create the superstructure of the new liner. Great care was taken with the attachment of the aluminum superstructure to the steel hull wherever the two metals might come into contact in order to avoid corrosion through electrolytic action. The firm of J ohn S. Craig & Co., Ltd., Glasgow, developed a flexible epoxy liquid that was applied to one of the two surfaces after an elaborate cleaning and curing process. The two metals were riveted together, and in the heating process a tight seal was formed, prohibiting contact between the two metals and the intrusion of water into the joint.

Four of the thirteen decks in the new ship are aluminum: the upper, boat, observation, and sports decks. These decks also include the two outdoor swimming pools toward the stern of the ship. Beneath the superstructure is the steel promenade deck, which was cleared and marked for the aluminum prefabricated units early in January 1967. The first unit of the upper deck was lowered into position on January 21. Within eighteen weeks the upper deck was well advanced, and within six months the superstructure clearly was emerging. When the aluminum superstructure was completed, the savings in weight to the new ship would give her a 7-foot reduction in draft over the older *Queens*, an incalculable asset in view of Cunard's desire to use the vessel extensively for cruising.

The main propulsion machinery was manufactured by John Brown Engineering (Clydebank), Ltd., and consisted of a twin-screw set of Brown-Pametrada turbines. Each unit would consist of a high-pressure and a low-pressure turbine driving a propeller shaft through double-reduction, double-helical, dual tandem gearing. At 174 revolutions per minute, the maximum output of the machinery was rated at 110,000 shaft horsepower, with the expectation that the normal service rating would be around 94,000 shaft horsepower, at which the highest level of efficiency would be achieved. The turbines were designed to receive steam at 800 pounds per square inch pressure and 940 degrees Fahrenheit. Among the cost-cutting economies made in order to bring the overall price of the ship down to what Cunard could afford was the deletion of an additional boiler from the specifications. The final contract called for three Foster-Wheeler E.S.D. II boilers, which also were built under license by John Brown. These were designed to produce 231,000 pounds of steam per hour under normal conditions and as much as 310,000 pounds at 850 pounds per square inch pressure and a working temperature of 950 degrees Fahrenheit.

A unique aspect of the new liner was the installation of a computer with a data-logging system. When the decision was made to see how much of the work of the liner could be handled by a computer system, negotiations were begun with the British Ship Research Association, resulting in equipping the ship with a Ferranti Argus 400 computer. A portion of the additional cost, regarded as experimental in nature, was underwritten by a grant from the National Research Development Corporation (NRDC), with the understanding that if the unit proved commercially advantageous in practice, Cunard could buy it, and if not, the NRDC could remove it. Cunard assumed the obligation of making the knowledge that it gained available to the shipping industry, and

The summer of 1967 sees the construction far advanced on No. 736 as the work force climbs toward 3,500. In this view from the Clyde River the majority of the superstructure has been assembled and the scaffolding has been removed on the port side.

in the long run this would pay major dividends in automation, navigation, and fiscal control.

A major jolt in the proceedings occurred in July 1967 when John Brown informed Sir Basil Smallpeice that the cost of the new ship would probably be in the range of £28½ million, up some £3 million from the original contract price. Simultaneously Philip Bates, Cunard's managing director, came up with the bad news that there would be another £3½ million loss on the passenger ships in 1967. Smallpeice had no choice but to inform the Board of Trade, overseeing the building aid program, that the sum guaranteed to the line by the government was no longer adequate and that construction of the ship would have to cease unless additional resources could be made available. Complicating the issue was the fact that the announced launching day was September 20, 1967, and Her Majesty Queen Elizabeth II graciously had consented to launch the liner in the proud tradition of her grandmother, Queen Mary, and her mother, Queen Elizabeth, the Queen Mother. The Cunard board of directors met under tense conditions on September 14 as they awaited word as to whether or not the government would agree to increasing the loan. The situation was so critical that a negative response might force the board to cease operations and sell off the assets for whatever they might bring rather than lose more money. To the relief of everyone concerned, Harold Lever, financial secretary to the treasury, sent Sir Basil a note while the board was in session indicating that the government would increase the loan to Cunard from £17,600,000 to £24,000,000, permitting the launch to go forward as planned.

The rumors about the name for No. 736 were as numerous as they had been for the launching of the *Queen Mary* thirty years before. The old story was trotted out about Sir Percy Bates, then chairman of Cunard, and King George V discussing the name for the first *Queen* liner. Supposedly Sir Percy was thinking of the name *Queen Victoria* (with an *ia* name ending) when he asked the king for permission to name the Cunarder after "our most illustrious queen." The monarch responded that he would be delighted to ask Queen Mary when they returned to the palace. That story almost assuredly is untrue, and many good authorities have tried to put it to rest. There would not be even the possibility of such a problem this time. There was no question what Sir Basil and

Near to the launching day in September 1967 the two massive six-bladed propellers are installed. The rudder also is in place for the launch. The force of the propellers against the water as she goes down the ways will assist in slowing her momentum as she makes her bow to the world. Note the tiny figure of a workman beneath the 70-ton rudder; others are clustered near the port propeller. (Photo courtesy of the Frank O. Braynard Collection.)

the Cunard board desired, although there was the British tradition that only capital ships in the Royal Navy were named for sovereigns. The name was discussed with Lord Adeane, the queen's private secretary, and it was decided to ask that the new ship be named *Queen Elizabeth*, because by the time of her commissioning both of the earlier *Queens* would be withdrawn from service and she could assume the name vacated by one of her predecessors.

Launching day on the Clyde was pleasant, as the crowds milled around the launching site or lined the river bank opposite to watch the show. Her Majesty Queen Elizabeth II moved to the front of the launching platform and was handed an envelope by John Rannie with the name of the ship inside. This was a traditional practice from many years before when someone had purportedly forgotten the name of the ship about to be launched. The envelope remained unopened as the Queen stepped forward and uttered the words:

> I name this ship *Queen Elizabeth the Second*. May God bless her and all who sail in her.

Her Majesty Queen Elizabeth II has just named No. 736 the Queen Elizabeth 2, *on September 20, 1967, and the giant Cunarder rushes toward her element without a hitch in the proceedings.*

Sir Basil Smallpeice was overjoyed at the sovereign's personal alteration of the name. He could not have been more delighted with having the third of the great royal Cunarders named in this manner. The decision promptly was made to style the giant *Queen Elizabeth 2* along modern lines and differentiate the ship from the sovereign. To maritime historians the name was entirely appropriate because of the fact that the *Queen Elizabeth 2* was the second liner to bear the name *Queen Elizabeth*. However, the name did not set well in all parts of Scotland, because the independent kingdom of Scotland had never been ruled by Queen Elizabeth I of England (1558–1603); thus the present monarch was not Queen Elizabeth II of Scotland.

The goal of Cunard and John Brown had been to get the *Queen Elizabeth 2* in

The tugs rush to secure the liner before anything can go wrong in what has been a picture-perfect launch. (Photo courtesy of the Frank O. Braynard Collection.)

service in time to make the most of the 1968 summer season on the North Atlantic, but that was not to be. By the launching date it was obvious that it would be impossible to complete the complex task of fitting out the huge liner in time for the late spring 1968 sailings. The schedule was pushed back to the fall of 1968, and this provided the opportunity for a major transformation in the ship.

A debate had been raging between those in favor of three classes (notably the New York office) and those who felt that because the future of the ship lay in cruising as well as the North Atlantic, she should be a two-class ship. The principal advantage of two classes over three was that the public rooms of a two-class ship could be so much larger. The feeling in America had been that in a ship carrying first, cabin, and tourist it was still possible to sell the cabin-class accommodations in sufficient numbers to warrant carving up the liner three ways. However, in Britain and among the Cunard staff at sea the two-class vessel seemed most practical and profitable.

Captain William Law of the *Carmania* wrote as early as February 6, 1964:

> Cabin class has no place in the future. The argument is often put forward that the Cabin class in the *Queens* is well booked; this is merely due to the fact that the Tourist class is well below standard and that a number of people who cannot afford the First class fare feel that they desire something better than the present Tourist class. In a new ship with a well designed attrac-

tive Tourist class there will be no need for the "Middle of the Road" passenger to look for anything beyond the Tourist class.

Law went on to discuss the fact that America had changed so much since World War II that the result was virtually a classless society wherein almost anyone in the vast middle segment could afford a substantial level of comfort.

Another telling argument was that as a three-class ship the *Queen Elizabeth 2* could accommodate between 1,860 and 2,000 passengers, depending upon the division of the three classes. As a two-class liner the new ship would be able to carry as many as 2,030 and, in spite of the increased payload, the number of staff needed would be less. Finally, under the direction of Sir Basil Smallpeice the two-class proponents won the debate because of the emphasis placed on cruising. The delay in the delivery schedule permitted this decision to be acted on carefully and thoughtfully.

The design team for the new liner was led by D. N. Wallace, chief naval architect for Cunard, whose life revolved around the new liner for nearly a decade before the launching. It was Dan Wallace who received the orders to change the ship from three to two classes when the hull was nearly completed, and it was Dan Wallace who made the philosophical statement that it was easier to redesign the ship with one fewer class than an additional one! Wallace received a vast amount of information from all over the world as hotels and liners were evaluated everywhere for ideas to make the new ship more efficient and more luxurious. The main requests for the new ship from all sources were the following: more single- and two-bedded rooms linked with adjoining rooms; elimination of upper bunks whenever possible; more outside cabins with natural daylight; private showers, baths, and toilets in every cabin; ample wardrobe and drawer space; good lighting in the cabins; efficient sound insulation and absence of vibration; a wide range of public rooms so that passengers may enjoy communal entertainment in the nightclubs and theaters, or solitude and quietness in the card room, library, or reading room; greatly enlarged exterior deck space and swimming pools for cruising; and carefully planned, colorful, and stimulating facilities for children.

The two design coordinators were James Gardner for the exterior of the ship and Dennis Lennon for the interior layout and appointments. The basic challenge, as Gardner saw it, was how to make a good shape for a ship out of what could end up as a three-block-long set of floating apartment houses—exactly what many modern ships have become! The horizontal lines of the *Queen Elizabeth 2* were kept severely straight because curves cost space and money, yet, by a delicate balance of converging lines fore and aft, the optical illusion of subtle curves and grace was created. In fact, there is not a single curved plate in the sides of the hull. From bow to stern the desire was to keep the blustery North Atlantic winds away from passengers who may not always have rejoiced at the invigorating nature of deck-chair travel. The funnel design of the

An aerial view of the John Brown Shipyard along the Clyde River, Clydebank, Scotland. Yard No. 736 dominates the shipyard and soars far enough into the air that airplanes approaching Prestwich Airport, Glasgow, regard it as a landmark. The hull rests on the same building berth used for the Queen Mary *and the* Queen Elizabeth.

Queen Elizabeth 2 was dictated by the practical desire to ensure that the fumes and soot from the furnaces were carried well clear of the liner. When the model of the liner was fitted with a traditional funnel, the appearance was unsatisfactory and the exhaust gases from the engine room simply rolled down the back of the funnel and smothered the broad open expanses of decks aft—a totally unacceptable result. Tailoring of wind scoops, exhaust pipes, and vents finally resulted in the upswept 67-foot, 3-inch-tall glory, towering a majestic 201¼ feet above the keel, the tallest funnel ever fitted on a *Queen* liner (the *Queen Mary*'s were 59 feet and the *Queen Elizabeth*'s 56 feet). The prominent mast forward did not have to be so massive, although it does serve as a wind scoop to carry kitchen fumes away; but it was created to complement the funnel, and anything smaller could not accomplish that design function. One of the greatest design challenges facing Gardner was the lifeboats, because, esthetically speaking, they mar the smooth lines of the ship. Nuances of color and design were combined in the color scheme of the lifeboats and their background in order to minimize their visual disruption of the clean lines of the ship. Initially the *Queen Elizabeth 2* was fitted with three bow anchors—port, starboard, and center–but a North Atlantic gale jammed the huge center anchor back into the bow and, following repairs, it was removed and stowed on deck as a spare. Reinforced steel plating covered the hole and strengthened the bow where the anchor had been.

Dennis Lennon, the joint coordinator for the *QE2* with James Gardner, was responsible for coordinating the work of the ten-man team of top designers involved in styling the interiors of over 1,400 public rooms and cabins on the liner. Their design created a unified and integrated effect reflecting the best of contemporary style and manufacture. Lennon's own team designed the restaurants, cocktail bars, a library, swimming pool, and all entrances, corridors, and staircases, as well as some of the cabins. Initially Dennis Lennon had been brought into the consultation process on the new liner through the invitation of Lady Brocklebank, when Sir John Brocklebank had been chairman of Cunard. There had been some disgruntlement over such an important appointment without first having held some sort of design competition. However, Lennon's achievements soon stifled all grumbling and made him one of the greatest successes of the Brocklebank period.

In addition to Lennon, Jon Bannenberg of Australia played a major role in fashioning the image of the *QE2*. Bannenberg designed a number of the premium-class cabins, a swimming pool, the card room, and the majestic panoramic Double Up–Double Down Room with its 20,000 square feet stretching the width of the liner and soaring through two decks. The main color schemes of red, silver, and clear glass have survived the test of time and made this one of the most successful public rooms on any liner afloat. The second-floor balcony area has gone through a number of transformations, but the room remains a remarkable utilization of space. David Hicks designed the initial tourist-class nightclub, the Q4 Room, and Michael Inchbald designed the quarterdeck library and the magnificent *Queens* Room, the principal first-class public room. Gaby Schreiber turned her considerable artistic skill to the creation of the largest theater afloat in the second of the two-deck-high public rooms of the ship. She also was responsible for the design of a series of suite rooms and the tour office. Stefan Buzas and his partner, Alan Irvine, were responsible for another nightclub, the 736 Club, a section of suites, the initial shops, and the boat deck gallery. Mrs. J. Pattrick undertook the decor of the

Late spring 1968 sees the bridge in place, still minus its wings, and the funnel has been seated, but there is no mast. The name Queen Elizabeth 2 *is emblazoned on the hull with the uniquely modern designation that would make the* QE2 *famous.*

officers' and crew's accommodations, as well as the hospital on the ship, with the goal of making all facilities as much as possible like a normal home in color and furnishings. It was fully realized that if the *Queen Elizabeth 2* was to go cruising a great deal, members of the crew would be serving extended periods of time away from Britain and that the off-duty areas of the ship should be made as attractive as possible. The partnership of Crosby/Fletcher/Forbes was responsible for all the graphics on the ship so that all signs and public notices everywhere were in the same basic style. They also designed the splendid observation lounge, or Look Out Bar, across the front of the ship, which was one of the most popular facilities on the liner when commissioned. Professor Misha Black, professor of industrial design (engineering) at the Royal College of Art, who served as coordinating architect for the public rooms in the P & O liner *Oriana*, designed the synagogue for the QE2. Two students from the Royal College of Art, Elizabeth Beloe and Tony Heaton, were commissioned to produce the designs for the children's play area on the *Queen Elizabeth 2*. In the future literally thousands of children were to enjoy this section of the liner, since it was not only a superbly stimulating center for young minds, but also included a miniature theater where cartoons and films were shown.

Significant of the change in philosophy in connection with the design and layout of the new ship was the desire to open as many of the public rooms as possible to a view of the sea. The attitude of the previous hundred years had been to make passengers crossing on a great transatlantic liner forget that they were at sea. Opulent public rooms gave the illusion of "life as usual" with the assumption that one might never have left port. When ships were the only means of crossing the ocean, the trip was often dreaded as much as appreci-

One of the giant cranes is working through the turbine hatch aft of the funnel that descends directly to the engine room of the liner. Lifeboats are in place on the starboard side of the Boat Deck, and painting is under way. A dry cargo bulk carrier can be seen under construction behind the Queen.

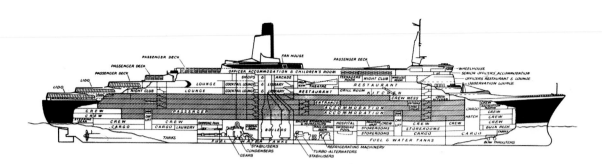

The "Q4" plans in a cutaway were available at the time of the launch on September 20, 1967, but, of course, no name could be attached to them; hence she could only be described as "the new 58,000-ton Cunarder." Later it would be realized that the Queen Elizabeth 2 would weigh in at well over 65,000 tons, which would create some cause for concern until assurances were given that this would not curtail the range of her potential employment.

ated; therefore, it was appropriate to camouflage the fact that the passenger was at sea. Millionaires could feel as comfortable in the great public rooms and suites of the *Aquitania* as in their own homes. It was possible, of course, to go out on deck, but it was desirable for only a few months of the year and even then was an invigorating, and for some unpleasant, experience. In contrast, the design team for the *Queen Elizabeth 2* was actively encouraged to emphasize the sea. The passengers who traveled by transatlantic liners, Cunard reasoned, did so by choice rather than lack of alternatives. Hence the great restaurants of the liner were placed high in the ship so that passengers dining on gourmet cuisine could have the best of both worlds: a grand hotel and an ocean vacation. Furthermore, the basic nature of the new liner was to be an "open ship" operating without class distinctions whenever she was cruising but with regard for them on the North Atlantic. Eliteness would be available through cabin selection and restaurant assignment for those who desired it. The overall expenditure for interior design work and outfitting was about £3,000,000 ($8,400,000), but, as Lennon said, "the public judge a ship by what has been done to the interior." The desire was to make the *QE2* second to none.

The interim report of the Cunard Line for the half year ending June 30, 1968, was the most encouraging news that Sir Basil Smallpeice, or any Cunard chairman for a decade, had been able to offer the employees and stockholders of the line. The slimming down of the passenger fleet by the removal from service and sale of the *Queen Mary, Caronia, Carinthia,* and *Sylvania* had resulted in a profit of £2,576,000 on a total passenger and freight revenue of £24,565,000. In contrast, the interim figures for the previous year had shown a net loss of £2,031,000 for an actual turnaround of £3.1 million! The high prices brought by the Cunard tonnage that had been disposed of also made it possible for the company to inform the British government that it would not need the remaining £4 million of the £24 million load made available to them in September

1967. It appeared that Cunard had instituted the twin management policies of rationalization of the passenger fleet and diversification of the firm's resources just in the nick of time. As a result of the profit posted, the board recommended a 7½ percent dividend for 1968 up from the minimum of 5 percent, which in a number of previous years had to be paid out of reserves instead of from profits. The financial position of the company was turned around even if there was still an enormous debt to service for the new ship. The future suddenly seemed very encouraging.

The fitting out of the ship went on as rapidly as possible, with an army of some 3,000 Scottish workers employed on the project at the actual building sight. By the time of the launch 17,500 tons of steel from Colvilles of Glasgow worth more than £1,000,000 ($3,000,000) had been used; so also had £500,000 ($1,400,000) worth of aluminum from Alcan; generators and other electrical equipment ordered from AEI were worth another £500,000; and air-conditioning equipment from Carrier capable of withstanding tropical sunshine was worth another £750,000 ($2,100,000). So the bills grew apace with the ship.

Considerable attention was paid to suggestions aimed at making travel more of a pleasure for handicapped passengers. A percentage of the *QE2*'s cabins were outfitted with bathrooms with lowered sills, larger doors, and plenty of swing room so that passengers traveling in wheelchairs could enjoy absolute mobility. Elevators also were adapted for handicapped passengers, and all public rooms, even if their main entrance was raised, such as the Columbia Restaurant, had convenient side entrances that were level.

A critical desire of Cunard was to have the *Queen Elizabeth 2* delivered on time so that the maximum advantage could be made of advanced scheduling and publicity. As early as December 1966 it appeared obvious that the liner would not be completely finished in time for the spring–summer 1968 season, and plans for that were scrapped. In determining the precommissioning schedule the two most critical problems were how much loading of stores on the ship could be done at the shipyard prior to delivery at Southampton, and how long a trial period would be required at sea after the ship's delivery (with guests on board but no fare-paying passengers) before the ship could begin commercial service. The hotel department, in particular, was concerned that all furnishings be placed on board before leaving the shipyard so that nothing would be lacking. Furthermore, a catering storing period spread over some three months was regarded as imperative before leaving the shipyard. The hotel department also felt that two eight-day cruises with company guests should be undertaken in order to get all systems fully operational. Each section of the passenger accommodations was to be locked and secured as soon as it was finished.

The technical director, Thomas Kameen, led a team of seven Cunard engineers responsible for coordinating the design of the main turbines and auxiliary power plant, as well as all other main and minor machinery, including

A brilliant day on the Clyde shows the fitting-out basin at John Brown's, with the QE2 nearing completion. Paint crews are at work on the port side and the ship looks remarkably complete, although there still is no mast forward.

generators, evaporators, and the computer. Foremost among Kameen's concerns was the operation of the sprinkler system, because more vessels have been lost from fires in yards and while fitting out than probably from any other single cause. The technical commissioning program was started nine months before the ship left John Brown's and included trials of all the major machinery as soon as possible. A proper sea trial had to include sufficient time to equal one North Atlantic round-trip voyage and take the ship into hot and humid weather so that the air-conditioning could be adjusted—a major problem on any new ship destined to operate both on the North Atlantic and in tropical waters. Cunard was under no delusions that the two-week shakedown cruise probably would produce a lot of adjustments and defects requiring an additional two weeks in port before acceptance. The goal in December 1966 was to have the *QE2* ready for commercial service by January 1969.

In the period between December 1966 and May 1968 the financial collapse of the Clydebank shipyards occurred and a new organization known as Upper Clyde Shipbuilders, Ltd., was created to salvage whatever might prove economically viable. The projected £2,400,000 loss of John Brown and Company, Ltd., on the *Queen Elizabeth 2* was the final blow to that old firm, although the writing had been on the wall for some time. This placed Cunard in the position of finishing a ship with a different firm from that which had contracted for the vessel. The instability of the times also produced substantial labor unrest, which did not make life any easier for A. E. Hepper, chairman of Upper Clyde Shipbuilders, as he tried to honor deadlines. In fact, Upper Clyde signed a contract for a smaller passenger ship for Fred Olsen Lines largely because of the desire to guarantee some work after the *Queen Elizabeth 2* left the yard and thereby maintain morale among the workers until the last great ship was safely delivered.

Sir Basil Smallpeice wrote to Hepper in May 1968 and emphasized the absolute necessity of maintaining the November delivery deadlines:

> I know full well that you are very anxious that the ship should be delivered on time because the publicity attached to the ship world-wide is such that a late delivery of it could not rebound on Upper Clyde Shipbuilders. As far as we are concerned, the revenue potential of the ship, even in the winter, is of the order of £¾ million a month, and even four weeks delay would therefore be a very serious matter from our point of view, to say nothing of your own.

Cunard was willing to accommodate Upper Clyde in almost any way if the *Queen* just could get to sea on time! Upper Clyde responded by making John Rannie, local director of UCS, solely responsible for the *QE2*, the power to do almost anything to get the ship ready for her trials. At the end of the summer Hepper set the tone for UCS by saying "Although we are living in a very difficult situation at the moment, we are all very conscious of the extreme importance of this contract."

To the infinite relief of all concerned, just as dawn began to break over Scotland on November 19, 1968, the magnificent new *Queen Elizabeth 2* slowly eased her way out of the fitting-out birth at Clydebank and into the narrow river. Western Scotland had declared a holiday to watch the newest of the *Queens* majestically weave her way down the Clyde on a high tide. She needed all the water nature could supply, even if she did not draw as much as her predecessors. On the bridge was Captain William Warwick and, besides the normal complement of Cunard and Upper Clyde Shipbuilders personnel, Prince Charles, the heir to the throne. The trip downriver was not to be a long one, because the destination was the Greenock Dry Dock, barely thirteen miles away. As the *Queen Elizabeth 2* completed her turn and prepared to move downstream, Captain Warwick fulfilled the fondest unspoken wish of the twenty-year-old prince when he asked his royal guest if he would like to blow the departure blast on the colossal horns of the liner. Prince Charles's eyes lit up, and he was clearly delighted to do so. Thus, the *Queen*'s parting salute to her birthplace, where Her Majesty Queen Elizabeth II had launched her two years before, was given by the Prince of Wales. Nothing could have been more appropriate.

Once in the Greenock Dry Dock, work on the completion of the *QE2* appeared to slow. Five hundred carpenters were let go one week and one hundred hired back the next, generating instability in the work force while the accommodations on the ship remained a shambles. Because the workers could sail with her, after a week the *QE2* left dry dock for her trials. The turbines steadily built up speed until she was racing along at 29½ knots, achieving this with two screws, whereas the older *Queens* had needed four, and with 50,000 less horsepower. The technical trials suddenly were interrupted by the discovery of an oil leak caused by a nonreturn valve that was contaminating the high-pressure steam system. There was no choice in the matter except to return to dry dock and completely clean the entire main and auxiliary steam circulating systems—a process that required the better part of two weeks. This delayed the resumption of the technical trials until the week before Christmas, and a holiday charity cruise for the benefit of the National Society for Cancer Relief was canceled. As a partial compensation to the Society, Cunard made a contribution to its treasury. When the sea trials were resumed, the *Queen Elizabeth 2* delighted everyone by reaching 32.46 knots at full speed with no sign of trouble.

Hurried arrangements were then made to take the ship on her final acceptance trials on December 23, with 500 members of the Cunard organization and their families along as "guests" and guinea pigs. Few "guinea pigs" ever ended up working so hard, because much of the passenger accommodation still required cleaning. Two hundred Clyde workers also went south with the ship in a desperate race to try to finish the most pressing carpentry work. Then, on the evening of December 24, as the liner steamed toward the Canary Islands, first the starboard high-pressure turbine and then the port turbine experienced problems. Initially the thought was that the rotor simply was imbalanced, but the fault was far more serious than that. Sir Basil Smallpeice, whose wife had been seriously ill, had missed sailing with the ship and he now flew out to Los Palmas with Anthony Hepper of Upper Clyde Shipbuilders to inspect the situation. This was a time for Cunard to be very firm and, after hearing the extremely uncertain engineering report, as well as seeing the unfinished state of the passenger accommodations, Sir Basil announced that Cunard would refuse to accept the liner until everything was corrected.

The *Queen Elizabeth 2* slowly steamed back to Southampton to something less than a triumphant arrival and brought with her a load of publicity, because nearly 200 reporters had joined the ship in the Canary Islands for the trip back to England. However, the nature of the coverage was quite well balanced;

The Queen Elizabeth 2 *offers a magnificent panorama in this official Cunard Line photo of the liner taken while on trials in the English Channel. The open expanses of deck toward the stern have never been equaled in any other vessel.*

most writers stressed the magnificence of the vessel, even if she was experiencing teething troubles. Very few complicated pieces of machinery do not require some adjustments, and it is commonly forgotten that the *Queen Mary* had her share of problems after commissioning. (The considerable duplication of units in the *Queen Mary's* propulsion system made it possible to continue whatever the difficulty.) The primary difficulty insofar as Cunard was concerned

The official visit of Her Majesty Queen Elizabeth II and His Royal Highness, The Prince Philip, Duke of Edinburgh, to the Queen Elizabeth 2 *occurred on the eve of the liner's maiden departure for New York, May 7, 1969. Captain William Warwick, master of the* QE2, *shows Her Majesty and Prince Philip around the bridge and while Lord Mancroft, a Cunard director, and Sir Basil Smallpeice, Cunard managing director, look on. (Photo courtesy of the Collection of Mrs. Evelyn Warwick.)*

was to stimulate UCS to take immediate and drastic action to discover and solve the problem. By January 16, 1969, no positive identification of the turbine problem had been made; and John Brown Engineering, the manufacturers of the turbines, was estimating at least another three weeks delay. On the face of that, Cunard canceled all future sailings. The company's position was very simple:

> Cunard cannot accept delivery until after the ship's turbines have been thoroughly re-tested and proved in further basin trials, speed trials and a prolonged acceptance trial under maintained pressure, followed by further inspection. It is impossible to say when this programme of correction, testing and proving of the ship's power plant can be completed.

The problem with the turbines may have been a blessing in disguise, because at least UCS could guarantee that during the next months the interior outfitting of the ship would be completed according to contract terms by the end of January. Investigation revealed that some of the blades vibrated at unacceptable pitches until they shattered and spread havoc everywhere in their path. Various strengthening efforts were made that solved this crucial problem, and the turbines could be reconditioned. The result was a long, drawn-out process that did not near completion until mid-March. By March 16 it could be announced by a greatly relieved Anthony Hepper that the *Queen Elizabeth 2* would undergo basin tests alongside her Southampton pier and then go to sea for speed trails in the Channel. The Channel trials were a success at full power.

The *QE2* went back into dry dock for cleaning and inspection, and then out

Majestic and regal, the Queen Elizabeth 2 *entered service with her sailing from Southampton for New York. Her maiden appearance remained unchanged until late 1972.*

on a shakedown cruise at the end of March during which all her machinery was given a workout, and finally the turbine casings were opened again for inspection. Everything being shipshape, or as Sir Basil put it, "Cunard-shape," the *Queen Elizabeth 2* finally was accepted by Cunard on April 20. Her final cost was £29,091,000 ($69,818,400).

The acceptance on April 20 permitted a mini-cruise to the Canary Islands from Southampton on April 22, which actually marks the beginning of commercial service. Upon returning from the Canaries, the ship was reprovisioned for her maiden voyage and spruced up for a royal visit. On the eve of her first transatlantic crossing Her Majesty Queen Elizabeth II and Prince Phillip renewed their association with the ship by visiting her for a royal tour. The visit heralded what Cunard was convinced would be the beginning of a brilliant career for Britain's largest liner. Captain William Warwick, master of the *QE2*, and staff captain George Smith received Her Majesty on board the ship. Among the ship's officers and heads of departments presented to the queen were Donald Wilson, chief engineer; Jack Marland, deputy chief engineer; Mortimer Hehir, chief officer; James Smith, hotel manager; John Morton, deputy hotel manager; and Dr. William Deely, principal medical officer.

The queen toured the bridge and the principal public rooms. The bust of Her Majesty, created by the sculptor Oscar Nemon, was in the Queen's Room. The queen told of sitting for the sculptor on several occasions when he could not get the nature and position of the head to suit him and had unceremoniously wrenched it off. After the tour of the ship a luncheon was served in the elite Grill Room, with cold salmon as the main course washed down with a 1962 Montrachet wine from the substantial cellars of the liner. The visit of Her Majesty to the *Queen Elizabeth 2* maintained a royal family tradition of three generations.

On May 2, 1969, nearly five years after her keel laying and two years after her launching, the *Queen Elizabeth 2* sailed from Southampton with 1,400 passengers for Le Havre and New York on her maiden voyage. What had appeared on occasion to be the impossible dream had become a glorious reality.

CHAPTER THREE

THE MAIDEN YEARS

The maiden Atlantic crossing of the *Queen Elizabeth 2* was an appropriate introduction to the solid, comfortable luxury that her passengers would enjoy in the
future. The steaming time from Le Havre to the Ambrose light tower was four
days, sixteen hours, thirty-five minutes, which gave an average speed of 28.02
knots. Early on the morning of May 7 the *QE2* was greeted by a flotilla of escorts as she neared the Verrazano Bridge. She was led into the harbor by the
U.S. Coast Guard cutter *Morgenthau* while the U.S. Navy destroyer *Conway*
took up position astern. Mayor John V. Lindsay of New York and a party of
dignitaries boarded the *QE2* in the Lower Bay before noon, along with numerous members of the press. The basic feeling among those who came to greet
her was that no vessel like her would ever be built again and that she represented the last of an era—the last great transatlantic liner. The gala parade up
the harbor soon included hundreds of yachts and pleasure boats, as well as a
chartered ferry boat. In New York tradition, the fireboats were present with
their fire pumps spraying water high into the air. The day had started cool and
overcast, but by noon the *Queen Elizabeth 2* was bathed in bright sunlight. She
passed the Statue of Liberty and slowly steamed up the North River exchang-
ing thunderous salute after salute with other vessels in the harbor. As the
afternoon started to wane, the *QE2* approached her berth at pier 92 and at
1512 hours "finished with engines" was rung. The maiden arrival of the *Queen
Elizabeth 2* at New York had been one of the most spectacular welcoming celebrations that anyone could remember in the history of the port.

Many "arrival celebration" dinners were held all over New York City, as
well as on the *Queen*. One thousand guests of Cunard Line at a supper dance

The Queen Elizabeth 2 *makes her majestic entrance to New York Harbor for the first time on May 7, 1969. Coast Guard cutters, fireboats, tugs, ferries, and yachts escort her as she exchanges salutes with other vessels. The crossing from Southampton to New York was accomplished in four days, sixteen hours, and thirty-five minutes at an average speed of 28.02 knots.*

enjoyed the amenities of the new ship and exchanged stories about her illustrious predecessors. The *QE2* certainly was the biggest "happening" in New York, and those who came to see her were divided into two groups: those who had traveled on the old *Queens* and were astonished by the modern look of the new ship, and those who were social trendsetters and were impressed that a ship could look so exciting. Among the guests were members of the diplomatic corps to the United Nations, including the ambassadors from Britain, France, Sweden, the Soviet Union, Ghana, and Morocco, and a generous selection of prominent men and women from industry, transportation, and finance. Other guests included Mrs. John V. Lindsay representing her husband, the mayor of New York, and the distinguished maritime author Walter Lord.

Many of the New York inaugural festivities on the *QE2* took place in the huge "Double Room," which, with its red, orange, chrome, and glass color scheme, was strikingly different from anything in the old *Queens*. It was impossible for the guests to realize that the Double Room was the tourist-class public room when the ship operated with two classes on the North Atlantic. In assessing the new liner, some illustrious individual noted that it was characteristic of the times that there was virtually no noticeable difference between the first- and tourist-class public rooms. The subtle class distinctions were handled by a few discreet signs reserving areas for first class rather than the locked doors and barriers of previous vessels. The comments and reviews were mixed, but there was no question about the fact that the *Queen Elizabeth 2* both broke new ground and was strikingly different from everything that had gone before. If the *Queen Mary* in 1936 had been "evolutionary," there was no questioning the fact that the *Queen Elizabeth 2* in 1969 was "revolutionary." She therefore achieved exactly the effect that Sir Basil Smallpeice, Lord Mancroft, the directors of Cunard, and the ship's design team had desired: She was unique. As John Quinn of the *Daily News* summed up his story, "the old queens are gone. Long Live the Queen."

Passenger bookings steadily improved as the summer season began on the North Atlantic. When the *Queen Elizabeth 2* sailed from New York for her second eastbound crossing on May 22, she sailed with 1,650 passengers on board.

Upon arrival in Southampton on April 29, 1969, the *QE2* had the pleasure of a second visit from His Royal Highness the Duke of Edinburgh. The purpose of the visit was to present the 1969 Council of Industrial Design awards. Among the 1969 winners were designers of the special dining-room chairs created for the *Queen Elizabeth 2*. While he was aboard, Prince Philip had a more thorough tour of the ship than he had had on his previous visit. He was shown some of the public rooms before being taken to the crew quarters, where he saw food being prepared for the crew mess. The tour also included the turbine control, engine, and boiler rooms.

The 1969 summer season passed relatively uneventfully, and the *Queen* carried an average of 1,550 passengers per crossing. The fortunes of the Cunard Line had begun to change for the better in 1968, even before the advent of the *QE2*, but now, with her increased earning capacity, everything began to look very promising indeed. The popularity of the *QE2* among families traveling with young children grew steadily as it became known that the liner had some

Docking in New York at the new North River passenger liner terminal is in some ways less challenging than at the old Cunard piers, but with any kind of a wind it still requires skill and practice to place the 963-foot Queen Elizabeth 2 *in her slip.*

The Queen Elizabeth 2 *has just cleared the Verrazano Narrows Bridge on her maiden arrival in New York Harbor, and an armada has gathered to escort her to her berth.*

of the finest facilities and best-organized entertainment program ever created for children of all ages. By 1972 it was not unusual for the ship to be crossing with 200 to 300 children. Furthermore, if one was returning from a year or more in Europe with a family and did not want to restrict the baggage, the *Queen* could end up as a bargain over the airline surcharges for overweight luggage. The *Queen* earned for herself an enviable reputation as a spacious ship with comfortable accommodations and superb cuisine for all travelers.

As far as her qualities as a good sea ship are concerned, the *Queen Elizabeth 2*

On the maiden arrival of the Queen Elizabeth 2 *in New York three Moran tugs were in attendance just to make sure that everything went perfectly as the brand new liner gracefully turned into her slip and came up against the old Cunard Line piers.*

Outward bound from New York, the QE2 *passes the Statue of Liberty and heads toward the Verrazano Narrows Bridge. Passengers traveling on her for the first time are always convinced that the towering mast and funnel will not clear the under deck of the bridge. Several feet of clearance do exist even at high tide.*

may well represent the ultimate achievement in naval architecture. The beautiful, sheer lines of her hull below the waterline gave her a smooth entry into virtually any sea and resulted in the most stable performance of any of the great Atlantic liners. In addition, her stabilizers were designed and contoured precisely to complement the hull lines of the ship and were able to operate under virtually any sea conditions and considerably reduce rolling, even in severe weather.

Her seaworthiness was put to the test in October 1969. The liner arrived in New York some ten hours late after having altered course several times during the North Atlantic crossing in order to avoid the worst of three major storm systems over the ocean. In meteorological terms, a complex depression with associated storm winds ranging up to force II and accompanied by very heavy west-southwesterly swells caused a speed reduction and delayed arrival. On October 18–19 relief Captain F. J. Storey took the *Queen* over 100 miles south and again on October 20–21, when this action was repeated and accompanied by reduced speed in order to minimize passenger discomfort. When yet a third storm in the same depression was encountered less than 600 miles from New York, there was not too much the ship could do to make up the time with the 110,000 horsepower at her command. The official Cunard report stated: "Considering the magnitude of the storms, it was considered that *QE2* made good headway and lived up to her reputation of being a good sea ship."

The news that the *Queen* had contributed £800,000 ($1,920,000) to the Cunard profits for 1969 certainly buoyed the satisfaction and expectations of the owners, because this represented less than a year's operations. Earlier, on October 18, 1969, it had been announced that before the *Queen Elizabeth 2* was nine months old Cunard would have repaid £2½ million of the government loans provided for the completion of the new liner and that they would be in a

Few ports in the world are more highly regarded by cruise passengers than Charlotte Amalie, St. Thomas, Virgin Islands. As the Caribbean sun begins to set the bow of the Queen Elizabeth 2 *points toward the resort hotel of Frenchman's Reef in an exquisite setting.*

position to repay £500,000 every six months of the outstanding balance of £12 million. Sir Basil Smallpeice commented:

> The fact that we have been able to make these repayments is clear evidence of Cunard's all-around progress and growing cash flow. I am glad that we are able to show in this practical way that the Government's confidence in Cunard's new direction and management was not misplaced.

Additional good news followed on November 3, 1969, when it was announced that the Cunard Line had decided to invite tenders for one, and possibly two, new 1,000-passenger liners for the leisure market. Although preference would be given to British yards, shipbuilders from all over the Continent were invited to tender for the ships, with Cunard reserving the right to make a selection on the basis of price, delivery date, and credit terms.

The plans for the 1969–1970 winter season were for the *Queen Elizabeth 2* to have a series of seven ten-day Caribbean cruises from New York. Wherever she went, the *QE2* was given a royal welcome in a fabulous series of "maiden arrivals" that delighted passengers and islanders. In Kingston, Jamaica, the governor-general, Sir Clifford Campbell, and an official party were entertained on board while passengers were greeted by bands, mounted horsemen, and a festival atmosphere on shore. The series of Caribbean cruises proved popular, although even the 28-knot speed with which the *Queen* rushed her passengers south could not eliminate the penetrating cold of a New York sailing.

When the *Queen* returned from the Caribbean on February 5, 1970, she encountered two problems: the New York tugboats were on strike, and her pier was choked with ice. Captain W. E. Warwick had to ease his 963-foot ship steadily in and out of the slip four times in order to crunch the 6-inch ice floes with her 65,000 tons and then, with the aid of the bow thrusters, berth her alongside the pier. Afterward the captain turned to his officers and said: "I never thought we would have to use a £30 million ship as an ice breaker."

Personal tragedy occasionally affects the life of those who go to sea, and sometimes in a dramatic way. The first instance of a "man overboard" occurred on March 30, 1970, when the *Queen Elizabeth 2* was on passage from Barbados to Madeira. The ship was steaming along at 28 knots when at 1202 hours it was reported to the bridge that a man had been seen falling overboard. Immediately the speed was reduced and the rescue launch crew alerted. Within sixteen minutes *QE2* had completed a "Williamson turn," a maneuver that brought the ship onto her reciprocal course. During the turn lookouts were scanning the area, and at 1249 hours an object was sighted floating in the water. Within five minutes the ship was stopped and the rescue launch was under way. At 1301 hours the body of a crew member was recovered from the sea, but efforts to revive him proved unsuccessful. The launch was recovered by 1316 hours and the ship resumed her passage. Although the incident was unfortunate, it did serve to demonstrate the maneuverability of one of the largest ships in the world.

By coincidence, it had been arranged for stop trials to be carried out the following week in the presence of British board of trade surveyors for the purpose of verifying and checking the ability of the ship to stop under emergency conditions. These "emergency stop trials" were undertaken on April 5, 1970, while on passage from Lisbon to Le Havre. At 0918 hours the *Queen* was steaming through the ocean at $29\frac{1}{2}$ knots when the full-astern order was given. Within 4 minutes at 0922 hours the forward momentum of the ship had been reduced to $8\frac{1}{2}$ knots and both engines were moving astern. By 0924 hours and $\frac{1}{2}$ minute, $6\frac{1}{2}$ minutes following "full astern," the *Queen* had stopped dead in the water and, within an additional 2 minutes, at 0926 hours and $\frac{1}{2}$ minute, she was making $4\frac{1}{2}$ knots astern. From full ahead at $29\frac{1}{2}$ knots to full astern at $4\frac{1}{2}$ knots in $8\frac{1}{2}$ minutes!

The hospital facilities on the *Queen Elizabeth 2* are the largest and most modern ever provided on a commercial vessel. The team of doctors and nurses is capable of handling virtually any situation. Sometimes their services are in de-

A scene of splendor as the majestic Queen Elizabeth 2 *slowly steams up the channel toward Southhampton with all her lights ablaze and a low cloud ceiling reflecting them back on the ship. The picture was taken from the* Nieuw Amsterdam *late on the evening of June 30, 1970, as the two passed "like ships in the night."*

mand from other ships, as was the case on a number of occasions during 1970.

The first such call was on June 26, 1970, when the *QE2* was on an eastbound passage from New York to Le Havre. A message was received from the 3,514-ton German motor vessel *Zosmarr* on a westbound passage to Boston requesting medical advice for a sick Spanish seaman, Jesus Ferreira. Radio contact was established with the master of the *Zosmarr* and the *QE2*'s principal medical officer, Dr. W. E. Deely, who, after hearing details of the illness, decided that the seaman's life could be in danger. The position of the *Zosmarr* was plotted, and a course was set to rendezvous with her. It was found that only an 8-degree deviation to the south was required and that the *QE2* should meet the *Zosmarr* shortly after midnight. At 2000 hours Captain William J. Law gave the order to steer the new course to close with the German ship, which was also instructed to steer a reciprocal course. While making for the rendezvous, the *QE2* encountered dense fog, and her high definition radars remained constantly manned as they scanned ahead. At 2345 hours the radars picked up the *Zosmarr* eighteen miles away, exactly on schedule. Contact was again made with the *Zosmarr* to give her instructions to enable the ships to maneuver together as close as possible. At 0025 hours the engines were stopped and, shortly after, a launch was under way with a doctor on board. Because of the dense fog and the pitch darkness, the *QE2* had to guide her launch across to the German ship. This was accomplished by the officer of the watch looking at a radar screen and giving instructions to the launch by walkie-talkie. The *Zosmarr* assisted by blowing her whistle periodically, and the launch sighted the little freighter at 0109 hours and soon thereafter went alongside. Fortunately there was only a slight swell, and the sick seaman was able to descend to the *QE2*'s launch by climbing down the pilot ladder. The launch sped back to the liner, was hoisted aboard, and by 0126 hours the *Queen Elizabeth 2* had resumed her voyage to Le Havre at full speed. Following treatment, Jesus Ferreira made a full recovery.

Under similar circumstances, assistance was also rendered to seaman K. Hopner from the trawler *Heinrich Kern* on July 27, 1970, while the ships were in mid-Atlantic.

On October 29, 1970, when on passage from Las Palmas to Dakar, the *Queen Elizabeth 2* diverted from course at 1236 hours to render assistance to an engineer officer injured on the S.S. *Cerinthus* of the Hadley Shipping Company, London. The fifth engineer, David R. G. Senior had suffered second-degree burns on the hands and face and was in critical need of expert medical assistance. The *Queen* reached the *Cerinthus* at 1332 hours and the lifeboat was away by 1350 hours, returning with the patient by 1422 hours, after which the *QE2* resumed full speed and the lucky man received the medical care that his wounds required. Happily, he made a satisfactory recovery.

In June 1970 the *Queen* made her fastest crossing to date, covering the distance from Cóbh, Ireland, to New York in three days, twenty hours, and forty-two minutes, at an average speed of 30.36 knots. Her reputation was growing. Evidence of the success of the *Queen Elizabeth 2* was in the eastbound crossing of July 23, 1970, when she carried her 75,000th passenger, who received a plaque in commemoration.

In October 1970 the *Queen* received a royal present of her own when Her Majesty Queen Elizabeth II presented portraits of herself and of Prince Philip to the officers' wardroom. The presentation at Southampton was made by Sir Basil Smallpeice on behalf of Her Majesty to the wardroom president, Chief Officer T. D. Ridley.

Cunard's decision to order additional passenger liners resulted in a partnership with Overseas National Airlines, which had ordered a 17,000-ton cruise ship from the Rotterdam Drydock Company. This arrangement enabled Cunard to take delivery of a new medium-sized liner by the summer of 1971 and a second vessel a year later. On July 15, 1970, the announcement was made that the line had acquired 100 percent ownership of the new vessels from ONA and that they would be owned and operated exclusively by Cunard. Sir

Sir Basil Smallpeice, chairman of Cunard (1965–1971), presents to Douglas Ridley, chief officer and president of the officers' wardroom, the picture of Her Majesty Queen Elizabeth II that was a gift of the queen to the ship in 1970. Looking on from the right is Commodore William Warwick, master of the QE2, *and to the left is Captain Mortimer Hehir. Warwick, Hehir, and Ridley were all masters of the ship.*

Basil Smallpeice, commenting on the decision, said: "It underlines Cunard's determination to re-establish a modern and profitable passenger fleet at an early date." In November 1970 it was announced that the first of the new 17,000-ton liners would be named *Cunard Adventurer* in line with the company's emphasis on the cruise and leisure aspects of the 700-passenger vessels.

One of the most dramatic experiences of the *Queen Elizabeth 2* happened the night of January 8–9, 1971. The giant Cunarder under the command of Commodore W. E. Warwick was anchored off Castries, St. Lucia, on a Caribbean cruise when an S.O.S. was received from the French liner *Antilles* stating that she had run aground and was on fire near the island of Mustique in the Grenadines. The distress signal was received at 1905 hours, and it was possible for the *QE2* to respond very quickly, as she was already preparing to sail for her next port of call. By 1954 hours the *Queen* had weighed anchor and was steaming at full speed to the rescue. In the meantime all departments on board were alerted to prepare for 500 survivors. Launch crews were mustered, gangway and scrambling nets were prepared, and volunteer parties of the *QE2* Scuba Divers' Club stood by. The hospital was on the alert, and in the hotel department chefs and waiters stood by to prepare and serve food and drink. Additional blankets were made available, cabins prepared, and a reception desk was set up near the gangway to allocate them to the rescued as they came aboard. A list was made of those passengers with special skills who offered their services and of those who volunteered to give up their cabins to any needy traveler. Since the *Queen* had only 1,000 passengers on board for the cruise, she had sufficient staterooms to accommodate the majority of the *Antilles'* passengers without inconveniencing many of her own.

Three and a half hours after sailing from St. Lucia the *Queen Elizabeth 2* reached the search area at 2230 hours. As she approached Mustique, the *An-*

The French liner Antilles *(1952, 19,828 tons, 599 by 80 feet). (Photo courtsy the John H. Shaum. Jr. Collection.)*

tilles could be seen as a pulsating glow on the horizon, ablaze from stem to stern and with flames soaring over 100 feet into the Caribbean night. The passengers on the *QE2* had a clear view of the *Antilles* as the *Queen* passed within a quarter of a mile of the stricken liner vividly marking the treacherous reef. The *Antilles*' captain apparently had wished to show the cruise passengers the beautiful sight of Mustique Island against a Caribbean sunset. The slightly different course took the *Antilles* toward an uncharted reef, and islanders tried to wave a warning. Hugo Money-Coutts also tried in vain to give warning from his private plane as he circled the ship. The *Antilles* steamed on until she struck the uncharted reef with such an impact that it caused fuel tanks to split open. Oil leaking into the engine room soon became ignited and attempts to contain the fire failed as it easily spread over the water in the flooded compartments. Passengers on the *Antilles* were ordered to their lifeboat stations. When the abandon-ship order was given, they proceeded ashore in lifeboats to the islands of Mustique and Bequia. The master and some of the crew remained on board in an unsuccessful attempt to fight the fire.

The *Queen Elizabeth 2* spent one hour in the search area near the burning inferno of the French liner and then sailed on to Grand Bay, Mustique, to take on survivors. It appeared as though there may have been a high loss of life because of the number of different places and ships to which passengers and crew of the *Antilles* had gone. The master of the *QE2* had in fact stated that anywhere from 50 to 100 individuals were unaccounted for, in response to an early request for news from the French line. The *QE2* was joined by other liners in the rescue area, including the *Empress of Canada* and the *Oceanic*, which, along with other vessels, searched for further survivors. The U.S. Coast Guard center in San Juan, Puerto Rico, the port from which the *Antilles'* cruise had-begun, was in continuous communication with the *QE2*, keeping abreast of the situation and ensuring that all possible assistance that could be used was available. In all, 635 individuals were transferred to safety from the *Antilles*: 501 to

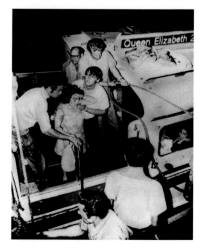

During the night of January 8–9, 1971, survivors of the French Line's Antilles *board the* QE2 *from her launches after being transported from the island of Mustique, following the wrecking and burning of the French liner on an uncharted reef.*

Mustique by lifeboat and life raft, 85 to the French ship *Suffren*, and 49 to the nearby island of Bequia.

At Mustique night conditions and a heavy swell made the transfer of survivors from the shore to the *QE2* difficult; nevertheless, between 0130 and 0530 hours the *QE2*'s launches moved back and forth between the island and the ship with the *Antilles'* passengers. By 0505 hours on January 9, Commodore Warwick was able to assure the French Line at Fort de France, Martinique, that everyone had been accounted for from the *Antilles*, but that, according to all reports and the assessment of the *Antilles'* purser, the French liner was a total loss. Having taken all on board from Mustique, the *QE2* sailed at 0530 hours for Barbados, where French Line agents commenced preparations to receive the *Antilles'* passengers. By the time the *Queen Elizabeth 2* arrived at Barbados the wind was too strong for her to go alongside in the harbor, so she anchored in the bay off Bridgetown. To assist with the ferrying of passengers and survivors ashore, seamen and launches from the *Carmania*, which was also in port, were directed to assist the *QE2*, as most of her crew had been on duty all through the night.

French Line officials boarded soon after arrival to arrange for the care and transportation of all those who desired it. Eighty-five passengers elected to remain on the *Queen* for a portion of her Caribbean cruise. These included sixty-seven Venezuelans who found it more convenient to disembark at La Guaira, Venezuela, and thirteen Colombians and five Dutch who elected to stay on board until Curaçao, Netherlands Antilles. The passengers who boarded the *Suffren* were also brought to Barbados. Captain Raymond Kerverde, the master of the *Antilles* and the last man to leave the burning liner, and the forty-eight other seamen on the little island of Bequia were picked up by another French ship, *Pointe Allegre*. To this day the burned-out hulk remains on the reef off Mustique.

Congratulatory messages soon began to flood into the radio room of the *Queen Elizabeth 2*. Michael Noble, British minister for trade, on an official visit to Venezuela, sent the following to Commodore Warwick:

> I have much pleasure in sending you and all your officers, staff, crew and passengers hearty congratulations on your magnificent achievement in coming to the rescue of the passengers and crew of the S.S. *Antilles*. This was in the best traditions of British seamanship. I am glad that my presence in Venezuela makes it possible for me to send you these congratulations direct.

> The U.S. Coast Guard radioed from San Juan: "Your cooperation in rendering assistance to the S.S. *Antilles* on 08 January 1971 is greatly appreciated and demonstrates the continuing high standards of the Merchant Marine in keeping with the best traditions of the sea. Thank you."

> Sir Basil Smallpeice radioed from London: Have received following message from President of the French Line; I want to thank you for the assistance which has been afforded to us by Cunard in the accident which struck our liner *Antilles*. Please convey to Captain of the *QE2* our deep appreciation for taking on board passengers which our crew had evacuated and put on Mustique Island.

When the *Queen Elizabeth 2* arrived at La Guaira, the president of Venezuela personally tendered his congratulations and thanks to the master and crew for their part in the rescue.

The remainder of the 1970–71 winter Caribbean cruise was relatively uneventful. But on March 15 the *QE2* was called on another mercy mission, en route from New York to Aruba, to aid a seaman who had fallen from the mast of the Norwegian vessel *Besna*. A launch was sent across from the *QE2* to pick up the seaman, and he recovered from his injuries.

The highlight of the early spring 1971 season was the maiden arrival of the *Queen Elizabeth 2* at Bermuda on March 26, 1971. Maiden arrivals always generate enthusiasm, but Bermuda has a special place in the hearts of many North Americans, and the Bermudians reciprocate these warm emotions as far as cruise ships and American and Canadian tourists are concerned. The *QE2* was too large to dock at Hamilton and had to anchor in the Great Sound.

Unfortunately, the financial situation of the Cunard Line deteriorated substantially during 1970 as a result of soaring costs. In Britain the president of the chamber of shipping noted increases at a pace far greater than for a generation or more. In Cunard's case, prices of fuel oil for ships increased by between 80 and 100 percent within one year, and other costs, such as seafarers' salaries and wages, port charges, baggage, and cargo handling, increased between 17 and 41 percent in a similar period. A total loss of £1.9 million was declared, which also included Cunard's associated companies.

The presence of an economic recession in the United States and a strong U.S. government publicity campaign aimed at encouraging Americans to stay at home had not helped Cunard revenues. However, the outlook for the *QE2* in 1971 appeared more promising, with cruise bookings running at around 1,300 per cruise in comparison with around 1,150 the year before. This was an increase of 13 percent and meant that the *Queen* would operate above the breakeven level for 1971.

CHAPTER FOUR

TRAFALGAR HOUSE, CUNARD, AND THE *QE2*

The summer of 1971 saw a fundamental change in the ownership of the Cunard Steam-Ship Company, Limited. Cunard, after an independent existence of one hundred and thirty-one years, was the object of a successful takeover bid by the British company, Trafalgar House Investments, Ltd. For some weeks Cunard shares had been rising on the London Stock Exchange, a clear indication of a takeover bid when a company has not announced any great profits or new endeavors to warrant optimism. News articles involved a number of potential suitors during the month of June, and Cunard was forced to acknowledge that negotiations were under way with an undisclosed party.

Trafalgar House was interested in the Cunard Line because it complemented their hotel and leisure interests. The acquisition also offered substantial tax advantages. Trafalgar House had a 10% holding in Cunard, which was the then-maximum allowed before the public disclosure of interest was required. They also knew that another company, Slater, Walker Securities, held 11.6 percent, so they arranged for brokers to obtain those shares on their behalf. On June 30, 1971, Nigel Broackes, the chairman of Trafalgar House, informed Sir Basil Smallpeice that they now had a holding of over 21 percent in Cunard and that they were going to make a bid for the shipping line.

The initial £24 million offer made by Trafalgar was met with resistance by Cunard and some of the shareholders, but this was overcome when the value of the company was increased to £27.3 million.

In a message to Cunard Line employees, the chairman stated that the Trafalgar House bid had been accepted because "Cunard Line have now received all the assurances they requested from Trafalgar about Cunard's future

The Queen *glides through the calm waters of the majestic Geiranger Fjord in Norway on her celebrated North Cape cruise.*

role in the British shipping industry." In addition, it was stated: "Trafalgar House have given assurances that if their bid is successful Cunard will remain as a shipping company within the Trafalgar Group and will continue as a major force in the British shipping industry and also that *QE2* will continue to operate under the British flag." Sir Basil Smallpeice closed by asking "all Cunard staff afloat and ashore to continue unabated their efforts to ensure the company's future prosperity and their own place within it wherever the future ownership of the company's shares may lie."

On August 26, 1971, Victor Matthews of Trafalgar House Investments, Ltd., took over as the chairman of the Cunard Steamship Company, Ltd.

The *Queen Elizabeth 2* was acknowledged by the new owners as a potential money-maker, and the orders that Cunard had placed for new tonnage were praised, even if some of the existing assets of the company did not appear so financially attractive—notably the *Carmania* and *Franconia*, both of which Cunard had been trying to sell. The new management of Cunard announced the withdrawal from service of the two ships in October 1971 and their subsequent lay-up awaiting sale.

During the summer season of 1971, The *Queen Elizabeth 2* continued to carry the rich and famous across the Atlantic. Mr. and Mrs. Blake Edwards and Mr. and Mrs. Michael S. Laughlin crossed in July, Mrs. Edwards being better known as Julie Andrews and Mrs. Laughlin as Leslie Caron–both famous

The transportation of passengers' cars can be a major draw-ing card for the Queen, *since she can accommodate around forty vehicles. Depending upon the facilities available and the nature of the tide, cars can be driven on through one of the nine shell doors in the sides of the ship, or lifted on by derrick and lowered through the hatch.*

members of the theatrical world. The holds of the *Queen* accommodate auto-mobiles and frequently have been occupied by vintage machines, stately lim-ousines, and racing cars. Robin Ormes, the motor-racing ace, shipped his Lola to participate in the Watkins Glen Six-Hour International Sports Car Race on July 24, 1971. The Lola previously had been owned by Roger Penske who had won the 1969 Daytona 24-Hour Race.

During passage from Cóbh to New York the *QE2* received a request for medical assistance from the ocean weather ship *Charlie*. The call was received at 1959 hours on September 12, and the liner altered course to reach the ren-dezvous at 2030 hours. At 0027 hours in pitch darkness the *Queen* hove to, and the United States Coast Guard cutter *Chase* transferred the seaman to the liner. Eighteen minutes later she proceeded on her way to New York.

The maiden arrival of the *Queen Elizabeth 2* in Boston caused quite a stir as the *Queen* stopped en route from New York to Le Havre on October 1, 1971, for the purpose of embarking approximately 300 members of the Honorable Artillery Company of Massachusetts. That organization was the first military company chartered in the Western Hemisphere when it was created in 1638 and has been in continuous existence ever since. In 1971 they decided to cross the ocean on the *Queen Elizabeth 2* to have their 334th Field Day Tour of Duty

The Souls Sheet provides the fundamental breakdown of passengers, officers, and crew for any voyage. The enormous carrying capacity of the Queen Elizabeth 2 *is dramatically underlined with the simple figures: passengers, 1,653; officers, 86; crew, 830; total souls = 2,569. Furthermore, while Voyage No. 93 (west) in August 1972 was well booked, she could, if necessary, accommodate nearly 400 additional passengers and almost another 100 crew.*

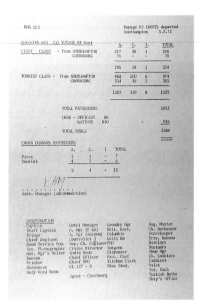

in England. The huge liner was suitably dressed for the occasion with all flags flying as an armada of small craft greeted her. Cunard's association with the port of Boston goes back to the very inception of the transatlantic service in 1840. There has always been a warm and close regard between the people of New England and the line. Everything went off without a hitch in spite of a dock strike, although Cunard shore personnel had to help with the loading of the luggage. The official welcoming ceremonies included the presentation of a Cunard flag to the city of Boston. The Ancient Honorable Artillery Company in full dress marched from Faneuil Hall, the upper floor of which has been the AHAC armory since 1746, to Commonwealth Pier where they were welcomed on board the *Queen*. Cunard had made arrangements for a flag of the Honorable Artillery Company to be broken out at the masthead upon their reception on board the *QE2*.

R. B. Patton, president of Cunard (North America), fitted his comments to the jocular nature of the occasion when he said "I also want to thank Commodore Warwick for his hospitality this morning. At this hour, the British often enjoy a different sort of beverage, but ever since another party on board a British ship got a little out of hand, we've made it a rule to put the tea under guard while in Boston Harbor. But this is truly an occasion that calls for champagne—to describe it in appropriate terms, the greatest ship in the world has come to the hub of the universe." Patton concluded: "To the Ancient and Honorable Artillery Company, welcome aboard and bon voyage; you honor us by choosing our ship. We're proud and happy to have such a distinguished send-off on our first sailing."

When the *Queen* docked at Southampton on October 6th the AHAC was

A Major transformation of the external appearance of the Queen *occurred in 1972 with the addition of ten penthouse suites on the sports deck slightly behind the mast. The prefabricated suites were lifted on board at Southampton during the annual refit at Vosper Thorncroft in the fall.*

The addition of the penthouse suites gave the QE2 *additional superlative accommodations, which are very popular. The preparations on the ship and the prefabrication of the units at Vosper Thornycroft had to be to a very high level of exactness for the pieces to fit.*

met by a Royal Marine Band and Regimental Colonel Brian Davis of the Honourable Artillery Company of London, the oldest British regiment, some of whose members in the seventeenth century had emigrated to New England and provided the nucleus of the AHAC. A highlight of the visit of the AHAC to the mother country was a meeting with Her Majesty Queen Elizabeth II and Prince Philip at Buckingham Palace where a silver tea set was presented to the queen and a silver plate to the Duke of Edinburgh.

In the first six months of their ownership, Trafalgar House undertook a complete survey of the *Queen Elizabeth 2* and the services she could provide. It was decided that £1 million would be spent on improvements to the ship. These included modifications to the restaurants and the construction and installation of the luxury penthouse suites on Signal and Sports Decks.

The 1972 season on the North Atlantic was made interesting by at least one violent storm and the presence of an enormous amount of ice in the steamer lanes. Captain Mortimer Hehir commanded the *Queen* on a memorable crossing from April 16–23, 1972, when a violent storm raged across the North Atlantic for 1,500 miles with 50-foot seas and 100-mile-an-hour winds. The horrendous conditions continued for four days. At times when one looked around there was nothing to be seen but spume and spray in all directions. The actors Robert Wagner and Natalie Wood were passengers and described the storm on the *Queen* as "a great experience—it was very exciting." On arrival at Southampton certificates were passed out to the 1,000 passengers who had "survived" the worst storm in memory, champagne was made available to all, and there were flowers for the ladies.

Certainly one of the most bizarre crossings that the *Queen Elizabeth 2* ever experienced began when the liner sailed from New York shortly after 2000 hours on Monday, May 15, 1972. The *Queen* was carrying 421 passengers in first class, 1,108 in tourist, and 907 crew members, with Captain William J. Law in command. In mid-Atlantic on Wednesday evening, May 17, the captain received a coded message from Mr. Charles Dickson of the New York office of the Cunard Line to the effect that there was a threat of some form of bomb explosion on board the 65,000-ton liner. The threat had been made known to Cunard in New York, and it was confirmed from London that there might be two accomplices traveling on the ship. Captain Law initiated every possible security arrangement in cooperation with his senior officers, and a discreet search was carried out. Nothing was found, however.

The Ministry of Defence in London was alerted and plans coordinated to enable bomb-disposal experts to board the *QE2* in mid-Atlantic. Captain Law made the following announcement to passengers at 1600 hours on Thursday 18 May 1972:

> Ladies and Gentlemen, we have received information concerning a threat of a bomb explosion on board this ship some time during this voyage. We have received such threats in the past which have so far always turned out to be hoaxes. However, we always take them seriously and take every possible precaution
>
> On this occasion we are being assisted by the British government who are sending out bomb disposal experts who will be parachuted into the sea and picked up by boat and brought on board.
>
> I will of course keep you fully informed about the situation. Cunard are taking every precaution ashore and on board and will take any necessary action to minimize risk. If there is any question of it being necessary to pay over money this will be done ashore in New York.
>
> I can only ask you to remain calm. On these occasions lots of rumors tend to circulate. Please only take notice of any information that comes from me direct or from one of my officers. That is all for the moment.

At 1636 hours the *Queen* began to reduce speed prior to rendezvousing with an R.A.F. Nimrod (jet reconnaissance aircraft) from St. Mawgan's in Cornwall in a position 740 miles due east of Cape Race, Newfoundland. The Nimrod was in sight at 1706 hours, positioning was verified, communication assured, and the *QE2* slowed to a stop at 1734 hours in a position 45.8 degrees north and 35.1 degrees west. A little less than half an hour later at 1808 hours an R.A.F. Hercules was sighted carrying the four members of the bomb-disposal team. Crews for two of the *QE2*'s launches were standing by when the Hercules was sighted, and one was immediately lowered with First Officer Robin Woodall in charge and accompanied by Second Officer Warwick. As the *QE2* and the launch headed into the wind, the pilot of the Hercules made a few preliminary runs to decide on the best approach. In addition to the weather being dull and miserable, the situation was further complicated by the fact that the height of cloud base was approximately 400 feet above sea level which was too low for a safe parachute jump to be made. It was therefore necessary for the pilot to bring his plane in below the cloud level, sight the launch, and then climb quickly up through the clouds to about 800 feet. A few seconds later, although it seemed like eternity, the first two parachutes drifted down out of the clouds. Two such runs were made, releasing two parachutists at a time and dropping them with great precision near the *QE2*'s launch. The *Queen*'s experienced boat crew had all four parachutists in the launch within 5 minutes of their landing in the water. The bomb disposal experts wore frogman suits and carried a considerable amount of equipment and, as a special consideration, a London newspaper for the captain. Most of the *Queen Elizabeth 2*'s passengers were on deck to view the splashdowns and cheer the successful proceedings. It would have been difficult not to have been thrilled by the operation and the courage of the individuals concerned. The Hercules turned back eastward to her base in England some 1,380 miles away, but the Nimrod stayed around until the *QE2*'s launch was safely aboard the liner. She then bade the *Queen* farewell and returned to Cornwall. The *Queen Elizabeth 2* was under way again at 1924 hours.

As the entertainment for the evening commenced, the bomb-disposal experts began a systematic search of the ship from stem to stern. Those courageous gentlemen were Captain Robert Williams (twenty-nine) and Sergeant Clifford Oliver (thirty-two) of the Royal Ordnance Corps and Lieutenant Richard Clifford (twenty-six) and Corporal Thomas Jones (twenty-eight) of the Royal Marine amphibious training unit at Poole. No explosive devices of any nature were ever discovered, and the *QE2* safely arrived at Cherbourg and Southampton with her passengers and crew.

In New York the scene had been one of considerable tension for Charles Dickson, Cunard's vice president who had received the anonymous telephone call about the supposed bombs and ransom demand. The caller appeared to know what he was talking about and commented that, although the gang had considered asking for $1 million, they had settled on a ransom of $350,000 in exchange for not blowing the ship up. The caller refused to say when he

Comparisons of the Queen Elizabeth 2 *with other vessels are difficult to envision, but in this scene of the old and the new, the Portuguese tall ship* Sagres *is shown passing the* Queen.

would call back, so the Cunard office telephones were manned day and night. In London, the chairman of the Cunard Line, Victor Matthews, was alerted in the middle of the night and agreed to the ransom payment which was assembled in New York and placed in a briefcase for delivery when so ordered. Charles Dickson was given a runaround by the anonymous caller, but no one ever appeared to collect the money.

The American police and the Federal Bureau of Investigation worked night and day on the case, although remaining in the background until the *QE2* safely reached Europe. Ultimately a man from New York was arrested and charged with extortion. He was tried in Manhattan Federal Court, found guilty, and given the maximum possible sentence of twenty years. Sentencing him, the judge said: "Your actions were reprehensible and unforgivable. You took deliberate advantage of a reign of terror for very substantial gain."

An unfortunate result of the bomb threat with all its ramifications was that Cunard decided no longer to permit unrestricted access to the liner for the general public or for individuals seeing passengers off. Accordingly, the long-standing tradition of the on-board bon-voyage party was canceled and future passengers would have to bid their fond farewells on the pier.

During the spring of 1972 reports were received from the United States

The Gare Maritime at Cherbourg plays host to the Queen Elizabeth 2 *on a number of occasions each year. Originally built to accommodate the* Queen Mary *and* Queen Elizabeth, *the French terminal is the only remaining one the* QE2 *uses regularly that served the older* Queens. *The giant passageways descend to meet the appropriate doors on the side of the liner.*

and Canadian meteorological offices that there was a large area of ice south of Newfoundland. The ice, drifting from the Labrador Basin, had not traveled so far south for over thirty years. Because of the warnings, the *QE2* had to take a course 100 miles to the south of her usual route.

On passage from Cherbourg to New York during the small hours of the 21st of August, 1972, the *Queen Elizabeth 2* reduced speed to rendezvous with the U.S. Coast Guard cutter *Hamilton*, which was being used as an ocean weather observing station known as *Delta*. One of her seamen, W. D. Emmett, received word that a member of his family was critically ill, and an inquiry had been made if there was any possibility of assistance from the *Queen Elizabeth 2*. On this occasion a launch was sent over from the other ship, and within eight minutes of her being alongside the *QE2* had ordered full speed ahead for her destination.

Toward the end of 1972, prosperity in the shipping division was underlined when Trafalgar House announced plans to build another cruise liner. During the naming ceremony of the *Cunard Ambassador* at Rotterdam on October 21, 1972, Victor Matthews said that the hull and engines of the new liner would be built by Burmeister Wein of Copenhagen and the fitting out would be accomplished in Italy by INMA of La Spezia because three British yards had declined to bid for the contract. The order for a sister ship was placed in January 1973. The two ships entered service as the *Cunard Countess* and the *Cunard Princess*.

Among the more interesting and exciting experiences that the *Queen Elizabeth 2* faced in 1973 were two "Silver Anniversary Cruises to Israel" under the auspices of Assured Travel Services, Inc., of Massachusetts, designed to cover

Summer storm clouds gather over Southampton, England, just before the departure of the Queen Elizabeth 2 *in 1972 from the old Ocean Terminal.. The starboard wing of the bridge with the bow thruster controls can be seen.*

the Passover/Easter (April 14–28, 1973) holiday and the twenty-fifth anniversary celebrations for Israel (April 28–May 13, 1973). They attracted a considerable amount of publicity because it was thought by many that the ship was vulnerable to an attack by Arab terrorists. As a result of these fears, and in consultation with the British Ministry of Defence, very strict security measures where taken throughout the cruise.

When the *Queen Elizabeth 2* arrived at Southampton from her Caribbean cruise on April 12, 1973, the Southampton Ocean Terminal was sealed off from the public and armed guards went aboard. Meanwhile Royal Navy skin divers kept vigil over the underwater hull of the *Queen* as she took on stores and awaited her passengers.

The *QE2* sailed from Southampton with only about 600 passengers, less than a third of her capacity, and returned from Israel on the second cruise with approximately the same number. Certainly adverse publicity and heightened security concern took its toll on the bookings. For those who did make the cruise to Israel, or back, there was a fabulous opportunity to enjoy the ship and be pampered with a crew-to-passenger ratio of two to one.

Special arrangements were made to provide a complete kosher service for the large percentage of Jewish passengers. The entire Columbia kitchen and restaurant were made kosher for the cruise conforming with the highest standards of kashruth.

First stop on the cruise itinerary of the *Queen Elizabeth 2* was a call at Lisbon, Portugal, on April 17, 1973. Portuguese authorities were very concerned about security and even went so far as to halt all traffic on the giant suspension bridge spanning the Tagus River while the *Queen* passed beneath the soaring span at precisely 0630 hours. The Lisbon passenger terminal was closed to all visitors and passengers were searched before being permitted to rejoin the ship if they went ashore. After leaving Lisbon the *Queen* set a course for Israel. The ship was under orders to complete the final day's voyage to Israel at her maxi-

A scene of awesome power and majesty: the Queen Elizabeth 2 *slices through North Atlantic swells during a crossing in August 1972. The penthouses have not been added yet, although work on them is underway; hence the* Queen *looks much as her original designers intended—sleek, modern, and powerful.*

mum speed and to extinguish all unnecessary external lights. Her arrival on April 21 marked the inaugural visit of the *QE2* to Israel and a unique occasion for the town of Ashdod–the first-ever visit of a passenger liner to the port. Ashdod is a convenient departure point for land tours to Jerusalem only forty-four miles away and other points of interest. The liner stayed at Ashdod for four days and then proceeded to Haifa for a similar period.

On April 29, the passengers from the Easter/Passover Cruise flew home and those who had booked for the Silver Independence Day Cruise joined the ship for a reversal of the itinerary until the *QE2* sailed from Ashdod on the 8th of May for the return voyage to Southampton via Palma de Mallorca. The liner returned safely to Britain on May 13, 1973, without incident.

Over a year later, on July 16, 1974, President Anwar Sadat of Egypt revealed in a BBC television interview with Lord Chalfont, former minister of state at the Foreign and Commonwealth Office that he personally had countermanded an order given to an Egyptian submarine commander by an Arab leader to torpedo the *Queen Elizabeth 2* during her cruise to Israel. Subsequently a debate ensued as to whether or not the submarine, an ex–Russia Romeo type had the capability to catch the 28.5-knot *QE2*. It was generally regarded that the submarine, with a maximum surface speed of 19 knots, could not have intercepted the liner.

The future for the *Queen Elizabeth 2* certainly brightened with the announcement that the liner would sail on her first world cruise on January 4, 1975, a ninety-two-day odyssey through the Panama Canal and around the world. The total cruise from Southampton to Southampton would cover over 38,000 miles and take the *Queen* on an easterly course to more than twenty major ports around the globe. Norman Thompson, Cunard's managing director at the time, told the press: "We think *QE2* is the best ship afloat for this type of cruise"–a remark subsequently acknowledged by the fact that a long cruise has been made annually ever since.

The *QE2* returned to the North Atlantic for the 1973 season with high hopes for her most successful season ever. Americans were preparing to travel more as the recession lessened and business conditions improved.

This was Captain William Law's last season as master of the *Queen*. He relinquished his command on August 5, 1973, after thirty-six years of service with the Cunard Line. Captain Mortimer F. Hehir was appointed master of the *QE2* in his place. Captain Peter Jackson became staff captain and relieving master of the *Queen*.

An unusual voyage was made by the *Queen Elizabeth 2* in the summer of 1973 when the ship was chartered for a cruise to Come by Chance, Newfoundland, in honor of the opening of the new oil refinery on the shores of Placentia Bay. The liner docked at the pier of the Newfoundland Refining Company, which soon would be hosting supertankers transporting the products from the 100,000-barrel-a-day refinery. John M. Shaheen, chairman of NRC, said,

A major event on any world cruise is the arrival in Hong Kong. The point of origin for many land tours to the People's Republic of China, the Crown Colony of Hong Kong also is a picturesque tourist center and a fabulous marketplace all of its own.

"Chartering the *QE2* allowed us to give everybody a firsthand look at the year-round, deep-water, docking facilities available in Placentia Bay, which is one of the major reasons for locating the refinery at Come by Chance." The invited guests aboard the *Queen* included representatives from major oil, financial, shipping, engineering, and construction interests.

The winter of 1973 brought a three-day cruise from New York to chase the comet Kohoutek, expected to be one of the brightest comets of the twentieth century. The cruise was completely sold out when the *Queen* sailed from New York on December 9 on the "Comet Watch." Guest of honor on board the liner was the Czech-born astronomer Professor Lubos Kohoutek, who first identified the comet in March 1973 and predicted its brilliance. Dr. Isaac Asimov, the famous science-fiction writer, was also booked as part of the enrichment program for the cruise. Unfortunately, in this instance, the weather did not provide much respite from overcast conditions and rain that made chasing the comet futile. Later Caribbean cruises were blessed with clear air and balmy weather, however, which permitted passengers to see the comet.

Trafalgar House was determined to make the *Queen Elizabeth 2* pay in every way possible. 1974 saw the introduction of free transatlantic airline tickets for

Entering New York at the end of an Atlantic run, the bow of the Queen Elizabeth 2 *is highlighted by the early morning sun. She has just cleared the Verrazano Narrows Bridge, and seasoned travelers may just be stirring from their beds while those who have not experienced an arrival by sea in New York Harbor will have been up for some time to see the sights.*

passengers booking one way in the more expensive suites and cabins on the ship. In all, twenty-one transatlantic crossings were planned for 1974, and the schedule, whenever possible, was integrated with that of the *France* of the French Line because it was felt that there was no point in having the two great Atlantic liners on the same side of the ocean at once.

The biggest headache that the Cunard Line faced in the mid-1970s was the enormous increase in the cost of bunkering oil, which went up from $20 to $70 a ton. Some critics complained that the *Queen* represented a poor use of a scarce resource. In a letter to the *London Times*, this argument was forcefully met by Norman S. Thompson, managing director of Cunard, who noted that the fuel consumption of the *QE2* over a 3,060-mile transatlantic voyage at a speed of 28-1/2 knots was approximately 1.55 tons per individual when she was carrying 1,500 passengers, which was relatively efficient in comparison with comparable vessels.

One activity that could generate good publicity and profit for the *QE2* was a "short-term" charter. When the Election Campaign Committee for New York Mayor Abraham Beame was casting around for a means of reducing the debt for the mayoralty campaign, they decided to hold a birthday party for His Honor on the *Queen* on the evening of March 21, 1974. Tickets for the novel "cruise" sold at $250 a head to 1,000 of Mayor and Mrs. Beame's closest friends. To make the whole thing more realistic, guests where given regular cruise tickets and "embarked" as though they were about to sail. Thus the ship became the scene of a very lively party and a spectacular salute to one of New York City's leaders.

The *Queen Elizabeth 2* appeared to be sailing toward a £2,000,000 profit for the 1973–74 fiscal year when she encountered misfortune. She was steaming some 200 miles off Bermuda around 0400 hours on April 1, 1974, when the alarm on an electronic probe designed to detect the presence of oil or other contaminants in the absolutely pure water of her boilers failed. The boilers consist of an arrangement of hundreds of pipes through which the water passes. A film of oil spread through some of these, and the furnace, instead of heating the water inside the tubes, heated the tubes themselves and damaged them. As a result, the propulsion system was shut down immediately before any further damage occurred. The ship's engineers worked hard to rectify the fault, but because there was a chance that this would not be done in a reasonable time, Cunard decided to leave nothing to chance and commenced making contingency plans. The president of Flagship Cruises in Oslo, Norway, was contacted and arrangements were made for the *Sea Venture*, which was on a three-day visit to Bermuda, to render assistance.

Captain Torbjorn Hauge, master of the *Sea Venture*, sailed his ship almost immediately for the *QE2*'s last position, leaving nearly four hundred of his own cruise passengers ashore. Two hundred and two passengers elected to stay with the officers and crew of the *Sea Venture* to experience the adventure and assist if possible. The Bermuda authorities assisted by providing hotel accommodations for the other Flagship Cruise passengers left behind until the *Sea Venture* returned. Meanwhile Cunard chartered aircraft to meet the *QE2*'s passengers in Bermuda and fly them back to the United States.

At sea the *QE2*'s passengers danced all night under the stars and regarded the whole experience as an adventure. Throughout their stay on board they were kept fully informed at regular intervals by the master, Captain Peter Jackson, over the public-address system operated from the bridge. By so doing, the captain undoubtedly contributed much to the well-being and peace of mind of the passengers and relieved them of any anxiety.

The *Sea Venture* reached the *Queen* at 0330 hours on April 3, and the plans for the transfer of the *QE2*'s passengers using the Norwegian ship's launches were formalized. The *Sea Venture* maneuvered as close as possible to the *Queen* and the two ships between them provided a calm stretch of water for the transfer of the 1,654 passengers.

A thousand life jackets and twenty inflatable rubber rafts were sent over to the *Sea Venture* because, with all the passengers from the *QE2* on board, the Norwegian liner would be way over her normal complement. Disembarkation took place from two gangways on Five Deck. The first launch departed with passengers at 0805, and by 1539 they had all left the ship. The discharge of baggage followed, and by 1745 the whole operation was concluded and the *Sea Venture* set her course for Hamilton.

The launches of the QE2 *do yeoman's duty carrying passengers back and forth from the ship in ports where she cannot berth. Designated units also serve as rescue vessels when called upon, while all, collectively, ensure the safety of the* Queen*'s passengers and crew.*

The towering side of the Queen Elizabeth 2 *stretches to the heavens in the view of passengers departing from the* Queen *by launch.*

The crew of the *Sea Venture* found accommodations for 700 in cabins, and the remainder were provided with blankets and deck chairs or portable beds in the public rooms.

An all-night buffet and free bar service was provided on the *Sea Venture* throughout the overnight trip. Additional doctors and nurses sailed with the

Sea Venture, but their services happily were not needed. Most of the passengers who were taken off the *QE2* gave her officers and crew high marks and were delighted with the services and total refund of their fares made by Cunard. The incident certainly ranks as one of the most difficult experiences that the *Queen* has ever faced, but the prompt, efficient manner in which all aspects of the problem were handled redounded very substantially to the goodwill of the line. Most passengers said that they hoped to travel again with Cunard in the near future.

Preliminary repairs were carried out at Bermuda, and then the *QE2* returned to New York where they were completed.

Captain Jackson and the officers and Crew of the *Queen Elizabeth 2* received a special radiogram from Victor Matthews, Managing Director of the Cunard Line:

> The following motion has been tabled in the House of Commons today by Mr. Robert Taylor conservative member of Parliament for North West Croydon which speaks for itself. That this House congratulates the management of Cunard for the exemplary manner in which it discharged every possible legal and moral obligation to the passengers of the *QE2* during the recent voyage and considers that in so doing it has maintained the highest reputation of British commerce.

Mr. Matthews commented that it was understood to be quite rare for a commercial organization to be so recognized in the House. He stated: "As your Chairman I would like to thank each and every one of you who have played a part in bringing this about. The strength of a team can only be judged in adverse conditions and I would particularly like to congratulate the Captain, officers and crew for their magnificent performance."

The *Queen* sailed on schedule from New York Tuesday, April 16, 1974 on her first transatlantic crossing for the season. On the way across Cunard and Dunhill sponsored the world's first backgammon tournament played aboard a liner. Players included Earl Lichfield, Liberal M.P. Clement Freud, and comedian Spike Milligan. The tournament was won by a Charles Benson, who collected £10,000 in prize money.

On April 25, 1974, the *QE2* sailed on a twelve-day cruise with 1,540 passengers to the Mediterranean. When she departed, she was given a farewell salute by the British army helicopter display team, the Blue Eagles.

At Cannes a rare event occurred when the *Queen Elizabeth 2* and the *France* anchored near each other for a day, and onlookers from shore could observe the two largest ocean liners in the world. It had already been announced by the French government that the giant *France* was to be withdrawn at the end of the 1974 season as an economy measure because the liner's deficit of $12 million a year had ballooned with the inflation in fuel prices. Accordingly Cunard announced that the *QE2* would increase the number of North Atlantic crossings to thirty-one for the 1975 season in a partial attempt to fill the gap and to benefit from being the only remaining transatlantic superliner.

On rare occasions, a New York Harbor pilot may get a longer ride than he bargained for when he takes a vessel to sea. Normally the pilot is dropped near the Ambrose Light, but on August 25, 1974, Captain John Cahill found himself a guest of the Cunard Line for an Atlantic crossing when the pilot cutter was engaged in a rescue mission and could not take him off. Accordingly, because steamship lines traditionally treat their pilots very well, indeed, he enjoyed a five-day ocean crossing to Southampton and a free trip back by air with all the trimmings.

Later on September 25, 1974, while on passage from Naples to Barcelona, the eternal watchfulness of the Cunard officers on the bridge paid off handsomely for some distressed seafarers. The *Queen Elizabeth 2* was steaming through gale-force winds and a rough Mediterranean Sea, when at 0215 hours red distress flares were sighted to the north. The *Queen* immediately answered so peremptory a summons of the sea and altered course through the heavy seas and the darkness to investigate. Fifteen minutes later, at 0230 hours, a small yacht in severe difficulty was sighted. The individuals on the yacht were incapable of doing anything, so the 963-foot *QE2* had to maneuver on her two engines in the gale conditions. Six male survivors of the yacht *Stephanie* of Toulon were rescued by 0345 hours and the *Queen* resumed passage to Barcelona. The fickleness of the sea takes some and leaves others to be rescued by a vessel beyond their wildest dreams.

CHAPTER FIVE

CRUISING THE WORLD

When the *Queen* sailed from Southampton on January 4, 1975, she set out on her maiden world cruise. She left England with 342 world cruise passengers, picked up another 570 in New York, and additional ones in Port Everglades, Florida. At various ports around the world other passengers joined or left the ship. One of the highlights of the world cruise was for 600 passengers to make a historic three-day excursion from Hong Kong into the People's Republic of China. Everywhere she went, the *Queen* was given a royal reception — from Cape Town to Singapore, Hong Kong to Kobe, Honolulu to Acapulco.

During the Pacific crossing a Country Fair was held on board to raise funds for charitable causes. The event is similar to those held each year during the summer months in towns and villages throughout England. The activities, to name a few, included raffles, tombola, a tug-of-war contest, fortune-telling, a human fruit machine, and an auction for the navigator's world-cruise chart. The fair has become an annual tradition on the *QE2*, and over the years hundreds of thousands of dollars have been raised by passengers and crew.

The last leg of the world cruise, Los Angeles to New York via the Panama Canal, had a waiting list of over 300 people. When the *Queen* made her first transit of the canal in March 1975, she became the largest passenger ship in the world to do so — surpassing the record held by the German liner *Bremen* (51,731 tons) in 1936.

The six locks that comprise the mechanical portions of the Panama Canal are 110 feet wide by 1,000 feet long. The *Queen Elizabeth 2* is just over 105 feet wide and 963 feet long. As the *Queen* leaves the Pacific and steams past Balboa toward the Miraflores locks, the impression is that she will never succeed in

The island of Tristan de Cunha issued one of the largest stamps in the world to honor the arrival of the Queen Elizabeth 2 *in one of the stops on a world cruise. Native vessels and the symbol of the Cunard Line, a gold lion rampant against a crimson background encircled by a golden rope, complete the design of the stamp.*

"threading the needle." Slowly but surely, the huge liner edges into the first of the three locks that will lift the ship 85 feet above the Caribbean to the level of Gatun Lake. Once locked in with a clearance of less than 30 inches on each side. 26,000,000 gallons of water will begin to flow from Gatun Lake by gravity into the lock. A short passage through the Miraflores Lake takes the *QE2* to the Pedro Miguel locks, which raise the liner in another two steps to Gatun Lake, which spans the continent.

Several hours' steaming is necessary to cross the 30-mile-wide Gatun Lake and pass through the picturesque Gaillard Cut, where the canal was excavated through the mountains of the Continental Divide. A monument marks the Continental Divide and is a memorial to those who lost their lives building the waterway. Once on the eastern side, the *Queen Elizabeth 2* enters the first of three locks that lower the ship to the level of the Atlantic Ocean.

The transit time of the Panama Canal ranges from six and half to ten hours, depending on the number and tonnage of ships scheduled. For passenger liners like the *QE2*, who want to cross during daylight, and other vessels whose schedules are critical, an advanced reservation system is available at extra cost guaranteeing a fixed time and date for crossing the continent. The transit fees for the Panama Canal are based upon the tonnage of the vessel as calculated by the Canal Authority. When the *Queen Elizabeth 2* crossed the isthmus for the first time, she set the record for paying the highest toll. Today the transit cost for the *QE2* are over $100,000.

By the time *QE2* returned to England on April 6, 1975, over 3,965 people had been on board at some stage of the cruise, and she had steamed 39,470 miles in ninety-two days to twenty-four ports in nineteen countries across four continents.

All voyages on the *QE2* can be tailored to suit individual preferences and time parameters. Today's marketing, aided by the speed of jet aircraft, makes it possible for passengers to experience the whole of a world cruise, or to enjoy sections of the cruise with air service to and from the *Queen* wherever she may be.

Traditionally, the year-long schedule of the *Queen Elizabeth 2* begins with the first Atlantic crossing of the regular season around the middle of April. Some individuals who do not like to fly will, in fact, have arranged their departure from Europe or the United States to coincide with this event. By planning a schedule of approximately twenty-five to thirty Atlantic crossings each season, the *Queen* succeeds in maintaining her position on the North Atlantic as the last of the great ocean liners and heiress to a tradition of service spanning more than a hundred and fifty years.

The provisioning of the *Queen Elizabeth 2* for crossings and cruising will involve loading a variety of items at the main ports of Southampton and New York. Computerized systems accurately monitor the stock levels of stores and the daily consumption. Provisioning is arranged many months in advance to ensure that the best quality is obtained in the quantities required. The following list gives the average consumption of food for one week with 1,700 passengers on board:

Baby food   135 jars
Bacon   2,625 lbs.
Beef   7,720 lbs.
Beer   4,780 cans, 18 brands
Biscuits   210 lbs.
Brandy   130 bottles, 12 brands
Butter   2,455 lbs.
Caviar   55 lbs.
Champagne   1,160 bottles
Cheese   1,275 lbs.
Chicken   2,750 lbs.
Coffee   600 lbs.
Cream   210 gals.
Duck   1,300 lbs.
Eggs   2,342 doz.
Flour   410 lbs.
Foie gras   19 lbs.
Fresh fish   2,010 lbs.
Fresh vegetables   16,410 lbs.
Fresh fruit   7,000 lbs.
Frozen fish   995 lbs.
Game hens   410
Gin   155 bottles   4 brands
Haggis   30 lbs.
Ham   795 lbs.

Ice cream   865 gals.
Jam   525 lbs.
Kippers   200 lbs.
Lamb   1,005 lbs.
Liqueurs   90 bottles, 26 types
Lobster   1,950 lbs.
Milk   1,600 gals.
Pork   1,100 lbs.
Port   15 bottles, 11 brands
Potatoes   6,700 lbs.
Prawns   595 lbs.
Rum   45 bottles, 5 brands
Sausages   1,840 lbs.
Sherry   55 bottles, 6 brands
Smoked Salmon   485 lbs.
Sodas   5,320 cans, 12 types
Suckling Pig   60 lbs.
Sugar   1,965 lbs.
Tea   26,500 bags
Turkey   990 lbs.
Venison   250 lbs.
Vodka   170 bottles, 5 brands
Whiskey   255 bottles, 35 brands
Wine   2,200 bottles, 203 labels

The size of the QE2 makes any transit of the canal an adventure; the maximum clearance is only 30 inches per side. The liner is 963 feet in length and the locks are 1,100 feet.

The QE2 pays the highest toll of any vessel using the Panama Canal on the basis of her size and the nature of her "cargo" as a passenger ship. In the case of the Queen the fees exceed $90,000 per transit, but this is still a bargain compared to the cost of steaming 11,000 miles around South America. (Photo courtesy of David Barnicote.)

There are only inches to spare as the Queen slips into a lock. The electrically powered cog-railroad "mules" pull the huge liner through the locks in tandem.

Twenty-six million gallons of fresh water from Gatun Lake supply the power through gravity flow to move the Queen *through the locks. No pumps are necessary.*

As the lock gates open, the Queen *prepares to continue her voyage.*

The three Gatun locks on the Atlantic side are all together and are not divided like the Pacific trio. In any crossing from the Atlantic to the Pacific passengers marvel at the wonders of the Panama Canal locks.

The QE2 steams through the Gaillard Cut 85 feet above sea level and over the Continental Divide. Over 25,000 men lost their lives building the Panama Railroad (1849–55) and then digging the Panama Canal (French effort, 1878–88, and American effort, 1903–14). (Photo courtesy of David Barnicote.)

Between North Atlantic crossings short cruises are sometimes made from Southampton to Spain, Portugal, and the Atlantic Islands. On the west side of the ocean cruises are usually made from New York to Canada and Nova Scotia and to Bermuda or the nearer Caribbean ports. Periodically the *Queen* will make a three-day cruise to "nowhere" from either New York or Southampton.

A popular mid-summer sailing is the North Cape Cruise from Southampton to the "Land of the Midnight Sun" and the fjords of Norway. The North Cape Cruise nearly always features the natural magnificence of the Geiranger Fjord along with a visit to the land of the Lapps and reindeer and lasts between eight to twelve days. Because of the tremendously long and varied coastline of Norway, the *Queen* has visited thirteen different ports in that Scandinavian country since she was commissioned.

There is always a Caribbean cruise over the Christmas and New Year holidays. The ship is decorated from stem to stern for the season, and a traditional festive atmosphere enables the year-end celebrations to be carried out in a tropical setting.

The *Queen's* 1975 North Atlantic season proved relatively uneventful until June 20, when on passage from Cherbourg to New York she received a call at 2204 hours from the Russian trawler *Luga* (2,690 tons) asking for assistance for a sick seaman. Aleck Sungayala (twenty-seven) of Latvia who was ill with a suspected burst ulcer. The *QE2* altered course and steamed 128 miles to rendezvous with the Russian ship, which was sighted at 0210 hours. By 0258 hours the sick seaman was on board the *Queen*, and four minutes later she resumed her voyage to New York.

On December 4, 1975, while on passage between Antigua and Boston, the *Queen Elizabeth 2* completed her first million miles of steaming.

Farther away in the Caribbean, Mrs. Neil Armstrong, wife of the astronaut and first man to step on the moon, was making maritime history when she became the first American woman to christen a Cunard Line passenger vessel.

The QE2's launch speeds away from the pier at Charlotte Amalie, St. Thomas, Virgin Islands, with another load of passengers returning to the ship at the end of a full day.

Anchored off the Caribbean paradise of Martinique, the QE2 dwarfs local yachts.

Following the ceremony at San Juan on August 8, 1976, the *Cunard Countess* put to sea on the first of many weekly Caribbean cruises.

On March 1, 1977, the company sold the *Cunard Adventurer* to a Norwegian company, and she was reregistered as the *Southward II*. Soon afterward, on March 30, Her Serene Highness Princess Grace of Monaco christened the Cunard Line's latest cruise liner the *Cunard Princess* at a ceremony held in New York.

The schedule for 1977 involved the Jubilee World Cruise of ninety-two days, and a series of European and Caribbean cruises in the spring and fall interspliced with thirty Atlantic crossings. In London, Trafalgar House had bought the venerable Ritz Hotel and completely refurbished it to bring the great hotel institution up to the standards of excellence for which its founder had been famous. The LaToc Hotel in St. Lucia and the Paradise Beach Hotel in Barbados continued to prove to be among the outstanding values in that region, with very high ratings from critics evaluating the opportunities for vacations in the Caribbean.

The June 27, 1977, sailing from Southampton coincided with the dress rehearsal for the Jubilee Review of the Fleet by Her Majesty the Queen. Passengers and crew on the *Queen Elizabeth 2* made the most of it by packing the rails as the cruise staff, aided by Royal Navy briefings, provided a detailed running commentary of the naval vessels as the *QE2* steamed past. The loudspeakers on the *Queen* played "Land of Hope and Glory" and "Rule, Britannia," which provided many emotional moments for those watching the proceedings. There were 180 vessels in the review line and hundreds of pleasure craft all over the water. Two Royal Naval vessels, H.M.S. *Ark Royal* and H.M.S. *Huron*, at the end of the line, had to be pushed apart by tugs as they

America's only major contribution to the superstructure of the QE2 was made in 1977 when the Queen Mary and Queen Elizabeth Suites were fitted forward of the 1972 penthouses during an annual refit at the Bethelhem Steel Shipyard, Bayonne, New Jersey.

Her Serene Highness Princess Grace of Monaco christens the new cruise ship Cunard Princess *during a visit to New York, March 30, 1977. Earlier Mrs. Neil Armstrong, wife of the first man on the moon, christened the sister ship* Cunard Countess *at San Juan, Puerto Rico, August 8, 1976.*

were swinging to the tide in order to allow the *Queen* to pass through a 700-foot space between them. The *Queen Elizabeth 2* exchanged salutes with vessels all the way down the line in a most majestic departure from Southampton.

For economic reasons, it was decided that the 1977 annual refit would be carried out by the Bethlehem Steel Corporation in Bayonne, New Jersey. By having the refitting in the U.S.A. the ship was able to start the winter cruise season earlier without having to make late-winter crossings of the North Atlantic at a time of the year when they are not very well subscribed. Work included the renewal of one of the turbines. The turbine weighing 17 tons had to be flown out in a Lockhead Hercules aircraft from the makers: John Brown Engineering of Scotland. The dockyard also constructed and fitted the two most luxurious rooms on the ship known as the Queen Elizabeth and Queen Mary Suites.

One more rescue can be listed to the credit of the *Queen Elizabeth 2*—during the hours of daylight for a change. On passage from Cherbourg to New York on August 16, 1977, a message was received at 1000 hours from the French trawler *Drakker* of Dieppe saying that they required assistance for an injured seaman. The *Queen* altered course and rendezvoused with the *Drakker*. A launch was sent from the *QE2* to pick up the seaman, who was safely on board by 1120 hours. The French seaman, Claude Leleu, was admitted to the ship's hospital and treated for leg injuries from which he fully recovered.

The desire to produce a variety in the *Queen*'s schedule resulted in a decision for the liner to make a Great Pacific and Oriental Cruise in 1978 rather than another cruise around the world. The history-making 39,057-mile cruise saw visits to Australia, New Zealand, and the Philippines during which the *Queen Elizabeth 2* visited thirty-one ports, including twelve that she had never been to before.

Captain T. D. Ridley, R.D., R.N.R., was in command when the *Queen Elizabeth 2* experienced one of the worst storms of her career during a North Atlantic crossing in September 1978. The liner encountered a storm front lying across the shipping lanes that gave little choice for maneuvering. The winds built up to force 12 (the maximum on the Beaufort scale), and the waves were 50 feet high. Captain Ridley commented that it was one of the three worst storms he had experienced in thirty-five years at sea. At one point a wall of water hit the liner broadside on the bow and crumpled the iron railing, and colossal waves occasionally reached as high as the bridge. According to a *Newsweek* article of September 25, 1978, a woman had asked Captain Ridley if he had considered asking the Coast Guard for assistance during the worst of the storm. Ridley had replied, "Madame, first there was no need for help. And, secondly, if there had been a Coast Guard cutter in the area, the *Queen* would have had to help the Coast Guard."

The *Queen Elizabeth 2* reached her tenth birthday in 1979, and the 1979–80 period was celebrated appropriately as a milestone in her career. The 1979 world cruise with the theme "For once in your life, live!" went to twenty-four ports in fourteen countries. Especially historical was the inaugural call at Darien, the first time in recent history that a passenger liner from the Western World has ever docked in the People's Republic of China. During the call, the Joe Loss band played at a concert attended by more than 1,700 Chinese — again, the first band ever to do so. Another inaugural visit was the island of Tristian da Cunha in the South Atlantic. In honor of the ship's arrival, they produced the longest British Commonwealth stamp ever issued!

During her tenth anniversary year the *Queen* was also the subject of a National Geographic film about the great ocean liners, which received enormous coverage in the United States and was shown by poplar demand several times on American television. The film, entitled *The End of an Era*, resulted in a new awareness of a vanishing piece of maritime heritage and of the fact that the *Queen Elizabeth 2* was the last great transatlantic liner. During her first decade in service the *Queen* had steamed over one and a half million miles and carried the British flag to sixty-three nations around the world.

The *Queen* has more than her share of heroes. On October 24, 1979, she was in the harbor of Las Palmas when an elderly passenger fell into the water. Four *QE2* crew members who saw the accident showed no hesitation in jumping to the rescue. They were Cruise Director Brian Price; cruise staff members Eric Mason and George Schofiled; and Deputy Chief Engineer Stanley Child. The four men dove between the ship and quayside in very deep water; and although they dragged the passenger to shore, he died approximately a month later without having left the hospital. Captain Douglas Ridley congratulated the men on their courage, and Bernard Crisp, Cunard's marketing director, presented them with awards. Mr. Crisp said: "Some of us go through life never having the opportunity to find out if we are really brave. I believe anybody on this ship would have done what you did—but the difference is that you actually did it."

The 1979 refitting was also undertaken by Bethlehem at Bayonne between November 21 and December 21, 1979, and resulted in extensive work on the boilers in cooperation with the British firm of Foster-Wheeler, Ltd., which had designed and built the units originally. The complete overhaul of auxiliary equipment was undertaken as well as work on one propeller, the stabilizers, and some bilge plating. What is most important to passengers, of course, is what they see and, perhaps, how they see it. The 1979 refitting saw the replacing of 25,000 fluorescent light bulbs to put a shine on the face-lift, along with 20 miles of carpeting, and the repainting of her hull with self-polishing paint.

During the Tenth Anniversary World Cruise in 1980, the largest number of passengers ever was carried on the ship. One of the highlights of the trip was the maiden crossing of the Suez Canal, which made her the largest ship ever to pass through both the Suez and Panama Canals during the same voyage. The inaugural call to Yalta on the shores of the Black Sea was unexpectedly short. As passengers were preparing to go ashore in the launches, the Russian authorities decided that every shore-going passenger must have a Soviet visa. As soon as this was brought to his attention, Captain R. H. Arnott knew right away that the process of carrying out their wishes would take so long that some of the passengers would never get ashore. Without any further ado, he ordered all the officials off the ship and put to sea again as the stirring music of "Rule, Britannia" played throughout the liner.

It was on a crystal-clear day in Geiranger Fjord on May 29, 1980, that the first known launching of a hot-air balloon was made from the deck of a British passenger ship. Mr. Ola Kalvatn brought his hot-air balloon on board the *QE2*, where it was inflated on the after end of One Deck, and with then–Chief Officer Ronald Warwick as crew lifted off. It made a twenty-five-minute flight across the fjord and landed in a field near the town.

The officers of the *Queen* were able to contribute something to the happy solving of an Atlantic mystery in June 1980. The two-masted schooner *El Pirata*, en route from Boston to Kristiansand, Norway, had not been seen or

One of the great cruises of the Queen Elizabeth 2 *nearly every year is the Canada and Atlantic Isles cruise. A frequent high point of this trip is the visit to Quebec, where the* Queen *now docks in the shadow of the Plains of Abraham and the Chateau Frontenac (August 1983).*

The Queen *slowly moves in toward the new quay adjacent to the Old Town of Quebec, which was founded by the French and dates back to the early seventeenth century. The docking operation against the current of the mighty Saint Lawrence must be handled with care. (Photo courtesy of James MacLachlan.)*

heard from since June 11 and was reported overdue by Portishead Radio. On June 22, the schooner was sighted 923 miles from Lands End. All was reported well except that problems had been experienced with their radio.

The 1981 world cruise of the *Queen Elizabeth 2* was dubbed the Six Continent Odyssey and began from New York on January 18, 1981. The *Queen* sailed around the world on an eastward course through the Panama Canal and across the Pacific for a total distance of 32,946 miles in eighty days.

Upon returning from the world cruise, the *QE2* sailed into a sea of labor troubles at Southampton Docks. As a result, she was unable to store much in the way of provisions and had to make arrangements to take on supplies at a

One of the most dramatic experiences a cruise or an Atlantic crossing can offer is a night sailing. These do not occur too often, but when they do the Queen Elizabeth 2 *is a dramatic sight as she slowly backs out into the North River, with all her lights ablaze and enough electricity being expended to supply a city of 20,000.*

number of cruise ports, notably Lisbon. In May 1981 she had to terminate a cruise at Cherbourg and turn around there when dockers, who had refused to handle the passengers of the P & O liner *Canberra*, also refused to serve the *Queen*. The 1981 transatlantic season began from Cherbourg as the result of Southampton labor unrest. On May 22, when the ship was preparing to sail, the crane drivers would not lift off the gangway. Captain Ridley instructed his sailors to cut it off with gas torches in order to permit the liner to sail on a Norwegian cruise.

A major modernization of the facilities at Southampton resulted in the closing of the old Southampton Ocean Terminal, which had served all three *Queens* and many other big ships for forty years. In its place, the new Queen Elizabeth II Terminal was created for the handling of the passengers and luggage from the *Queen* and opened in April 1981.

During the summer 1981 season the *QE2* called at Bar Harbor, Maine, on a Canadian cruise that proved very popular with some 1,750 passengers on board. Cunard designated the July 25–30, 1981, crossing from New York to Southampton the *QE2* Royal Wedding Commemorative Voyage. The ship was decorated in honor of the Prince and Princess of Wales, and special programs and lectures were given during the crossing. As a finale, a specially made film of the royal wedding in St. Paul's Cathedral was flown out to the *Queen* by helicopter for showing in the theater during the last day out. Passengers were delighted with the experience and expressed their appreciation to Cunard for ensuring that they did not miss the wedding of the century.

Four television camera crews and several news reporters were on the quay to meet the ship when she arrived in New York with a stowaway from a Bahamas cruise. Piccolo, a mongrel that lives near the pier at West Forty-ninth Street had slipped aboard the ship in search of food. He was smart enough to have picked a voyage when there were no other dogs aboard, so he enjoyed the luxury of his own kennel maid and a choice of quarters.

In 1982 the *Queen Elizabeth 2* was invited to Philadelphia for the celebrations in connection with the three hundredth anniversary of the city, "Century Four." The events in connection with this maiden voyage to Delaware Bay and what followed would make for one of the most exciting episodes in the life of the *Queen*.

CHAPTER SIX

THE FALKLANDS

The maiden arrival of the *Queen Elizabeth 2* in Philadelphia on April 25, 1982, was all that anyone could have desired. The special occasion was the grand opening of "Century Four," the year-long tricentennial celebration (1682–1982) of the founding of the city of Philadelphia by William Penn. The reception given the *Queen* was exuberant, even if security precautions were tight. In addition to the normal concern about Northern Ireland, the outbreak of hostilities between Great Britain and Argentina over the Falkland Islands (Malvinas) some 8,000 miles away in the wintry South Atlantic had heightened concern. The *Queen Elizabeth 2* put out to sea again on April 29, for what everyone thought would be a normal run to England.

All the *Queen*'s officers were concerned about developments in the South Atlantic, but few thought there was much likelihood of the *QE2* taking part in the hostilities. First Officer Philip Rentell and Second Officer Paul Jowett were on the bridge for the 8-to-12 watch when they became interested in calculating the fuel, time, and distance factors at various speeds for a run from England to the Falklands. These calculations were filling a note pad when Captain Alexander J. Hutcheson came up behind the two junior officers and saw what they were doing. Laughingly Hutcheson said, "You two will have us down there yet!" Within days the statistical information would be of value. The officers on the bridge calculated that the *Queen Elizabeth 2* would cover the 8,000-mile route at a speed of $27^{1}/_{2}$ knots over $10^{1}/_{2}$ days, during which her engines would gulp an awesome 6,000 tons of oil. That oil would have a retail value of £1,080,000 at $180 per ton for the one-way trip.

The news that the *Queen Elizabeth 2* actually was to be requisitioned for

Preparing the Queen Elizabeth 2 *for her duties as a troop transport/helicopter carrier included the construction of an after flight deck for helicopters on the stern of the ship.*

Below the new flight deck it was necessary to strengthen the structure in order to provide firm landing platforms for the helicopters and their loads.

trooping duties came as something of a shock and through unofficial channels. On May 3, as the *Queen* steamed along the southern coast of England bound for Southampton, those on the Cunarder listening to the 1230 BBC news heard that their ship had been requisitioned by the government. One of the radio officers came up to the bridge with the news, but when Captain Hutcheson was phoned by an enterprising BBC reporter and asked about the requisitioning, all he could say was that he knew nothing about it officially. Needless to say, there was some feeling that the ship's officers could have been given some forewarning of these developments, but it was learned later that the news had been prematurely released in London. Following confirmation, Captain Hutcheson made a formal announcement to passengers and crew that the *QE2* would be withdrawn from commercial service upon arrival at Southampton. The *QE2* was due to dock late that evening at the Queen Elizabeth II Terminal and, as she steamed up the Channel with all her lights ablaze, there was considerable excitement on board. The *Queen Elizabeth 2* officially came alongside her berth at two minutes past midnight on May 4, 1982, and was immediately requisitioned for war service. The run from Philadelphia to Southampton was 3,203 miles and had been accomplished at an average speed of 27.19 knots. Later that morning 1,600 passengers disembarked after breakfast between 0900 and 1030 hours, and various normal cleaning-up chores were done for the remainder of the day. At 2200 hours that evening tugs carefully swung the 963-foot liner/troopship around in the turning basin so that her starboard side lay against the quay.

The conversion work began on May 5 to prepare the ship for her trooping assignment. The amazing adaptability of large modern helicopters made the broad open expanses of the *Queen*'s decks both fore and aft perfectly suited for the aircraft with just a "few, minor" alterations. Then Chief Officer Ronald Warwick and First Officer Rentell went over the plans of the ship with Lieutenant Commander David Poole of the Royal Navy and then escorted him around the open decks. Suddenly the immensity of the task sank in as decisions were made to slice off the upper deck Lido in line with the Q4 bar (now the Club Lido Bar), as well as all the associated superstructure down to the quarterdeck level. This would enable the after end of the *QE2* to be converted into one huge landing pad and service area for helicopters. Forward the decision was made to extend the quarterdeck toward the bow and over the capstan machinery in order to create a landing pad there. The question of what would support the enormous weight of the steel pads and the 18,626 pounds (8,499 kilograms) of a Sea King helicopter plus whatever it might be called upon to carry was critical. The two outdoor swimming pools aft were the answer; they were designed to hold tons of seawater and therefore could supply the foundation for the flight deck. Steel plates were laid over the bottoms of the pools to support and distribute the weight of a network of vertical girders.

Communications in any war situation always remain critical, and an independent radio room was especially constructed behind the bridge. Because the *Queen* could not carry fuel for much more than a one-way trip, provisions had to be made for refueling the giant liner at sea. Pipes were laid from the starboard midship's baggage entrance on Two Deck to the huge tanks of the liner six decks below. The potential peril involved in refueling the *Queen* at sea with heavy oil coursing through piping that ran through prime passenger areas and then down to the vulnerable propulsion system was considerable and caused some trepidation.

Between May 5 and May 9 most of the decorative pictures and valuable furniture were removed from the ship and stored in warehouses ashore. All plants also had to go, as well as the casino equipment—definitely not needed on this voyage, when Lady Luck would have her hands full with other matters. The *Queen*'s own china, glassware, and silverware were collected, packed, and stored. In an effort to protect the carpeting, sheets of hardboard were laid over all carpets in the public rooms, passageways, stairways, and in some of the cabins. The boards were successful only in areas experiencing light usage. During the voyage it became necessary to remove the hardboard covering in the vicinity of "D" Stairway near the entrance to the Columbia Dining Room because the boards were deteriorating under heavy use and the carpet was being destroyed. Some of the famous deep blue carpet of the "D" Stairway was taken up and stored, exposing the bare deck, which could better withstand the beating. In other areas the carpet would have to be replaced when the *Queen* returned from trooping duties.

As the *Queen* received tons upon tons of military stores and equipment, the news was received that H.M.S. *Sheffield*, a British destroyer, had been hit by an Exocet missile fired from an Argentinian Super Etendard plane. There were heavy casualties as a result, including twenty dead. The sinking of the *Sheffield* followed by two days the torpedoing of the second largest ship in the Argentinian navy, the *General Belgrano* (ex-U.S.S. *Phoenix*), which sank in the icy waters of the South Atlantic. The war clearly was heating up for both sides with grievous losses in men and ships. Suddenly Cunard officers and crew who were being given sporadic leave began to be more concerned about writing wills and setting their personal affairs in order.

The equipment coming on the *Queen* included hundreds of extra life jackets and additional safety appliances of all nature. The ammunition assigned to the ship for transport was stored primarily in No. 1 hold, although additional quantities in containers were also loaded on the sports deck forward of the funnel, near what was normally the kennel. Equipment too large for convenient stowage or that might be needed quickly for off-loading by helicopters ended up on the open decks aft, on the raised boat deck, and on what was left of the upper deck. This included land rovers, trailers, helicopter parts, fuel, and rations. The combination of high-octane aviation fuel and ammunition in containers on open decks with the possibility of an Exocet missile attack was hair-raising, but virtually no location on the *QE2* offered much security against an attack.

In manning the ship for the voyage to the war zone, Cunard sought volunteers. Approximately 650 were chosen out of over 1,000 who had stepped forward. Finally, after eight whirlwind days of creating a fighting unit from the chaos of conversion, the *Queen Elizabeth 2* was ready to receive her most important military cargo. Preparation parties arrived on the afternoon of May 11, and the formal embarkation of troops began at 0545 hours on May 12, with regimental bands on hand to pipe the men aboard. Not unexpectedly, a large number of high officials wished to see the *Queen* off. Representing the owners were Lord Matthews and Ralph Bahna, president of the Cunard Line. A selection of military brass saw their compatriots off, including an admiral and four generals plus staff. Finally, John Nott, minister for defense in the British government, arrived at 1430 hours for a quick tour of the bridge and a short address to the troops. The *Queen* had on board approximately 3,000 men of the Fifth Infantry Brigade comprising units of the Scots Guards, the Welsh Guards, and the Gurkha Rifles, in addition to naval personnel and her own crew. Departure time was scheduled for 1600 hours, and at 1603 hours the *QE2*'s siren heralded the fact that all wires and ropes were clear fore and aft. With the tugs *Albert*, *Calshot*, and *Clausentum* fast forward and *Romsey* and *Brockenhurst* fast astern, the 67,000-ton liner/troopship under the command of Captain Peter Jackson slowly headed upriver to turn. This was achieved within twenty-three minutes in spite of force 4/5 south-southeasterly winds, and the *Queen Elizabeth 2* proceeded to sea, past the terminal bearing her name, which was crowded with families and well-wishers, to the wail of a Scottish bagpipe rendering "Scotland the Brave."

A view of the QE2, *taken from a Sea King helicopter as it circles the huge liner in the South Atlantic and begins an approach to the stern landing area.*

The departure was majestic, but not without anxiety. The routine maintenance on two of the three boilers still had not been completed on schedule, but, because of the enormous wartime propaganda value of an on-schedule departure, it was decided that the ship should sail on time.

The *Queen* had three massive boilers as part of her propulsion machinery, and she could do up to 30 knots on all three, around 21 knots on two, but much less, 6 to 10 knots, on only one. With only one third of her boilers in service, the ship was not capable of sudden stops or quick maneuvers, let alone much speed. While in port for an overnight stay or longer, only one boiler normally would be in use.

As the *Queen Elizabeth 2* steamed slowly down the Eastern Solent, passing Cowes and the coast of the Isle of Wight, the helicopter landing pads received their first baptism as two Sea King helicopters made their cautious approach and touched down. They were speedily secured in their appointed positions for the voyage, with their rotors folded back. As one Cunard officer commented, "it all appeared so practised and proficient that one would imagine we had been doing it for years."

The *Queen* anchored for the night, as planned, along the Isle of Wight, but away from curious onlookers. Early in the morning the tug *Bustler* brought still more stores on a quick trip, being alongside and away between 0120 and 0130 hours. Matters certainly looked much better by breakfast on May 13, and shortly after 0900 hours the order was given to "stand by engines." The anchor was weighed, and to everyone's relief full power was soon available on the boilers.

The safety of all on board was the prime concern of the *QE2*'s officers, as well as the various military staffs. Shortly after getting under way on May 13 and before the Isle of Wight had dropped from view, the first full-scale boat drill was held at 1030 hours for the 3,000 troops. All lifeboats were swung out to the normal embarkation level so that everyone could see the full procedure.

The principal job for the afternoon of the first day at sea was to experiment with at-sea replenishment of the *Queen Elizabeth 2*'s fuel bunkers. She sailed from Southampton with 5,969 tons of fuel oil, but that was, in fact, barely enough to get her to the destination in the South Atlantic. Somewhere and somehow much more fuel would be needed. The *Queen* headed south to a rendezvous point in the Channel with the Royal Fleet Auxiliary (R.F.A.) tanker *Grey Rover*.

The *QE2* made rendezvous with the tanker *Grey Rover*, which approached from astern on the starboard side and fired a rocket line across to the troopship. The lightweight rocket line was attached to a second, intermediate line, which was attached to the "messenger." The two ships took up position about 150 feet apart, and a distance line was run across from the two forecastles. *Grey Rover* had the responsibility for station keeping in a reversal of the traditional refueling roles. Approximately 100 soldiers took up position on Two

Critical to the success of the Queen Elizabeth 2 *as a troop transport and helicopter carrier was the ability to refuel the vessel. A practice refueling exercise with R.F.A.* Grey Rover *occurred along the south coast of England soon after the* Queen *began her voyage.*

A pipe was installed on Two Deck amid-ships leading down to the liner's fuel tanks. The critically needed fuel supplies in the thousands of tons came gushing in through these pipes and descended through the ship to the bunkers.

Deck near the baggage door, which had been modified for fuel replenishment, and they took up the slack in the "messenger" and then pulled over the 8-inch flexible fuel line. With great difficulty this feat was achieved and the hose was connected to the *QE2*'s new bunker line, permitting the system to be tested by the passage of several tons of oil from the tanker to the *Queen*'s bunkers. With the success of the experiment, the line was cleared, disconnected, and paid back out to *Grey Rover* for retrieval. Because the refueling system was work-able, the giant Cunarder could go anywhere and remain at sea indefinitely. As the two ships peeled away from each other, their horns thundered the tradi-tional three-blast salute. In this instance the salute marked a job well done.

The *Queen Elizabeth 2* proceeded south, avoiding the normal sea-lanes on a 3,000-mile track toward Freetown, Sierra Leone. The second day out a French Atlantic reconnaissance plane buzzed the liner and wished her well. Thereafter it was felt that security from any sea-based unit was probably com-plete, although the problem of "spy satellites" makes all precautions under cloudless skies somewhat questionable against an enemy with such capability. Various news media quoted American intelligence reports as confirming that at least some of the twelve Soviet radar, photographic, and communication satellites were being used in a search for the liner as she steamed south. In a television interview former chief of naval operations Admiral Elmo Zumwalt said that he fully expected the Argentinians to make an attempt to destroy the *QE2*. "It is one big fat target," the admiral said.

The troops on the *Queen Elizabeth 2* were obsessed with physical fitness from the very beginning, both for the need to remain fit and as a means of reducing nervous energy. Every unit was given an assigned time period for jogging around the boat deck, starting at 0630 hours. All day long some of the 3,000 troops went around and around the boat deck, and the noise of hundreds of men in full kit and boots jogging around the open deck was deafening. Some Cunard staff began to hate the whole process with a passion, because the noise was omnipresent and thunderous. Within a short time the vibration from

One of the most important reasons for requisitioning the QE2 was her ability to deliver physically fit troops and pilots to the war zone. Soldiers exercised in full kit so that their training and conditioning would make them fit for whatever challenges might materialize.

A portion of the ammunition carried by the Queen *was intended for troop practice sessions. Firing exercises frequently took place from the boat deck, at small floating targets released from a forward shell door as they swept by the liner. Care had to be taken to restrain enthusiasm so that no bullets came too near the liner.*

thousands of heavy footfalls began to lift the caulking right out of the teak deck. Streamers of caulking were everywhere, and, long after the *Queen* returned to commercial service, it was still lifting out in many areas.

Some of the ammunition on the ship was intended for firing practice, and this daily routine commenced on May 15. Bags of garbage made the best targets, but strong protests had to be lodged on occasion against random shots that destroyed railings. Every part of the ship was utilized for some form of training. Giant wall maps of the Falklands and the South Atlantic were spread across the Blue Staircase wall, where the tapestries of the launching of the *Queen* previously had hung. A newfound interest in South Atlantic geography was noted on the part of passers-by. The church service on Sunday morning, May 16, was well attended in the theater, with Captain Peter Jackson presiding.

Another daily routine as the *Queen* steamed southward was flying practice for the crews of the Sea King helicopters. From Friday, May 14, onward, several hours a day were devoted to this, in part because no one actually knew where they would be required to disembark the troops or in what manner the disembarkation might be accomplished. Some of the pilots from the new 825th Squadron had never flown on and off a merchant ship before, even if their expertise in basic flying was unquestioned. Every ship is different, and even the veteran pilots of naval maneuvers had to learn where the air pockets and downdrafts would add extra challenges to landing on the *Queen*. It was necessary to practice not only fore and aft landings, but also athwartship touchdowns. If both the aft landing pads were in use at once, then one helicopter might come in from one direction while the other employed a different flight approach. The Number One landing position forward of the bridge in some ways was the most difficult of all because of air currents slamming into the front of the huge ship and being deflected upward and sideways, while the bow area also would be subject to more pitching. As one Cunard Officer com-

The most dramatic part of the training sessions as the Queen Elizabeth 2 *steamed southward was the Sea King helicopter take-off and landing exercises, which always drew an admiring crowd. The pilots found that the aft landing pads required some time for familiarization. The landing pad guidelines ultimately were extended to the sides of the ship in order to increase visibility.*

mented, "One can appreciate that to land on a heaving deck in rough, rainy weather, with a ship doing 25 knots, would be difficult enough; however, to land sideways is a whole new ball game." The goal had to be to keep the ship in one's mind as a solid landing pad, match speed with her, maintain position, and ignore the millions of tons of water rushing by the hull. The South Atlantic would provide an icy grave for anyone forgetting their priorities, and no one wanted that!

After six days at sea at 0900 hours on Tuesday, May 18, the Cape Sierra Leone Light was sighted, and pilots Kenokai and Jones boarded. By 1145 hours all lines fore and aft were secure, and the *Queen* was alongside a berth for what would be the last time in three weeks. The passage from Southampton to Freetown had taken five days, one hour, and twenty-four minutes over a distance of 2,956 miles and had been accomplished at 24.35 knots. The engines, even at that economical reduced speed, had consumed 1,919 tons of oil, leaving 4,050 in the bunkers, so that 1,867 tons were taken on board, as well as additional water and supplies. The stop at Freetown was a calculated risk, but it meant that the *Queen* could proceed to her destination without danger of running low on fuel and using the pipeline system. Furthermore, security was such that the *Queen Elizabeth 2* slipped in and out of Freetown unnoticed by the world's press. With the tugs *Sena* forward and *Interman* aft, the liner sailed from the West Coast of Africa with her bunkers topped up. The destination for this leg of the trip south was Ascension Island. The late-night departure from Freetown featured as crew and troop entertainment a film on deck. The scene of a large military troopship showing a film on deck during a hot tropical night as the ship sailed from an African port took some viewers back forty years to another conflict.

One of the most critical tasks on the *Queen Elizabeth 2* after leaving Freetown was the creation of a total ship blackout. In the words of Captain J. James, R.N., senior naval officer on the *Queen*, the giant liner had to be converted from "the brightest star on the ocean, to the darkest." There are an awful lot of portholes on the *QE2* and hundreds of large floor-to-ceiling public-room windows. At the same time, in tackling the problem there was no desire to apply black paint everywhere if anything else would do. Black plastic, such as that used in garbage bags, came to the rescue for temporary service.

On Sunday, May 23, as the *Queen Elizabeth 2* headed southward on the last leg of her outward voyage, the radar was turned off and the ship was electronically silenced. Modern radar is a great boon to navigation, but in wartime a dead giveaway as to the location of a ship. Therefore the officers on the bridge had the clock turned back on them some forty years, and the importance of a sharp watch was never more critical. From dawn to dusk military lookouts were posted on the bridge wings as well as near the funnel. The watertight doors on decks 6, 7, and 8 had been shut earlier, but as the ship steamed closer to the war zone all other watertight doors were closed as a safety precaution.

The closer to the war the *QE2* came, the keener attention was paid to the news. Before May 21 not too much happened, but after that, with the landing on San Carlos by the British on the twenty-second and with the news of the successful Argentinian strikes against H.M.S. *Ardent*, *Antelope*, and *Coventry*, as well as the *Atlantic Conveyor*, the war was suddenly a reality. To those listening on the *Queen* the air raids against British ships seemed incessant, even if the Argentinians were taxing their men and planes to the limit. The loss of the *Atlantic Conveyor*, a Cunard ship, caused particular concern for those who had friends on her, because the loss of life was substantial.

On May 24 two platforms on the bridge wings were finished to hold the mounting for .5 Browning machine guns. The Browning machine guns could fire about 800 rounds a minute. In addition, 7.62-millimeter general-purpose machine guns and Blow Pipe Air Defense missiles were located in a few strategic positions. These were the only armaments carried for the *Queen*'s own protection. The firing exercises added to the din, although there were fewer helicopter flights in order to conserve fuel. Some exuberant marksman managed to damage the No. 5 raft-launching davit fall wire, which had to be replaced, while bullet holes in the forward rails met with strong protests by the

Cunard representatives at the daily afternoon conferences.

By noon on May 26 the ship was in position, latitude 47°59' south, 25°20' west, and the air temperature, which had been steadily falling, was now 5 degrees Celsius. Soon it would be below zero with a wind-chill factor far lower than that, and cold weather gear was in demand all around. The troops continued their routines in spite of the cold.

May 26 had also placed the *Queen* near enough to the active war zone that she began to zigzag rather than just steering variable courses as before. During the night of May 26–27 mist settled in around midnight, and visibility was reduced substantially while the presence of ice became ever more ominous. The situation in the darkness rapidly deteriorated to such a critical level that the danger from the numerous icebergs was considered far greater than that from hostile forces. Captain Jackson had gone to the bridge as the fog settled in. He consulted with the naval authorities as the *QE2* was forced to reduce speed and to weave in and out between the giant bergs. Finally, in spite of the danger of revealing the ship's position, the radar was turned on at 0340 hours. The possibility of the *Queen*'s becoming trapped by icebergs or colliding with one was a more imminent risk than discovery by the enemy. During the next six hours many icebergs of monstrous proportions suddenly loomed out of the misty darkness, and at one time over 100 bergs large enough to be seen by the radar were on the scan. Each of those great masses of ice could sink a ship. The largest of the gigantic bergs was over a mile long—six times the length of the *Queen*—and at 300 feet high must have weighed in at several million tons— many times the liner's gross tonnage. Captain Jackson described the time on the bridge as he took his charge through the ice field as the most harrowing experience he had had in nearly forty years at sea. With visibility less than a mile and sometimes even less than that, expert seamanship and the legendary Cunard luck saw the *Queen Elizabeth 2* through the icefield. As dawn broke, the iceberg danger was past, although one huge berg could still be seen seven miles from the *Queen*, soaring above the low-lying mist and probably towering 200 to 300 feet above the rolling South Atlantic. It was so huge that it looked like the Cliffs of Dover, while another appeared like cathedral spires rising from the turbulent sea. As the sun rose, the icebergs reflected a rainbow of colors in magnificent shades of red, orange, and yellow. After what the individuals on the bridge of the *Queen* had just been through, it was difficult for some not to think of 1912, of another great luxury liner, and another iceberg.

A rendezvous with H.M.S. *Antrim* was planned for noon on Thursday, May 27, in order to transfer Major General Moore and Brigadier Wilson with their advanced headquarters. Before Brigadier Wilson left the *QE2*, he penned a parting message for publication in the "5th Infantry Brigade/*QE2* News" that summed up the role of the soldiers and the liner to that date:

> Very shortly we shall all transfer to other ships off South Georgia and start on the last phase of our move to the Falkland Islands. It looks as if the Brigade will be there about 1st June, that is early next week.
>
> Once there, we shall join 3 Commando Brigade. We shall sort ourselves out; and then start joint operations to recapture the islands.
>
> Orders will be given out on landing. It is too early yet to issue a detailed plan, for it would be bound to change over the course of the next five days.
>
> This is the final issue of this newspaper, and to the Master and ship's company of *QE2* I would say `Thank You' for the way you have looked after us on this voyage. We have come to know you well, we admire you, and we shall always be proud that we sailed with you in your magnificent ship.
>
> To the Brigade I would simply say this: "We shall start earning our pay as a team shortly; and we are in this game to win!"

Major General Moore and Brigadier Wilson left the *QE2* on schedule for the rendezvous with H.M.S. *Antrim*—a remarkable achievement, considering the ice of the previous night. The general and his staff went by helicopter, but two of the *Queen*'s launches were used to transport the brigadier and the 5th Brigade Party. The goal was to have General Moore rendezvous with Admiral Sandy Woodward at sea en route to the Falkland Islands so that additional plans could be formulated. The sea was calm when the *QE2* launched her boats, but the swell was several feet high and this made disembarkation alongside *Antrim* treacherous. One warrant officer suffered a broken leg when it became trapped between the launch and H.M.S. *Antrim*. The war was over for him, and he returned to the *Queen*'s hospital by helicopter. The recovery of the *QE2*'s launches proved difficult because of the swell. Considerable stress was placed on the falls as the weight of the launch came on them quite suddenly when the swell subsided.

When the *QE2* had neared the H.M.S. *Antrim*, it was evident that she already had seen considerable action both in South Georgia and the East Falklands. Her exterior was distinctly weatherbeaten, and the battles she had fought were highlighted by the line of cannon shell holes down her sides. The Seacat missile launcher was out of commission as the result of an unexploded Argentinian bomb that had lodged itself in the missile magazine. Fortunately the bomb had been defused before it could explode, or the *Antrim* would have had her stern ripped off.

At 1804 hours on May 27, Right Whale Rocks, South Georgia was 4$^{1}/_{2}$ miles away but visibility was virtually nil; the short South Atlantic winter day had already given way to night and there was thick fog. As the ship approached the planned anchorage, the cable was walked back two shackles. By 1922 hours the vessel was safely at anchor approximately 1 mile from Grytviken. The passage from Freetown, Sierra Leone, had been over a distance of 5,025 miles and had taken eight days, twenty hours, and twelve minutes, with an average speed of 23.9 knots in spite of ice. During that period the *Queen*'s engines also had consumed 3,570 tons of her precious fuel. South Georgia represented as much of the war zone as the liner would see, because other vessels would tend to the transfer of her critical troops to the Falkland Islands, themselves some 200 miles to the west. The *Queen*'s anchorage was in Cumberland Bay East near the old whaling station at Grytviken, the origin of the whole conflict.

Among the other vessels in Cumberland Bay East was the P & O liner *Canberra*, the North Sea ferry *Norland*, and H.M.S. *Endurance*, as well as a number of trawlers outfitted as mine sweepers that had arrived from England just the previous day. They served as transports for the troops from the *QE2* to the other ships. Soon after anchoring, Captain Barker, R.N., of H.M.S. *Endurance* and the senior naval officer, Captain C. Burr, R.N., of the *Canberra* came on board to meet with the S.N.O. *QE2* Captain James, and the senior military of-

The famed Gurkhas of the British Army made up one of the contingents traveling south on the QE2. *They had accommodations deep in the liner on Five Deck and practiced reaching their lifeboat stations blindfolded in order to be prepared for any eventuality.*

The fastest means of transferring large numbers of troops from the QE2 *to the other waiting transports was by the trawlers, and one is shown leaving the side of the liner. The trawlers also worked relentlessly around the clock trans-shipping stores brought by the* Queen *to other waiting vessels*

ficers present. The meeting held in the Queen Mary Suite was to agree on a plan for disembarkation. The communications blackout had seen the development of two alternative plans that now needed to be resolved. Those on the *QE2* wanted to start unloading the cargo immediately, because it was going to take at least forty-eight hours. Those coming on board wanted the troops to begin transferring immediately, with the movement of cargo to go forward simultaneously. All involved had well-thought-out arguments that, as befitted strong personalities, were expressed in firm, straightforward opinions. Eventually agreement was reached and about 700 troops commenced disembarkation at 2345 hours for transfer to *Canberra* and *Norland*. The requisitioned British trawlers did yeomen's service, transporting the troops in the dark between the blackened ships. H.M.S. *Leeds Castle*, sister ship to the *Dumbarton Castle* at Ascension and one of the North Sea vessels, was the first of the smaller ships to try to come alongside the *QE2* in the darkness. The *QE2* was visible at only 100 feet, and the approach of the *Leeds Castle* was foiled when her mast hit the bridge wing of the *Queen* as she tried to maneuver forward to be underneath No. 1 hatch. The *Cordella*, one of the converted trawlers, was the first vessel to make it alongside successfully. She was one of five trawlers requisitioned and outfitted as the new 11th Mine Countermeasures Squadron. Her sister ships in the squadron were the *Northella, Farnella, Pict,* and *Junella.* They were manned by Royal Navy officers and ratings and adapted to act as mine sweepers in the Falklands, but they had many other uses.

Despite the late hour, the soldiers were in good spirits. The trawlers came alongside the *QE2* with difficulty because of the low visibility. Security dictated that no lights were to be used. No doubt the liner and the trawlers lost some paint during the night. A start was made on discharging No. 1 hatch, but it was just too difficult in the blackness, and the bulk of the work had to be put off until daylight.

The first real view of Cumberland Bay East and South Georgia came with the dawn on May 28. Snowcapped mountains spawned glaciers that flowed to the sea, forming numerous small icebergs in the waters of the bay. Discharge of the troops and stores began at 0800 hours with helicopters and trawlers. The work proceeded quickly because of the uncertain weather conditions and the desire of all concerned to get the *QE2* out of the anchorage as expeditiously as possible. The transfer of baggage, equipment, and personnel continued all day by helicopter and trawlers. The Admiralty tug *Typhoon* also assisted in transfers to the waiting *Norland.* It soon appeared that, even with all the

The morning sunlight brilliantly lights one of the snow-capped peaks of South Georgia as seen from the afterdeck of the QE2 *in Cumberland Bay. A few crew members stop to admire the breathtaking beauty of the landscape.*

As dawn broke on May 28, those on the QE2 *had their first view of Cumberland Bay, South Georgia, with the* Canberra, *dubbed the "Great White Whale" by her troops, at anchor nearby. The 45,000-ton P&O liner would see a great deal of service in the South Atlantic before her return to Britain.*

smaller vessels working full-time, not all the troops would make it to their assigned ships on schedule. One of the 7th Gurkha officers asked if he could use the *QE2*'s launches to transport his men to the North Sea ferry. This request was granted, and just before noon the *Queen*'s launches began to load the Gurkhas and their nearly overwhelming bulk of equipment. When the boats reached the *Norland*, they found that she had no pontoon alongside and that her hatch, normally used for disembarking cars, was eight feet above the water and higher than the Gurkhas were tall by a very good measure. There is no question that the Gurkhas are among the finest fighting troops in the world, but this represented a very substantial challenge. The troops could not even see the *Norland*'s deck, let alone reach it, from the *QE2*'s launches. The solution was to use the cab of the launch plus a good boost to get the soldiers on their way.

Snow started to fall on May 29 at 0400 hours, and by daybreak it had settled everywhere, blanketing South Georgia with a couple of inches. The snow was very beautiful to see, but treacherous to work in. Nevertheless, more than 100 tons of cargo still had to go. This was loaded into trawlers for transfer to H.M.S. *Stromness*, which had arrived shortly before noon. The Sea King helicopters had been permanently transferred to *Canberra* the day before. As matters were being tidied up there was time to think of others, and a *QE2* launch was sent ashore to take some Cunard and army personnel for a visit and to bring some of the Royal Marines who were garrisoning the bleak base at

The principal human settlement from the days of the whaling industry in South Georgia was Grytviken, although the site had been abandonned as a working community. The spark that started the war occurred when Argentinian workers, brought here to dismantle the whaling station for scrap, raised the Argentine flag and thereby produced a chain reaction which resulted in hostilities.

Grytviken back to the liner for lunch and a much-appreciated break. When the Cunard group reached shore, the captain in charge took them around the old whaling station. Nearby was the wreck of the Argentinian submarine *Santa Fe*, which was sunk in shallow water with the conning tower still above the water. The whaling station had been closed for twenty years and most of the timber buildings showed the ravages of numerous South Atlantic hurricanes, but the church was well preserved. The tradition of the island was that anyone remaining on South Georgia for any period of time repaired and maintained the church. Chris Haughton, one of the *QE2*'s second officers, walked ahead toward the church, and as the others approached they were astounded to be greeted by Bach's Toccata and Fugue in D floating heavenward from the old pump organ. The impression was breathtaking to the visitors. Outside of town near the shore was the old cemetery with the grave of the famous Antarctic explorer Sir Ernest Shackleton which was decorated with the crested shields of visiting ships in tribute to the gallant adventurer.

During the afternoon of May 29 some 640 survivors of H.M.S. *Ardent*, *Coventry*, and *Antelope* were transferred to the *QE2*. The *Queen* thus became the largest hospital ship in the world. Many of the survivors of the lost Royal Navy vessels had little more than the clothes on their backs, and some of those were ragged. These men had been through the fiery furnace of war, and they were a very stern-faced and determined group of Royal Navy sailors. The officers and crew of the *QE2* did their best to make them feel welcome and to assist in the unwinding process from the high level of tension that these warriors had endured. Most of the survivors could be accommodated in normal cabins, but the hospital of the *Queen* was soon filled with the more critical casualties, who were, according to the medical staff, very lucky to be alive.

The barometer was falling steadily throughout the day, and the weather was

A dusting of snow blanketed the flight decks of the QE 2 on her second day at Grytviken, South Georgia. Graffiti instanta-neously appeared in the new-fallen snow on the flight decks of the QE2, as few could resist the impulse to be creative.

giving cause for concern. The swell coming in the entrance to Cumberland Bay East caused the *Queen* to yaw wildly. This made it increasingly difficult for the trawlers to come alongside safely. The port gangway and pontoon were damaged beyond further use by the buffeting they received. In order to mini-mize the exposure of the smaller vessels, the *QE2* weighed anchor and turned to create a lee shore for the last disembarkation of troops. Meanwhile, during the afternoon a report was received that the tanker *British Wye* was under at-tack 400 miles due north. An Argentinian aircraft dropped a series of bombs that fortunately missed. The incident was a particular cause for concern, be-cause the tanker was a considerable distance from the mainland and to the north of South Georgia. By deduction, this meant that the *QE2* was in range and a sitting duck while anchored at Cumberland Bay. (Later it was learned that the Argentinians had used a Boeing 707 with a very substantial cruising range to survey the South Atlantic at 18,000 feet searching for the *Queen Eliza-beth 2*.) That afternoon it was deemed judicious to get the huge liner out of Cumberland Bay East in order to reduce her vulnerability. She put out to sea at 1727 hours with 60 tons of ammunition still remaining on board.

The *Queen* increased speed to 18 knots and headed into the icefield that had been so terrifying on the way south. By 1930 hours the liner passed the first of the giant bergs in darkness, but the feeling this time was that night and the ice would make it all the more difficult for the Argentinians to find the ship. Fur-thermore, within 2½ hours the *QE2* was clear of the main icefield and in-creased speed to 25 knots, with more in reserve should danger strike. Although no one knew it, she was on her way home.

On Sunday, May 30, Captain Jackson held the Sunday service with Cap-tain James reading the special lesson and prayers. The weather deteriorated substantially, with rough seas slamming against the ship and heavy swells

The QE2 *is shrouded in an icy fog in Cumberland Bay East, South Georgia, as trawlers work energetically to remove men and supplies from the liner. The photograph was taken from one of the* Queen's *launches taking a small party of Cunard personnel to see the whaling station at Grytviken.*

churning the South Atlantic. Even some strong-willed souls felt moderate discomfort from this weather, although the good news was that under such conditions the *Queen* could still maintain speed and stand a much better chance of escaping detection from hostile submarines and aircraft.

The fuel situation was becoming increasingly acute as night fell on May 31. Rendezvous was made with the R.F.A. tanker *Bayleaf*, but conditions on Monday and Tuesday, June 1, had been too wicked for any attempt at fuel transfer. The arrangements on both days had to be canceled. By Wednesday, June 2, the options were severely reduced, with the giant liner down to less than 1,000 tons of fuel (1½ days steaming at full power).

Speed was reduced to 10 knots and course set at 300 degrees to facilitate

The grave of the intrepid British Antarctic explorer, Sir Ernest Shackleton, lies in the wind-swept cemetery at Grytviken. Many naval visitors have paid their respects at the site and left their ship emblems in tribute.

After leaving South Georgia, the Queen Elizabeth 2 *encountered gale-force winds that made refueling operations with the fleet oiler* Bayleaf *treacherous. By June 2 the* Queen *was down to less than 1,000 tons of fuel (less than two days' supply at full speed), and it was imperative to attempt transferring the precious fuel from the tanker to the liner.*

pipeline connecting. The *Bayleaf* came up on the *Queen*'s starboard side shortly after 0900 hours, and the pipe was secured by 0905 hours on the first try in a miracle of precision work under horrendous conditions. The two ships were rolling along, 150 feet apart, with the sea boiling between them. The violent movements of the ships at times made the hose appear to be almost horizontal. There was more than one near miss, and Captain Jackson grew a few more gray hairs as the fate of his ship was taken out of his hands once again. All day the two ships kept position, with the tanker captain having the additionally demanding responsibility of keeping station on the *Queen Elizabeth 2* rather than the other way around, as was normal when refueling takes place between naval vessels. At 1835 hours, after 12 1/2 hours, the decision was made to cease refueling because the pipeline clearly was chaffing and night was descending fast. By that time the *Queen* had taken on board almost 3,834 tons of fuel, which would be sufficient to sustain operations for quite a while at 25 knots. The decision to stop replenishing was fortuitous—it was discovered that the joining shackle supporting the weight of the hose within the ship had almost worn away and would have given out in another few minutes.

Initially the feeling was that the survivors of the lost British ships would disembark at Ascension Island for the long flight home. Therefore the navy opted to give the *QE2* a crew show to remember. Acts were assembled quickly and the Double Up–Double Down Room (now the Grand Lounge) of the *QE2* rang with raunchy jokes and hilarious nonstop routines as everyone unwound to the best medicine ever invented—laughter. There were few unaffected as the officers and sailors wound up the program with a rousing, full-throated rendering of "God Save the Queen!" A naval mess dinner was given by the resident naval party for the officers of the *QE2* in the Princess Grill. Clothes were still at a premium, but spirit was not and the officers retired to the Queen's Grill Lounge for traditional mess games. Such levity served to break some of the strain for all concerned and to help those who had experienced the trauma of losing their ships regain stability and peace of mind.

On June 3 the orders were received from the Ministry of Defence to return to Southampton. The *Queen Elizabeth 2* had succeeded so well in her assignment that she was no longer required in the war zone and could best serve the Crown by bring the survivors home. This news was received with mixed reactions. Many of the crew were emotionally prepared to spend at least two months away, and they felt that they had not participated enough in the cause. The *Canberra*, it seemed, had done so much more, and the crew of the *QE2* were prepared to make additional sacrifices. Such was the *esprit de corps*. Yet, as Captain Jackson and others explained, the *Queen Elizabeth 2* had accomplished something that no other vessel could have by delivering the majority of the 5th Brigade to the war zone within two weeks, safe and sound.

On Friday, June 4, as the *Queen* neared Ascension Island, she rendezvoused with H.M.S. *Dumbarton Castle* at 1500 hours and then turned her bow northward, leaving the South Atlantic behind. Six survivors of a helicopter crash departed the ship at Ascension with two severe casualties to be flown home, but the bulk of the survivors remained on board for the voyage home. Twenty-five tons of ammunition also were transferred by helicopter for potential use in the war. Good weather continued, and the operation was carried out smoothly. June 5 saw the normal morning lifeboat drill as the *Queen* steamed northward at 23.89 knots. The sea was moderate and the weather fair as a balmy cruise climate prevailed. A survivors' competition on June 8 for the title "Miss QE2" was won by a sailor with a beard, and daily sports competitions kept the troops active and occupied. One group from one of the lost ships even built a temporary pool on the aft deck. There was nothing like ten days at sea on the *QE2* to restore the health and minds of war-torn individuals, but the biggest thrill lay ahead.

On June 6 a signal was received by Captain Jackson informing him that the liner would be returned to Cunard immediately upon her arrival in Southampton, but the refitting was not expected to be completed until August 14 — eight weeks later. The news also arrived and spread like wildfire through the ship that the *Queen Elizabeth 2* would be greeted in the Solent by the Royal Yacht *Britannia* with Her Majesty Queen Elizabeth, the Queen Mother, on board to welcome them home. Therefore the "boys" had to be dressed properly. The "hands to flying stations" sounded yet again at 1540 hours on Thursday, June 10, and helicopters from the Royal Naval Station, Culdrose, Cornwall, landed with all sorts of gear for the 640 survivors of the *Ardent*, *Coventry*, and *Antelope*. A few important military personnel also arrived to give orders about secrecy and how to handle the press. At 1830 hours the *Queen Elizabeth 2* passed Mounts Bay near Penzance, and by 2200 hours the helicopters lifted off for Culdrose once more while the liner steamed slowly up the Channel to her well-earned welcome home.

The homecoming to Southampton on June 11 was spectacular, with welcoming escorts in the Solent. The survivors from the Ardent, Antelope, *and* Coventry *lined the decks of the* Queen Elizabeth 2 *to greet Her Majesty Queen Elizabeth, the Queen Mother, on the royal yacht.*

Her Majesty Queen Elizabeth, the Queen Mother, stands on the aft deck of the Britannia *to welcome the troops home.*

The timetable for the *Queen Elizabeth 2*'s arrival in her home port on June 11 was carefully orchestrated. Captain Driver, the *QE2*'s frequent pilot, boarded at 0848 hours, and the Needles were past at 0900 hours. Admiral Sir John Fieldhouse, commander in chief of the Royal Navy, landed on board at 0800 hours and, after addresses to the crews and a press conference, he left by 0935 hours. Lord Matthews also arrived as the senior Cunard representative and made his way around the ship, speaking to personnel. Admiral Fieldhouse's use of the Q4 Nightclub for the press conference was one of the last official events held in that room which was subsequently transformed into the Club Lido. Following Admiral Fieldhouses's departure, the survivors of the *Ardent*, *Coventry*, and *Antelope* mustered on the upper deck aft (flight deck) as the *QE2* slowly steamed up the Solent and *Britannia* came into view with Her Majesty Queen Elizabeth, the Queen Mother, waving to the ship from the afterdeck of the yacht. All those on the *Queen Elizabeth 2* gave three resounding cheers to Her Majesty.

The exchange of radiograms between Her Majesty and Captain Jackson has been immortalized on two large silver plaques that now grace one of the

Following the return to Southampton on June 11, 1982, the QE2 was returned to the Cunard Line. The restoration of the ship as a five-star passenger liner took place at Southampton in the huge dock originally built to accommodate the Queen Mary *and the* Queen Elizabeth. *The ship is shown in dry dock during the reconditioning.*

The removal of the aft helicopter landing pads from the liner is under way in this dry dock photo. Although reconstruction to prepare for the Falklands was accomplished in less than a week (May 5 to May 12, 1982), reconditioning consumed the better part of nine weeks (June 12 to August 7, 1982).

lobbies of the liner bracketed by the standards of Queen Elizabeth II and Queen Elizabeth, the Queen Mother. The message sent to Captain Jackson read:

> I am pleased to welcome you back as *QE2* returns to home waters after your tour of duty in the South Atlantic. The exploits of your own ship's company and the deeds of valor of those who served in *Antelope, Coventry,* and *Ardent* have been acclaimed throughout the land and I am proud to add my personal tribute.
>
> Elizabeth Regina
> Queen Mother

Captain Peter Jackson's reply was:

> Please convey to Her Majesty Queen Elizabeth our thanks for her kind message. Cunard's *Queen Elizabeth 2* is proud to have been of service to Her Majesty's forces.

As the *QE2* passed the Fawley oil refinery, every tanker and vessel, great and small, thundered, whistled, or shrieked a salute to the liner, filling the air with the cacophony normally reserved for a maiden voyage. Southampton Harbor was crawling with small boats out to view the historic occasion of yet a third "*Queen* liner" returning from a war. The *QE2* was assisted to her berth by the tugs *Albert* and *Culver* forward and *Ventnor*, *Chale*, and *Calshot* aft. The huge liner swung in the basin as people became visible out of the enormous throng and all lines were made fast by 1156 hours, with the port side to the QEII Terminal. Some of the *Queen*'s officers took the opportunity to walk into the Wardroom and watch their ship as she was being shown live on television. A gangway was down within minutes, and the naval survivors walked ashore over a red carpet, were handed red roses, and directed to a quiet area inside the QEII Terminal for a private reunion with their families. The *QE2*'s own crew disembarked via the forward gangway, where hundreds of happy family members had gathered to greet them in a wild rush. It was a very emotional day for everyone. The *Queen Elizabeth 2* was home safe and sound.

Passage from South Georgia to Southampton: 12 days, 12 hours,
  18 minutes
Distance: 6,976 miles
Average speed: 23.23 knots
Fuel: 1,076 tons (remaining); 4,798 tons (consumed)
Arrival draught: 26 feet, 4 inches forward; 31 feet, 10 inches aft
Total distance steamed: Southampton to Southampton: 14,967 miles
Value of fuel at $180/ton: $1,851,660

CHAPTER SEVEN

THE NEW *QE2*

On August 7, 1982, the *Queen Elizabeth 2* put to sea for twenty-four hours of engine trials following her refitting after service in the South Atlantic. It had only taken seven days to convert the *QE2* into a troopship, but to restore her took the better part of nine weeks. Following the removal of the two helicopter pads, a considerable amount of structural restoration had to be carried out, as well as internal refurbishing.

The time that the government required to restore the ship gave Cunard a unique opportunity to make several improvements of their own. Among the new facilities installed was the Golden Door Spa at Sea. This provided to be very popular with health- and weight-conscious travelers of all ages, and the idea was ultimately extended to other Cunard ships. The Queen's Grill was redesigned and the casino expanded and redecorated. The first stage of the new Club Lido was carried out, which involved the repositioning of the bar and the fitting of glass doors at the after end leading out onto the open deck. The results were striking and received many favorable comments.

Certainly the most noticeable change was in the color scheme of the liner. The dark gray hull was repainted a light gray that was almost white, and the funnel was painted in the traditional Cunard red with the two black bands. The goal was to give the *QE2* a new appearance after her return from trooping duties; however, the gray hull was very difficult to maintain in pristine condition, and some paint was always lost when using tugs or from dock-side fenders. After a reasonable trial period, it was decided to revert to the original dark gray. She was repainted in June 1983.

The "Pride of the British Merchant Fleet" sailed from Southampton on August 15, with a full complement of passengers destined for New York. Thousands of well-wishers gave her a rousing send-off. Wessex helicopters flew overhead in salute, and a flotilla of small boats accompanied her out into the Channel. Prior to her departure Cunard chairman Lord Matthews hosted a reception on board. In his speech he stated that Cunard was delighted to have the *Queen Elizabeth 2* back in service and that it would take nearly £200 million ($300 million) to replace her. The *Queen*, he said, was unique and, given existing commercial conditions, was likely to remain so for the rest of her life. She was the last of the great transatlantic ocean liners. Ten years later, the replacement cost of the *QE2* was estimated to be about ($630 million).

At the end of the 1982 season Her Royal Highness Queen Elizabeth, the

The reconditioning of the QE2 following her return from the Falklands is nearly completed. The most striking aspect of this was the repainting of the hull to pebble gray as part of her new image. Astern of the 67,703-ton QE2 lies the 44,807-ton Canberra, *the second largest passenger liner in the British Merchant Marine, which also was being reconditioned after service in the South Atlantic.*

Pristine in her new color scheme, the Queen Elizabeth 2 *returned to service in August 1982. In June 1983, the decision was made to return to a darker, gray hull that was substantially easier to maintain.*

The first arrival of the QE2 *to New York in August 1982 virtually qualified as a second maiden arrival as New Yorkers celebrated the return of the largest ship to use the North River passenger ship terminal on a regular basis. The scene when she sailed was a little quieter. The* Queen *passes the twin towers of the World Trade Center, which, at 1,250 feet, are only 25% taller than she is long.*

Queen Mother, paid a personal tribute to the liner when she visited the ship at Southampton on December 2, 1982. The queen mother toured the ship with Lord Matthews and Captain Peter Jackson and spoke to many members of the ship's company who had sailed to South Georgia. She presented a handsomely embossed silver plaque to the ship to commemorate the vessel's service in the Falkland campaign. The plaque records the messages exchanged between the queen mother and Captain Jackson while the *QE2* was steaming past the royal yacht in the Solent on her return voyage. The plaque is now on display between the royal standards situated between the Casino and the Theatre Bar on Upper Deck.

In January 1983 the *Queen Elizabeth 2* set forth on her annual long cruise, which was named The Great Pacific and Oriental Odyssey. The liner sailed from New York to Florida and the Caribbean and then via the Panama Canal to the west coast of Mexico and as far north as San Francisco before heading south toward the Tahitian Islands in South Pacific and on toward New Zealand and Australia. Following a maiden call at Brisbane, the *QE2* turned northward through the Great Barrier Reef to Indonesia and the Orient. The visit to China and Japan remained one of the key attractions of the cruise. The *Queen* is regarded as a great tourist attraction in Japan, and thousands of people visit the docks to see her when she is in port. The homeward leg of the cruise across the North Pacific is one of the single longest stretches of the cruise, but the great speed of the *Queen* turns it into a pleasurable break before the call at the Hawaiian Islands and the return to California. A west-to-east Panama Canal cruise brought the second passage of the waterway for the year and placed the *Queen Elizabeth 2* in New York for the beginning of the 1983 transatlantic season.

In May 1983, Trafalgar House and the Cunard Line announced the completion of successful negotiations to purchase the fleet and goodwill of Norwegian American Cruise for $73 million. The two prizes gained were the magnificent five-star-plus passenger liners *Sagafjord* and *Vistafjord*, which enjoy reputations second to none, among the finest ships of their kind. Both liners were built to exacting standards and are designed to cater to the highest class of discerning world travelers. The quality of their staterooms, the superb design of their public rooms, and the gracious nature of their staff have earned the *Sagafjord* and *Vistafjord* one of the highest percentages of repeat customers in the cruise industry. By this acquisition, Cunard was able to avoid the high costs of new constructions and at the same time increase their fleet with two ships that consistently received the "five star plus" rating given by the prestigious Fieldings Guide to Cruising. When Cunard wanted to expand, no finer acquisition was possible than Norwegian American Cruises, which instantaneously gave the *Queen Elizabeth 2* two medium-sized "sisters" with accommodations and reputations comparable to her own.

Also in May 1983, Trafalgar House, Cunard's parent company, announced that they had acquired a 5 percent holding in the Peninsular and Orient Steamship Company (P & O). P & O operates a large fleet of passenger liners and other vessels and is the only other major British line engaged in the passenger business. The subsequent takeover bid received a lot of publicity and

San Francisco is one of the most magnificent natural harbors in the world. The passage under the Golden Gate Bridge heralds the arrival of the Queen *in one of the most cosmopolitan cities in the world.*

was eventually referred to the Monopolies Commission in Great Britain for evaluation. The commission ultimately decided in the spring of 1984 that it would not be against the public interest for the bid to proceed. However on September 11, 1984, Trafalgar House announced that it was selling its shares in P & O.

In the summer of 1983, the *Queen Elizabeth 2* set course for Skarsvag, Norway, in the land of the midnight sun. When the ship anchored in the evening, passengers were able to go ashore by tender and then take a forty-minute bus ride to the summit of the North Cape Plateau. Here, sheer cliffs rise over 1,000 feet above the Arctic Ocean. From this point one can watch the sun, at the midnight hour, nearly touch the horizon and slowly begin to rise. The entire face of the sun can be seen twenty-four hours a day from mid-May until the end of July. Norway's most dramatic monuments are the fjords; and the Geirangerfjord, where the cliffs tower above the ship and the famous Seven Sisters Waterfalls can be seen cascading into the sea, is the most favored of all. While the *QE2* was at anchor in Geiranger on July 16, 1983, an old naval tradition took place on the bridge. At a ceremony attended by Captain Arnott and Chief Officer Warwick, the ship's bell was used as a font to christen six-week-old Cybelle Lisbeth Kalvatn.

Each fall the world's premier marathon race takes place in New York City. The race was set for October 23, 1983, and it attracted some 17,000 runners from all fifty states and sixty-eight foreign countries to compete in the event. Among the vast throng of runners at the start of the marathon were five members of the *QE2*'s crew, who had been training on board and at various ports around the world whenever the opportunity arose. The *Queen* was scheduled to dock in New York on the morning of the marathon, but in order to be at the start on time, arrangements had to be made to pick up the runners as the ship passed under the Verrazano Narrows Bridge. A launch came alongside the *QE2* to take on the runners and ferry them to Staten Island, where, after a quick BBC interview, the five were rushed by limousine to the assembly point for the start of the race. Those taking part were Grenville Cartledge, Brian Marshall, Mike Burgess, Barry Brennan, and Peter Burge, all of whom completed the course. Many of the *Queen*'s crew members sponsored the New York Marathon runners, and as a result £1,778.11p ($2,700) was collected and shared between the National Lifeboat Institution and the Guide Dogs for the Blind Association. A guide dog was christened Marathon and his picture can be seen in one of the showcases on board the liner.

On November 28, 1983, the *Queen Elizabeth 2* arrived at Bremerhaven, West Germany, for her annual refitting. The announcement that the work costing some £2½ million ($3,750,000) was being carried out in Germany generated adverse reaction in the British press. Very little attention was given to the fact that the major British shipyards had admitted that they could not carry out the work on time, nor was there much focus on the fact that Cunard already had

The Queen Elizabeth 2 *has visited more ports along the long Norwegian coastline than in any other country. The annual North Cape cruise to the Land of the Midnight Sun always proves popular. One of the highlights of this cruise is the transversing of the Geiranger Fjord, with some of the most magnificent and rugged scenery in the world.*

The slate gray hull scheme was restored in June 1983, but the traditional Cunard Funnel was retained. The Queen *is shown as she was from late June 1983 to late December 1983 when the Lido Deck was reconstructed at Bremerhaven.*

spent £11 million on the ship in British yards since June 1982. A huge passenger liner cannot lie idle and wait for a berth to come along. She must receive the needed services promptly and be back on the line earning revenue as quickly as possible. At Bremerhaven, the Magradome was fitted over the quarterdeck swimming pool, making it available for use in all weather. Powerful new launches were added to assist in the transfer of passengers from ship

The QE2 rarely remains the same for a long period of time. A recent major improvement involved the covering of the Lido Deck pool with a retractable Magrodome, making it into an all-weather facility and vastly expanding the amenities of the ship. The work was done at Bremerhaven, West Germany, and involved both extensive preparations and precision handling.

The aft end of the Club Lido (ex-Q-4 Room) was sliced away on the North Atlantic by workmen who had joined the ship for the voyage. Then the Lido Deck was prepared for the Magrodome.

to shore at anchorage ports. Various sections of the ship were redecorated and refurbished in line with Cunard's ongoing program of maintaining the *QE2* as a vessel second to none.

By April 15, 1984, the *Queen Elizabeth 2* had visited 145 different places around the world during the first fifteen years of her career. The most frequently visited port was New York, with 325 calls, and Southampton, the *Queen*'s home port, was second with 240 dockings.

The world belongs to the *QE2*, as much as the *Queen* does to the world, because she is and remains unique. The 1984 great cruise was called the Quintessential World Cruise. One of the highlights of this voyage occurred on February 29, at Port Kelang in Malaysia when—at the invitation of His Royal Highness, the Sultan Salahuddin Abdul Aziz Shah of Selengor, and Her Royal Highness, the Tengku Ampuvan of Selengor—a banquet and entertainment in observance of the fourth annual *Queen Elizabeth 2* World Cruise Society was held for over 300 passengers at the royal palace. A fitting indication of the importance of the *Queen* to other nations and their people was given by the message of His Royal Highness, in which he said:

> I am privileged and honored to be given the opportunity to host this special function for the distinguished members of the World Cruise Society. Whilst it brings singular honors to me, it is equally an honor for all Malaysians and the State of Selengor in particular.

After the Queen Elizabeth 2's *return to the yard, the huge Magrodome was lifted from the yard by a powerful crane and positioned over the Lido Deck.*

Once the positioning appeared exact, the Magrodome could be lowered onto the liner and welded in place. What had been one of the Queen's *two outside pools and rarely usable on the North Atlantic was transformed into a universal asset.*

On behalf of the people of Malaysia and the State of Selengor, I wish you all a very warm welcome and hope your stay here will be a pleasant and memorable one. We sincerely hope that this magnificent ship will call at Port Kelang on all its round-the-world trips, so that many more people can enjoy our warmth and hospitality, and, that whilst this beautiful vessel makes our world smaller, we can in our journeys mutually help to bring peace, understanding, and happiness.

An Easter-egg hunt was the special event arranged for children when the ship arrived in New York on April 22, 1984. But when a five-year-old girl found a silver Easter egg worth a free cruise on the *QE2*, she was heard to say that what she really wanted was a chocolate one!

The *QE2* is like a city at sea, but when that city reaches port it must rely on a considerable amount of support for its survival. Occasionally the shore-operations department is taxed to the fullest extent to make arrangements that would normally be a routine event. Such was the case when the *QE2* was scheduled to arrive at Southampton on July 13, 1984, after a cruise with over 1,800 passengers on board. A sudden strike by dock workers in her home port of Southampton meant terminating the voyage across the channel at Cherbourg. This forced change in itinerary created a logistical challenge for the Cunard Line staff ashore as well as those on board. The purser's office was inundated with inquiries. Air transportation had to be chartered to take passengers and their baggage to England, and similar arrangements had to be made

At Bremerhaven the hull was thoroughly cleaned and painted as part of the annual refit. The anchor chains are payed out so that each anchor and all the links may be checked and painted. Note the bulbous bow that reduces water friction and the bow thruster doors on each side of the hull, open for inspection.

The Queen's *original propeller dwarfs the workmen in the drydock. Each of the six-bladed propellers weighed 31.75 tons and had a diameter of 19 feet. These propellers were replaced in 1987 by variable-pitch units with five blades each.*

for those joining the ship for the transatlantic voyage to New York. It was a mammoth undertaking trying to contact all the passengers and crew—plus some dogs, cats, and cars—joining the ship, many of whom were already heading for the scheduled departure port of Southampton. The store managers both ashore and afloat had their own problem to deal with as provisions and technical equipment for the following voyage also had to be air-freighted across the channel. Yet despite all the difficulties, the *QE2* managed to sail on time, maintaining her schedule. Unfortunately, for a ship the size of *QE2*, these operations do not come cheaply and the company had to face excess bills of hundreds of thousands of pounds.

To provide the ultimate combination of travel, the *Concorde* continues to be extensively used by the Cunard Line to carry passengers to and from the *QE2* and their other cruise ships. On February 13, 1985 one of the supersonic aircraft was chartered to take passengers from London to Sydney, Australia, to join the world cruises of the *QE2* and the *Sagafjord*—both in port together. The *Concorde* made the record-breaking trip in seventeen hours, three minutes, and forty-five seconds—including refueling stops at Bahrain, Colombo, and Perth. The following evening the *QE2* hosted a St. Valentine's Day ball, to which the passengers of the *Sagafjord* were invited.

The *Concorde* made her first commercial flight to South Africa the same year

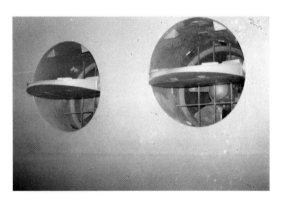

Bow thrusters enhance the Queen's *maneuverability. With the doors open, two variable-pitch propellers can be seen in through-hull tunnels. Each is 6.55 feet in diameter. When not in use, the doors fit flush against the hull.*

when she flew in to Cape Town with ninety-eight passengers who were joining the ship for the voyage to South America.

While off the coast of South Africa on March 25, 1985, the South African Air Force came to the assistance of the ship when they evacuated a sick crew member by helicopter and flew him to a hospital in Durban, where he later made a full recovery.

During the world cruise, the traditional country fair was held, and over £16,100 ($21,500) was raised by passengers and crew. The selected charity for 1985 was the Jubilee Sailing Trust Fund. The charity was dedicated to building a sail training ship for the handicapped named the *Lord Nelson*. The three-masted 150-foot-long barque was designed and built to carry a crew of twenty physically handicapped and twenty able-bodied passengers. It is often seen sailing around the coast of England and the Continent.

Most maritime cities regard the first visit of a ship to their port as an important occasion and, events are arranged to make the arrival a special one. Such was the case when the *QE2* made her inaugural visit to Baltimore on May 5, 1985. With a flotilla approaching 2,000 boats as well as helicopters and planes circling overhead, the ship passed under the Chesapeake Bay Bridge and made a stately entrance into the port. The city of Baltimore gave a regal wel-

The Queen Elizabeth 2 *steams into the Caribbean at the beginning of the 1984 World Cruise. The European, New York, and Florida passengers are on board for the trans-Canal section of the world cruise, which was totally sold out. The* Queen *is fresh from her annual overhaul and the installation of the new Magrodome and cruise launches at Bremerhaven.*

come to the ship and presented the passengers and crew with 5,000 long-stemmed red roses.

Three marvels of British technology came together in the English Channel on May 18, 1985, when the *QE2*, *Red Arrows*, and the *Concorde* were all photographed at the same time from a Hawk jet aircraft. It took months of careful planning to take this historic picture as the ship and airplanes had to rendezvous in daylight hours in good weather conditions.

On May 27, 1985, Captain T. D. Ridley, R.D., R.N.R., was appointed commodore of the Cunard Line. He was the first master to be appointed to this rank since Commodore W. E. Warwick retired from the sea in 1972.

Like any city, a ship the size of the *QE2* cannot be without the occasional mystery. A British vacationer was reported missing by his wife when he had not returned to his cabin by 2000 on October 29, 1985. Captain Lawrence Portet ordered a thorough search of the ship and, when convinced that the man was not on board, had the ship turned around and the course retraced. Although searchlights were used in the approaching darkness, the search was abandoned when the captain considered that there was no chance of ever finding anyone in the choppy sea.

History was made during the 1986 world cruise when the first-ever TV transmissions were received at sea. Programs received included *NBC Nightly News* with Tom Brokaw and even the U.S. Super Bowl—the highlight of the American football season. The television transmission was received from the Comsat satellite network on a gyroscopic antenna. The 1,100-pound antenna, over seven feet in diameter, was lowered in place by helicopter while the ship was in New York on January 14, 1986.

Another milestone in the life of the *QE2* was recorded while bound for New York on June 5, 1986, when a baby was born to Mrs. Kim Holtvoigt. The baby was delivered by the ship's medical officer, Dr. Mike Beeney. She was named Lauren and took United States citizenship, like her parents.

The *Queen Elizabeth 2* participated in the Statue of Liberty centennial celebrations in New York harbor on July 4, 1986. Cunard commissioned Garrards, the crown jewelers of London, to make a "freedom torch" as a gift to the American people. The torch, four feet high, made of copper, and decorated with gilt, is a contemporary copy of the torch held by Miss Liberty. The gift left England on June 26 sailing from Southampton and was presented to the National Maritime Historical Society in New York. It was escorted to the U.S.A. by a Polish immigrant family of four, Ryszard and Magdalena Olesiak and their two sons Karol (age 7) and Jakub (age 3). Like many immigrants to the United States, this family viewed America for the first time from the decks of a ship—but theirs was the *Queen Elizabeth 2*. As the *QE2* sailed under the Verrazano Narrows Bridge escorted by an armada of thousands of boats, a 100-foot American flag was unfurled over the side of the ship. Red, white, and blue balloons were released into the sky while red, white, and blue carnations were tossed into the river saluting America as the ship passed the Statue of Liberty. With the traditional fireboat welcome she then anchored off Liberty Island, joining many other naval and commercial ships from several other countries also there for the celebrations. It is estimated that Cunard has carried over two million immigrants to the U.S.A. since the company was founded in 1839.

In August 1986, the Cunard Line added two more ships to the fleet by taking over the operation of the *Sea Goddess* I & II from Norske Cruises. The two yacht-style cruise ships entered service in 1984 and 1985. They were built by Watsila in Finland, and each has fifty-eight staterooms for 116 passengers with a crew complement of 89. The two ships are built like private yachts and designed to provide an all-inclusive voyage in a private and luxurious atmosphere. Their itineraries are worldwide and they often call at remote and exotic ports inaccessible to larger ships.

When the *Queen Elizabeth 2* sailed from New York on October 20, 1986, with Captain Portet in command and John Chillingworth as chief engineer, another milestone was reached in the history of the Cunard Line. This was the last transatlantic crossing before replacing her steam-turbine propulsion plant with diesel engines. Thus ended 146 years of continuous steam service which began with the paddle steamer *Britannia*, the first ship to establish a scheduled transatlantic service. By the time the *QE2* arrived at the dockyard in Bremerhaven she had steamed 2,622,858 nautical miles since December 23, 1968, which represents over 120 times around the world.

CHAPTER EIGHT

THE END OF STEAM

Several well-known engine designers and shipyards from around the world were invited by Cunard in July 1983 to submit bids for the re-engining of the *QE2*. The decision to make this move was due to rising fuel costs, high maintenance and repair expenses, and the risk of engine failures in service. Extensive research by Cunard had revealed that replacing the steam turbines with a completely new engine plant would result in a reduction in engine-room manning and a saving in fuel consumption in the region of 200 tons per day. Although the designers had the freedom to propose the type of plant and the general arrangement of it, there were some strict criteria. The successful bidder would have to demonstrate that noise and vibration levels would not be higher than with the steam turbines, simultaneously carry out the upgrading of passenger and crew facilities, and complete the conversion work in less than six months against penalty clauses for late delivery. By the summer of 1985 the Cunard Line had decided that MAN-B&W diesel engines would be used and soon thereafter, on October 24, 1985, a contract was signed with Lloyd Werft Shipyard in Bremerhaven to carry out what would be the biggest marine engineering conversion job in merchant shipping history. No United Kingdom shipyard submitted a bid to carry out the work; however, approximately 30 percent of the contract price was spent in the U.K. on various parts of the propulsion plant. Despite requests to the British government for financial assistance, they refused to provide any contribution to the project. The contract valued at £180 million included the removal of the existing turbine plant, installation of new diesel engines, conversion of public rooms, improve-

One of the nine new diesel engines lies in the manufacturers' workshop. Each engine was assembled and tested ashore before being lifted into the ship through the access made by the removal of the funnel. (All photos on these pages courtesy of Martin Harrison.)

Before the new engines could be fitted at Bremerhaven in 1986, 4,700 tons of metal had to be removed. Here a section of the original 250-foot propeller shaft has been cut and drawn out of the stern tube.

ments in the kitchens, refurbishing of passenger cabins, upgrading of crew accommodations, and overhaul of the lifeboats and davits.

The *QE2* arrived at Bremerhaven on October 27, 1986, and soon thereafter stripping out of the old propulsion plant began. The first major item to be removed was the funnel, to provide access down through the center of the ship to the engine room. Most of the old machinery was lifted out through the casing, and the new engines were lowered down the same way. Over 4,700 tons of metal was removed from the ship within the first five weeks.

After an estimated 1.7 million man-hours of work, the ship was delivered back to the owners 179 days later on April 25, 1987.

Fitted with her new engines of 130,000 horsepower, the *Queen Elizabeth 2* became the world's most powerful marine propulsion plant. During the trial she

One of the steam turbines that helped to pro-pel the Queen *over two million nautical miles lies on the dockside at Bremerhaven, destined for scrap.*

The final section of the new 230-foot long port propeller shaft is being lined up to be in-serted into the stern tube (at left). The outer end of the shaft is covered to protect the mech-anism of the variable-pitch propeller blades.

reached a speed in excess of 33 knots and demonstrated an emergency stop in three minutes and eighteen seconds in a distance of 1.1 miles.

To achieve this performance, the *QE2* is fitted with nine medium-speed diesel engines. Each engine weighs 217 tons and has an output of 10,620kW (14,236 hp) at 400 revolutions per minute. They are arranged athwartships in two groups: four in the forward engine room and five in the after engine room. The engines are secured in position on antivibration mountings.

Each diesel engine is connected with a flexible coupling to an alternator to produce electricity. Any axial movement of the rotor caused by the rolling and pitching of the ship in rough weather is overcome by thrust pads fitted to the front end bearings. A brushless excitation system provides the field for the eighteen pole generators using a permanent magnet exciter. The power from

New highly polished variable-pitch propeller blades on the dock ready to be fitted to the shaft. Controls situated on the Bridge can vary the angle of the blades which enables the ship to be maneuvered in either direction without the need for a gear box or by reversing the engine. (Photo courtesy of Martin Harrison.)

all nine generators is fed directly to a common 10kV busbar system divided into two separate main switchboards. Each switchboard is installed in a separate compartment. The common busbar supplies the electricity to the two main propulsion motors. For domestic and ship's services use the voltage is transformed to 3,300 volts for distribution throughout the ship. Further voltage reduction to 415v, 220v, and 110v is performed by transformers local to the sub-switchboards for various uses.

The propulsion motors, made by GEC Large Machines, Ltd., England, are believed to be the largest single-unit propulsion motors in commercial service. Each weighs 295 tons and is rated at 44MW synchronous running at 144 rpm. The motors have a diameter of about 30 feet, and due to space constraints they were made especially for the ship. A variable-frequency synchro convertor starting system makes it possible to start the motors without the high current that would be required directly from the generators. To allow for the ship to operate at maximum efficiency at slow speed, the constant propeller speed can be reduced to 72 rpm with the use of the 11MW convertors. Each motor is connected to a 230-foot-long propeller shaft inclined downward at 1.5 degrees to the horizontal extending sternward to each side of the rudder.

This picture shows the seven-bladed Grimm Wheels, which rotated freely on the propeller shaft and were designed to improve efficieny by recovering energy lost in the slip stream. Unfortunately some of the blades broke off during trials so the wheels were removed entirely and have never been replaced.

The two controllable-pitch propellers, 22 feet in diameter, were made by Lips BV., Holland. They have five blades shaped to provide maximum thrust and at the same time reduce tip vortexes and cavitation. The design, to absorb 44MW at 144 rpm makes them the most powerful CP propellers in the world. The pitch of the blades can be controlled from the engine control room or from the bridge.

The propellers were designed to function with Grimm Wheels. The seven-bladed vane wheels are fitted behind the propellers and freely rotate on the same shaft. These wheels are in use on other ships to reclaim part of the energy normally lost in the slipstream of the propeller and convert it into additional thrust. They were predicted to do the same on the *Queen Elizabeth 2* and to save 2 to 4 percent in fuel costs. Unfortunately, some of the vanes were lost during trials so the remainder of the blades on both shafts were removed and not replaced.

The operation of the engine plant is fully automated by electronically controlled governors which help to ensure optimum efficiency and safety. In port, one diesel will remain on line for domestic services with another on standby which will activate automatically should the need arise. When the ship is preparing to sail, the operator selects the "ready to sail" mode, which causes three more diesel engines to come on line and a further two diesel units to come on standby. Lubricating oil pumps and ventilators are automatically started.

When all the conditions have been satisfied, the computer will indicate the "ready to sail" condition and maneuvering can commence. The next stage is the "combinator" mode. This starts the two propulsion motors running at a speed of 72 rpm. At this time the propeller pitch is at zero. The power now available is about 11 MW per shaft for ahead and 8 MW per shaft for going astern. This will give about 16 knots speed ahead.

After the ship has left the harbor, the "free sailing" mode is selected. This will cause the speed of the propulsion motors to be increased to 144 revolutions per minute and automatically synchronized onto the main busbar. The propeller pitch commensurate with the desired speed is selected by the telegraph unit, and additional diesel engines will automatically be activated as required to achieve the required power.

The Engine Control Room (ECR) was redesigned during the refitting to permit the machinery space to be left unmanned. With the aid of computerization, data is centrally collected in this one room. About 4,000 pieces of data such as oil pressures, water and oil temperatures, voltages, and currents can be requested and displayed on screens. Critical values are highlighted. Closed-circuit television cameras monitor the machinery space in twenty-six locations. A panel is centrally located to indicate the rudder and propeller pitch angles, the speed and engine revolutions. Nearby are the levers to control the propulsion and associated machinery. These controls are duplicated on the bridge so that the ship can be operated from either position.

As far as possible, machinery is divided between the forward and after engine rooms—either of which can be operated independently to run the ship in

Data from the engines and ancillary services is fed electronically to the Engine Control Room which enables the officers on duty to monitor all aspects of the machinery. Closed-circuit television provides a constant visual surveillance of the machinery in twenty-six locations. (Photo courtesy of Robin Ebers.)

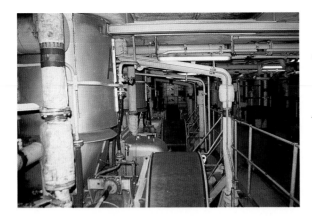

The turbo-charger casings in the center of the picture are situated above the couplings connecting the engines to the alternators. Exhaust gas from each engine is carried to the funnel by the large trunkings on the left. Within the funnel, heat from the exhaust is recovered in specially designed boilers to provide steam to heat the fuel and domestic water. (Photo courtesy of Martin Harrison.)

the event of serious damage in the other engine room. Emergency shutdown systems operated from the ECR include electrical switching to stop all pumps passing flammable liquid, ventilation fans, dampers, main engines, and boilers. A Halon gas system is fitted for use in an emergency. In the event of fire, the gas can be discharged from the storage cylinders in about twenty seconds after shutting down the machinery and sealing the compartment. This gas breaks the chain reaction in the combustion process and thus extinguishes the fire.

As part of the re-engining, the whole of the inside of the funnel had to be replaced, so it was removed to carry out this work. Exhaust gas pipes and silencers for the nine diesel engines and space ventilation ducting were all fitted into a metal framework prefabricated ashore in two parts and then assembled on the ship. The original funnel casing, considerably widened, was then replaced over the new stack.

Twenty-four exhaust and supply ventilators have been fitted for ventilation to the engine rooms for the supply of combustion air and heat removal. The ventilators can supply 2 million cubic meters per hour and remove 1.4 million cubic meters per hour.

For domestic power and services, any combination of the nine alternators can be operated to supply power to the common busbar. Via transformers, some of this power can be directed to the domestic busbar (up to 3,300 volts) to operate the heating, lighting, fans, and other auxiliary machinery throughout the ship.

Steam is still used for domestic heating and for heating water and fuel. When the ship is at sea, the steam is provided by exhaust-gas boilers fitted to each of the diesel engine uptakes. Two auxiliary oil-fired boilers with a capacity of twenty-five tons per hour provide a backup supply. An estimated 74 percent of all waste heat will be recovered. The new boiler plant was manufactured by Sunrod International AB of Sweden.

Fresh water is made by four SERCK vacuum evaporators having a total daily output of 1,000 tons per day. Heating for the evaporators is mainly pro-

This view of the Queen's bulbous bow makes it hard to believe that its design improves the hull's efficiency. In the drydock, the damaged paint is scrapped away and recoated with primers and then the entire bottom is repainted with a special paint that gradually wears away so that the hull remains smooth and free of barnacle growth.

At each drydocking the anchors and chains are lowered out on to the dock for inspection. Each chain is 1,080 feet long and it is made up in lengths of 90 feet. The joining shackle of each length is painted white to identify the amout that is to be used when the ship is at anchor.

vided by cooling water from the diesel engines. It can also be provided by steam-heated booster heaters so that output can be maintained if the ship is on reduced speed or if all the diesel engines are not running. In addition, there is a reverse osmosis plant that can produce up to 450 tons of fresh water a day.

The bilge and ballast pumping systems were completely renewed in the conversion areas, and some tank modification and repairs were carried out. Pumping operations are activated from the Safety Control Room on Two Deck.

The two bow thruster units, one of which is twelve feet to the rear of the other, were supplied by Stone Manganese Marine, Ltd., London. Both are contained in separate tunnels that pass laterally through the hull about 18 feet below the water line. Each unit has four variable-pitch blades 6.55 feet in diameter driven by an AEl 1000hp electric motor controlled directly from the bridge. Steel flush-mounted hydraulically operated tunnel doors preserve the streamlining of the hull when the thrusters are not in use.

The semibalanced rudder, which weighs seventy-five tons, was manufactured in Norway by A/S Strommens Vaerksted. It is controlled by a four-ram electro hydraulic steering gear supplied by Brown Brothers of Edinburgh. Although one is sufficient, it has two pumping units. Under normal conditions the steering gear is operated automatically from the bridge, but in an emergency the rudder can be controlled from a position local to the machinery.

The Denny-Brown AEG stabilizers were manufactured by Brown Brothers. Each of the four retractable fins has an area of seventy square feet. Fully extended, they protrude about twelve feet out from the ship's side. When not in use or when entering port, the fins are hinged forward into recesses in the ship's hull. All four fins are controlled from a central point but are hydraulically independent of one another and are fully automatic in action. In use, the stabilizers work in pairs, on each side of the ship, pivoting in opposite directions to counteract the roll.

Passive resistance to the rolling motion is present in the form of bilge keels which are fixed to the turn of the hull on each side of the ship.

The re-engining of the *QE2* was continually supervised by the Cunard Line team of shore-based staff and, most importantly, by the shipboard engineer officers who take the ship to sea. The ship's officers come under the leadership of the chief engineer who's responsibilities are far-reaching and rarely fully appreciated by the crew, not to mention the passengers. The achievements of his department are more often overshadowed by the grandeur of the ship. His expertise, and those of the design engineers, led to the successful completion of yet another episode in the continuing technical challenge that the Atlantic Ocean has provided since Samuel Cunard's first pioneering voyage of the *Britannia* in 1840.

CHAPTER NINE

INTO A NEW ERA

The *QE2*'s return to service in April 1987 coincided with an important accolade to the company — The Queen's Award for export achievement was presented to the Cunard Line. Presenting the award, Field Marshal the Lord Bramall, the Lord-Lieutenant of Greater London said: "Cunard was selected for this honor because the company has not only generated and sustained a significant increase in overseas income, especially from the U.S.A., but has achieved it in an industry noted for over-capacity and ferocious competition."

On April 29, The Princess of Wales made her first visit to the *Queen Elizabeth 2* when she embarked off Cowes, on the Isle of Wight to join a party of over 400 schoolchildren from the Southampton area who had boarded the ship at the dock. During her tour of the ship, Princess Diana visited the bridge and sounded the ship's whistle — as Prince Charles had done in the Clyde nineteen years previously. There was a fly-pass by the *Concorde* and a display of R.A.F. Harrier jets. While on board Princess Diana unveiled a silver plaque commemorating her visit, which is on display in the midships lobby on Two Deck.

The month of May saw the North Atlantic gales initiate the newly commissioned *QE2* on her way back from her first trip to new York since the engine conversion. The storm, with winds up to fifty knots and forty-foot seas, was encountered during the evening and was unexpected. As a result there was considerable damage, especially in the kitchens where racks of china broke adrift. In the lounge, the piano and numerous items of furniture were overturned. It was one of the worst crossing in years, and not surprisingly the ship arrived several hours late.

A new United States Customs policy subjecting all vessels and airplanes

QE2 carried a message for the citizens of New York as she steamed up the Hudson River into her berth on the west side of Manhattan. On this occasion four Moran tugs were required to assist her to dock against strong tides. (Photo courtesy Francis J. Duffy.)

Shortly after docking in New York a bunker barge is positioned alongside the Queen to replenish the supply of oil fuel used during a trans-Atlantic crossing. Over 4500 tons of fuel can be kept in various tanks along the bottom of the ship. (Photo courtesy J. R. Murphy.)

coming from Colombia to intensive searches caused many of the passengers and crew of the *Queen Elizabeth 2* consternation when she arrived at Los Angeles on January 28, 1988. A six-hour search for drugs delayed the disembarkation and postponed crew leave for hours while five trained dogs ran through the ship and sniffed luggage on the quay belonging to the 1,265 disembarking passengers.

Captain Alan Bennell had the honor of entertaining Her Majesty Queen Elizabeth, the Queen Mother, for lunch on board in Southampton on December 14, 1988. The occasion was to celebrate the fiftieth anniversary of Her Majesty's launching of the *Queen Elizabeth* at Clydebank, Scotland, on September 27, 1938.

To celebrate the 130th anniversary of the city of Yokohama, a consortium of Japanese companies chartered the *Queen Elizabeth 2* for seventy-two days. The charter commenced on March 27, 1989, and the ship docked alongside the passenger terminal in the port as a central attraction. Although she did not go to sea, she maintained her status as an ocean liner throughout her stay. Every day several hundred visitors arrived to spend the night aboard and another twelve hundred or so would just spend a few hours having lunch, looking around, or shopping. All the usual events took place—the bars, casino, swimming pools, beauticians, and shops were open, and there was a full program of entertainment. The atmosphere was kept Western, but it was supplemented by Japanese staff with signs and menus translated into their language. The authorities permitted wedding ceremonies to be carried out on board, but the captain only acted as a witness. In December the *QE2* returned to Japan for a similar six-month charter for the World Exposition in Osaka. After Expo, the ship made short cruises to Hong Kong and other nearby ports.

Under the command of Captain Robin Woodall, R.D., R.N.R., in July 1990 the ship made her fastest-ever eastbound crossing of the Atlantic Ocean. Her average speed was 30.16 knots in four days, six hours, and fifty-seven minutes—99 minutes less than the previous fastest passage.

To commemorate 150 years of achievement and to mark the maiden voyage of the *Britannia* in 1840, Cunard planned a series of special voyages and cruises in 1990. The most colorful cruise began from Southampton on July 22, when the *Queen* sailed for Cóbh, Liverpool, Greenock, and Cherbourg.

About 60,000 people turned out to greet the ship when she sailed into Cóbh at dawn on July 23. It was he first time the *QE2* had docked in the Irish port. She berthed at the new Ringaskiddy container terminal which was then officially opened by the Irish premier, Charles Haughey. After the ceremony, the premier joined Captain Woodall and other distinguished guests for a reception on board.

When the *Queen Elizabeth 2* arrived at Liverpool the following day on her very first visit ever, she received the most spectacular of welcomes. Hundreds of thousands of spectators cheering and waving banners from the riverbanks and a flotilla of boats of many shapes and sizes greeted the *QE2* as she approached her anchorage. Throughout the day people came out to greet the ship and sight her from the banks of the Mersey during the day. The *Queen* was anchored in the River Mersey near the spot where the paddle steamer *Britannia* had sailed on her historic maiden voyage to Boston and Halifax 150 years previously. An inaugural party was held on deck shortly before noon, and to mark the occasion 10,000 balloons were released from the quarterdeck swimming pool. Many of the crew had gathered in the Magradome the previous evening and worked well into the night inflating the balloons. The port of Liverpool bid farewell to the liner amid a spectacular fireworks display and the twinkling flashes of light from thousands of cameras.

The nostalgic arrival at Greenock on July 25, marked the first return of the *Queen* to Scotland since she had been launched in 1967. Again she was greeted by thousands gathered at every vantage point as she docked to the sounds of the Strathclyde Police Pipe Band.

When the *QE2* sailed from Cherbourg on July 26, Captain Ronald W. Warwick was in command, having taken over from the senior master, Captain Woodall, in order to release him for the events of the following day. This event was another historic occasion in the Cunard Line because it was the first known time that a Cunard master had captained the same ship as his father, Commodore W. E. Warwick.

The climax of the 150th anniversary year celebrations took place in Southampton waters on July 27, 1990. This was the royal review of Cunard and Royal Navy ships at Spit Head by Her Majesty Queen Elizabeth II from H.M.Y. *Britannia*. The royal yacht was led by T.H.V. *Patricia* with the Elder Brethren of Trinity House lining her forecastle. The long-standing tradition of the Elder Brethren escorting the monarch while in pilotage waters was started by George IV in 1822. (The corporation has been closely associated with the royal yachts since 1660.) The parade of ships was followed by a fly-past of the *Concorde*, a Britannia B747, a Virgin Atlantic B707, Sea Harrier aircraft, and the Trafalgar House Dauphine helicopter which had been carried on the deck of *QE2* for the cruise.

Shortly before noon the royal yacht stopped nearby, and Her Majesty and H.R.H. Prince Phillip transferred by tender to the *QE2*. As Her Majesty stepped on board, her personal Standard was broken out at the truck to indi-

Her Majesty Queen Elizabeth II listens with interest to Captain Warwick on the bridge during her visit commemorating the 150th anniversary year of Cunard Line. Cunard Line's senior master, Captain Robin Woodall R.D., R.N.R. (right) talks with His Royal Highness, the Prince Philip while he inspects the steering wheel. (Photo courtesy Ocean Pictures.)

The highlight of the 150 anniversary year celebrations in 1990 was the royal review in Southampton. The royal yacht Britannia, *bearing the same name as Samuel Cunard's first ship sails past the* QE2 *as she lies majestically at anchor in the River Solent. (Photo courtesy Glyn Genin.)*

cate her presence on board. Sir Nigel Broakes, chairman of Trafalgar House, and Captain Woodall were at the gangway to meet the royal party and to escort them to the Queen's Room for a reception. Her Majesty the Queen then went in to the Grand Lounge to unveil a plaque commemorating her visit on board. As the queen made her way to the Columbia Restaurant, she took time to speak with passengers. During lunch the *QE2* weighed anchor and, led by the T.H.V. *Patricia* slowly cruised toward the docks. Her Majesty arrived on the bridge in time to witness the liner she had launched and named after herself in 1967 dock gently alongside the terminal. Her Majesty the Queen made history when she became the first reigning monarch to sail on a commercial liner with other passengers.

When the *Queen Elizabeth 2* arrived in New York from Southampton on August 9, 1990, she had completed her five-hundredth scheduled transatlantic crossing since coming into service. At an average speed of 28½ knots the crossing takes about four and a half days, depending on the route taken. The weather forecast and reports of the presence of icebergs in the region of the Grand Banks of Newfoundland will have a bearing on which course is set. If the ice has drifted well to the south, an extra hundred and fifty miles could be

When the QE2 *went to Germany for repairs in 1992 she was comfortably accommodated in one of the largest floating drydocks in the world which is situated on the river in the heart of the city of Hamburg. (Photo courtesy Ian Denton.)*

added to the overall distance.

On August 20, 1990, the *QE2* was heading against gale-force winds for the North Sea on the first day of the Norwegian cruise. Shortly after midday, the chief radio officer informed Captain Warwick that the automatic radio receiver had picked up the international distress signal, MAYDAY, from the accommodation platform West Gamma. The message said that the rig was adrift with forty-nine persons on board, the helicopter landing platform was damaged, some lifesaving appliances had been destroyed, and the rig was in danger of capsizing. They requested immediate assistance. A few minutes later the situation was confirmed by the Danish Coast Guard, and the *QE2* altered course for the distress area forty-seven miles away. Although proceeding at full speed, the *QE2* was still battling against high seas and force-nine winds, thus it was not until two hours and eighteen minutes later that the rig was sighted in the overcast sky ahead. By this time, rescue helicopters and other vessels had appeared on the scene. On arrival, the *QE2* was put in charge of the rescue operations, but soon thereafter the captain of the rig informed Captain Warwick that they had their situation under control and did not wish to be evacuated. The rig captain then re-

During a world cruise the QE2 lies peacefully at anchor in the tranquillity of the Tahitian Islands. The ships tenders lay alongside ready to ferry passengers ashore.

leased the *Queen Elizabeth 2* from the obligation to stand by and passage to Bergen, Norway, was resumed. Unfortunately the West Gamma did capsize later that same night, and fortunately all the crew were rescued from the sea by helicopters.

Rounding off the 150th celebration year, the *QE2* made calls to Halifax and Boston—the first ports visited by the paddle steamer *Britannia* in 1840. Governor Michael Dukakis of Massachusetts declared September 4 "Cunard Day" throughout the state in honor of the company's anniversary.

The year 1990 came to a close when the *QE2* proceeded to Hamburg for her refitting in December. The yard selected to carry out the work was Blohm and Voss located, in the heart of the city. The *QE2* entered one of the largest floating dry docks in the world and, within a few hours of arrival, was lifted out of the water. In addition to major overhaul of the hull and machinery, the casino, which had been designed by Graham Faye, was extended and remodeled and a new restaurant, the Princess Grill Starboard, was added.

Meanwhile in Malta, the *Cunard Princess* was chartered by the United States Army for service in the Persian Gulf. The cruise ship was based in Bahrain as a rest-and-recreation facility for U.S. troops involved in Operation Desert

Storm. Every three days 850 soldiers would come aboard and enjoy all of the facilities available to passengers on a cruise, in particular hot showers and cold beer. There was only two differences: There was no casino, and the ship never sailed. General Norman Schwarzkopf visited the *Cunard Princess* and paid tribute to the crew. Later the ship was issued a certificate of commendation for "Outstanding Performance and Meritorious Service" toward the 50,000 troops that spent time on board.

His Royal Highness, the Prince Edward, made his debut on board the *Queen Elizabeth 2* on June 15, 1991, when he attended the *QE2* Royal Ball with his father, the Duke of Edinburgh. The Prince is the chairman of the Duke of Edinburgh's Award Special Projects Group.

Shortly after the *QE2* returned from her 1992 world cruise, a celebration was held on board to commemorate the tenth anniversary of the Falkland Campaign. The guest of honor for the luncheon was the Right Honourable Margaret Thatcher, O.M., F.R.S. In a speech after lunch, Sir Nigel Broakes welcomed Mrs. Thatcher and said the company was pleased that the *QE2* had been able to be of service for the campaign. In response, Mrs. Thatcher gave a stirring speech in which she spoke of the events leading up to the war and emphasized the importance of the *QE2*'s participation in it.

Misfortune came to the *QE2* on a cruise a few months later when she was sailing westerly along Vineyard Sound off the New England coast bound for New York. Shortly before 2200 on August 7 when passing south of Cuttyhunk Island, the captain, pilot, and officers on the bridge felt a rumbling, heavy vibration and the ship shaking. The captain's first reaction was to think that the ship had struck a floating object or there was a problem in the engine room. These thoughts were quickly eliminated and the least-expected conclusion was that the ship must have struck an uncharted object or rocks on the sea bed. Captain Woodall immediately stopped the ship and ordered some of the crew to emergency stations to inspect for any possible damage. The chief engineer soon reported that the steering gear and propulsion machinery was not affected and remained in full working order.

From other parts of the ship it was reported that the vibration was either more noticeable or not even felt. Some passengers seated for dinner noticed a slight discomfort, but it was not enough to stop a group of waiters in the Columbia Restaurant from singing happy anniversary to a celebrating couple. There was no panic, and most people were untroubled by the incident. The evening's cabaret continued, the musicians played on, and the roulette wheel kept spinning in the casino.

Meanwhile information was received on the bridge that there was water in some of the double-bottom tanks that should have been empty. It was then concluded that two freshwater tanks, one saltwater ballast tank, and an empty fuel tank had been breached. However, calculations established that the stability of the ship was not in any danger and that any ingress of water could be adequately taken care of with the water ballast pumps.

As a formality, the captain notified the United States Coast Guard by radio and was informed by them that the liner must anchor nearby for further investigation until they were satisfied that there was no danger to passengers or a threat of oil pollution to the environment. These procedures took a long time, and the *Queen* had to remain where she was until 1700 hours the following day.

On hearing the news, Cunard Line personnel in New York swung into action to prepare for a mass disembarkation of passengers. Obtaining transport at short notice over the weekend was no easy task. One enterprising bus owner telephoned the head office and offered to send five busses from as far away as New Jersey, which were gratefully accepted. Local ferry boats were chartered to take some passengers ashore to Newport, where they were met by bus and transferred to trains for onward travel to New York. The baggage was discharged from the ship when it arrived at Boston and was sent to the owners by air services. The *QE2* arrived in Boston the following Monday and later entered the drydock.

An inspection of the hull commenced as soon as all the water was pumped out of the drydock. The damaged area was found to be mainly confined to the forward section of the ship near the keel where the steel is one and one-half inches thick and constructed to withstand the inclement elements of the North Atlantic in the winter. A series of intermittent gashes were sighted up to seventy-four feet long and three inches wide running in various areas between the bow and amidships. The after part of the ship including the propellers and rudder were unscathed. Temporary repairs, which included welding over of the small cracks and fitting steel patches over the larger ones, were carried out by the General Ship Corporation of Boston. Meanwhile after inviting bids from several shipyards in the U.S.A. and Europe, Cunard chose Blohm & Voss of Hamburg, Germany, to carry out the permanent repairs.

As a result of the accident, the first survey in fifty-three years of Vineyard Sound was carried out by the National Oceanic and Atmospheric Administration (NOAA). The NOAA survey discovered the presence of uncharted rocks in the position of the incident and also other previously uncharted ridges in the seabed in the general area.

The repairs were completed by October 4, and the *Queen* resumed service for a brief period with a cruise from Southampton. By the end of the following November she had returned to Hamburg once again to have one of the engines replaced. This work had been scheduled long before the incident at Martha's Vineyard, but unfortunately the replacement engine could not be made available at the same time as the hull repairs because it was still under construction.

Both the drydock periods provided an opportunity to carry out further upgrades of the internal accommodations. This included refurbishing of the movie theater and the commencement of a major redesign and rebuilding of the Spa at Sea. By mid-December the *Queen* was back in service on the Atlantic heading for New York and the 1993 world cruise.

The *Queen Elizabeth 2* has traveled over three and a quarter million miles and visited 201 different places around the world during the twenty-five years since she was launched on September 20, 1967. She represents one of the most complex integrations of design and machinery ever constructed by man—a vessel capable of going almost anywhere on the globe covered by oceans, seas, and rivers carrying nearly 2,000 passengers and a 1,000-member crew at a speed in excess of 30 miles an hour in the height of luxury. When she went into service in 1969 she was revolutionary in many ways. Today, two and a half decades later, she remains technically modern, and continued efforts will be made to keep her so. Her voyages have taken her through many contrasts of cultures and civilizations. Every journey is different, memorable, and important in one way or another to those who sail on board her. The *Queen* is the last of the great luxury liners and when she goes, an era will end. While she remains, and continues to carry the flag of the world's first and oldest transatlantic steamship company, she is the most majestic and sophisticated passenger liner ever built and bears testimony to the traditions that Cunard signifies: luxury, elegance, life enrichment, and international friendship.

The *Queen Elizabeth 2* sails on as a living memory and monument to the founder, Sir Samuel Cunard.

CHAPTER TEN

GUIDE TO THE *QUEEN ELIZABETH 2*

The guide to the *QE2*, starting on the uppermost deck and working down and forward to aft on each deck, describes the *QE2* as she presently exists with the various alterations that have been made since she first went into service in 1969. The majority were incorporated to upgrade the standard of passenger life on board. Other alterations, such as those to accommodate the health spa and Computer Learning Centre, reflect the requirements of modern living.

The Mast

Next to the funnel, the top of the mast is the highest part of the ship, being 169 feet, 1 inch above the waterline when the draft is 31 feet. Because the aerial for the satellite navigation system was situated at the top, the mast was 5 feet higher when the ship was commissioned. This aerial was removed when the satellite receiver was updated. Unlike the old liners, the *QE2* does not have a crow's nest, but there is access to the navigation lights and whistles provided by a 40-foot ladder inside the mast. Part of the mast also acts as a duct to ventilate air from the kitchens.

A closed-circuit television camera is installed on the mast, which is directed astern. This enables the engineer officer on watch in the engine control room to monitor the engine exhaust from the funnel.

The Funnel

The funnel, 204 feet, 1½ inches above the keel, is 4 feet higher than the mast and from an external view probably the most noticeable feature of the *QE2*.

The original black-and-white color scheme of the funnel was a breakaway from Cunard tradition, but at the time it was felt that the red with black bands would not look appropriate with the modern functional design. However, in 1982 when the hull color was changed to a very light gray, the funnel was painted in Cunard colors and remained as such when the hull was sprayed again in 1983 to its present-day dark gray.

The design of the funnel was the result of many months of research carried out by Cunard's technical department and wind-tunnel tests at the National Physical Laboratory at Teddington, Middlesex. With so much open deck space on the *QE2*, it was paramount that fumes and the occasional soot ejected from the funnel be carried well clear of the ship. To achieve this, used air from within the ship is ducted up behind the main boiler vents to create an area of high pressure and keep the exhaust up and away from the decks. In some wind conditions, however, this would not be sufficient, and the smoke would swirl back down again over the decks. To overcome this, the shovel-shaped scoop was designed and introduced to direct a stream of air up and behind the vents.

During re-engining in 1986, the funnel was removed and modified to accommodate part of the new propulsion equipment. The exterior shape is slightly wider than the original design.

Signal Deck

The Signal Deck is the highest deck on the ship. Forward, the most important area is the bridge, which consists of the wheelhouse and chart room. The bridge of the *QE2* contains some of the most advanced, as well as the more traditional, navigational equipment used today. There are two state-of-the-art Krupp Atlas radars. These afford both daylight viewing, with a computerized

The mast of the QE2 towers 200 feet, 1 inch above the keel of the liner, and 169 feet, 1 inch above the waterline, when the Queen is drawing her normal 31-foot draft. Next to the funnel, the top of the mast is the highest part of the ship.

facility for plotting targets automatically, as well as the capability to superimpose maps on the screen when approaching a harbor or coastal areas. There are Decca and Loran navigators, a Marconi direction finder for coastal position fixing, and a Magnavox Satellite Omega Navigator and Global Positioning System (GPS) for ocean passages. Other equipment includes depth recorders, magnetic compasses, a Doppler speed log, Tyfon whistles, and Sperry Gyro compasses coupled to an automatic pilot for steering. Facilities are available for receiving weather reports from meteorological stations ashore. The standard compass is situated on the roof of the bridge so that it is as far as possible from any magnetism generated by electrically operated equipment.

Consoles in the center of the bridge house controls for the variable-pitch propellers, bow thrusters, steering, and stabilizers. There are numerous indicator lights and dials showing the state of the propulsion plant and the operational status of the console controls. The propeller pitch, bow thruster, and steering controls are duplicated in the smaller consoles situated on each wing of the bridge.

The bridge is always manned by at least one qualified officer twenty-four hours of the day throughout the year. When the ship is at sea, there are always two officers on duty. In addition to his navigation duties, the officer on watch is responsible for the safety of the ship. In an emergency, he can close the watertight doors from the bridge. He also has direct communication with the

The area aft of the funnel on Sports Deck is usually referred to as the "helicopter deck." This photograph would have been taken during a chilly trans-Atlantic crossing when the deck stewards traditionally turn the chairs to face the sun and provide passengers with thick blankets and warm drinks at their request. (Photo courtesy Robin Ebers.)

safety control room, the engine room, and the fire equipment lockers.

The chart room is situated behind the bridge. This is mainly the navigator's domain and, as the name implies, is where all the charts are stowed when not in use. Charts are kept on board covering all the principal ocean routes and leading cruise ports of the world. Nearby is the Captain's Sea Cabin. This is a small room for his use in bad weather or in other circumstances when it is necessary to be immediately available to the bridge.

Astern of the mast is the upper level of the penthouse suites (described below), which is reached by a secluded elevator or stairway from either one of the two decks below. In 1987, eight more suite rooms were added, filling in the open deck space that had existed forward of the funnel base.

Farther astern are the pet kennels. This area is reached from the inside by a stairway on the starboard side of the Boat Deck, astern of the "D" stairway. There are accommodations and an exercise area on deck for eleven animals. Dogs, the most frequent travelers, are more privileged than the rest—they have their own lamppost.

Sports Deck

Reached from the stairs leading up from each side of the Boat Deck is the foremost observation area on the Signal Deck. The whole of the foredeck can be seen from this point. Immediately behind it are the captain's and senior officers' quarters.

Continuing aft is the lower level of the penthouses. The penthouse accommodations did not exist when the ship was commissioned. They replaced an area of deck enclosed at the sides but open to the sky.

The penthouses were added in three stages—the first at Southampton during the 1972 refitting. The suites were prefabricated ashore and then lifted on board in two halves. Each room was given a distinctive atmosphere of its own. The two premier units on each side forward are two story, spanning the Signal

The bridge on Signal Deck sweeps across the ship from wing to wing, providing the officers on duty with a commanding view of the ship fore and aft. Beneath the bridge is the Sports Deck observation area, and beneath that the long line of windows indicate the officers' wardroom. The white boxlike shape in the center was added in 1972 and houses a portion of the kitchens. On either side of the Quarter Deck forward are the QE2's cranes, capable of lifting 5 tons each, and forward of them on One Deck are the capstans and anchor chains.

and Sports Decks, each with its own private internal stairway. The port-side penthouse was named the Trafalgar Suite and was originally designed and furnished to resemble Lord Nelson's quarters on the H.M.S. *Victory*, even to the inclusion of a contemporary portrait of Lady Emma Hamilton. The starboard duplex, the Queen Anne Suite, was furnished in the style and period of the name that it bears. Each of the luxury suites has two bathrooms and private verandas overlooking the sea. The Queen Mary and Queen Elizabeth

Captain Warwick joined the Cunard Line as a junior officer in 1970. Twenty years later he is on the bridge in command of the Queen Elizabeth 2 standing in the same spot that his father, Commodore W. E. Warwick C.B.E., R.D., R.N.R., stood during the ship's maiden voyage in 1969.

suites were added when the ship was having her annual overhaul at Bayonne, New Jersey, in 1977. These two split-level suites are more luxurious than any others available at sea, and in addition to verandas they have their own individual sun decks with panoramic views forward over the bridge and ocean.

The majority of the suite rooms are totally refurbished approximately every two years when the ship goes into refitting. Additional features subsequently fitted included whirlpool baths and video-cassette players.

Continuing aft is the Children's Playroom, which was designed by Elizabeth Beloe and Tony Heaton while they were students of interior design at the Royal College of Arts. The room, staffed with an English nanny, retains its original design and includes a nursery for young children and a movie theater with a sloping floor for those that are older. Although inboard, the room is bright and gay with lots of colorful cupboards. Curvy fiberglass screens that divide part of the room make it an attractive play area for children's games.

Farther astern on each side of the deck are the radio and engineer officers' accommodations. The cabins are single berth, and each has its own adjoining bathroom.

Doorways lead out onto the open deck—commonly referred to as the "helicopter deck." The large cross painted on the deck is a guide for helicopter pilots when making their approach.

Boat Deck

Right forward on the Boat Deck is the officers' wardroom and dining room, the windows of which look out over the foredeck. The wardroom houses a splendid array of nautical memorabilia collected since the ship came into service. Situated in a prominent position are signed prints of Her Majesty Queen Elizabeth II and the Duke of Edinburgh presented to the wardroom in 1970. Below the prints is the original brass bell from the Cunarder R.M.S. *Aquitania*.

On the starboard side aft of the wardroom are accommodations for the navigating officers, which also include a duty room for use by the officers when the ship is in port.

Outside the wardroom is the top of the "A" stairway. For those not put off by heights, there is an impressive view from the top all the way down to Five Deck. Nearby can be seen the *Britannia* figurehead. This was originally situated at the forward entrance to the Britannia Restaurant by "A" stairway one deck below. The figurehead is carved out of Quebec yellow pine by Cornish sculptor Charles Moore and was presented to the ship by Lloyds of London.

The radio room is situated on the port side of the square. This department is manned twenty-four hours a day. The officers are constantly in touch with the outside world by radio telegraphy, telex, FAX, and satellite links. The ship's newspaper is received via satellite daily from the U.S.A. and the United Kingdom. Since the ship was launched there have been many equipment changes in the radio room reflecting the advances in communications technology. In 1989, a Magnavox system was installed enabling passengers to dial directly

The Penthouses on QE2 are amongst the most spacious ever to be made available at sea. They are arranged on two decks and can be reached by a private stairway or elevator.

The most prestigious cabins on the ship are the Queen Mary and Queen Elizabeth suites. They are arranged on a split level and the sitting room opens out into a secluded sun deck.

The Penthouse suites are attended by some of Cunard's longest serving and most experienced stewardesses and butlers. Service is available twenty-four hours a day from the moment a passenger steps on board.

The adventurous atmosphere of the Children's Playroom has entertained youngsters since the ship came into service in 1969. It is one of the few rooms on the ship that has never been altered from the original design. (Photo courtesy Robin Ebers.)

from their cabins to virtually anywhere in the world.

Double glass doors lead from the square to the Queen's Grill Restaurant. When the ship was commissioned, this was known as the 736 Club, the number 736 being the one given by the ship's builders to identify the "job." The *QE2* did not have a casino when first in service due to restrictive laws that existed in the U.S. When the laws were relaxed, the 736 Club was used as the casino for a brief period before being permanently located on the Upper Deck.

At the time of the installation of the penthouses in 1972, the 736 Club was converted to the Queen's Grill Restaurant. This area has enjoyed various decors over the years, but the Queen of England's coat of arms carved out of wood has remained on the after bulkhead. The restaurant was extended to accommodate the passengers from the penthouse suites that were added in 1986. The Queen's Grill kitchen is located directly behind the restaurant and is totally dedicated to the 240 people dining there.

Doors on the starboard side lead to the Queen's Grill Lounge. This room replaces the areas once known as the Coffee Shop and the Teenage Juke Box Room. Here coffee and light meals were available throughout the day and into the night. The Juke Box Room had an area set aside for the jukebox, pinball machines, and other teen amusements such as distorting mirrors.

The Queen's Grill Lounge has also enjoyed a variety of decors. In 1982 it was remodeled along with the Queen's Grill by Dennis Lennon, who was the original coordinating designer of the interior of the QE2.

The top of "D" stairway is the entrance to the movie/theater balcony with seating for 136 people.

To the port side of the stairway is the Business Center, established in 1987. This replaced the Computer Learning Center, which had been installed during the 1983 refitting. The Business Center has a thirty-foot-long boardroom table and full conference facilities. This part of the ship was originally the London Gallery, where works of art were on display and for sale. When the penthouses were installed, it was converted to a quiet reading room and housed interesting pictures depicting old Cunard Line ships.

Astern of "D" stairway on each side are suite rooms, once the site of the original shops. The QE2 probably has the largest selection of shops at sea. A full range of clothing is available in both traditional and the latest fashions, in addition to jewelry, cameras, perfume, souvenirs, books, and duty-free liquor. Items indigenous to the countries that the ship visits are also made available. In 1972 the shopping arcade was moved to its present location, which previously had been a lounge served by an island bar amidships. Windows on either side and at the after end looked out over the Boat Deck. The interior design of the shops has changed periodically over the years, reflecting whatever might be in fashion. In 1987 more shops were added at the after end, and what was previously an open-air space known as the Raised Boat Deck, is now called the International Shopping Concourse. Doors on each side at the after end lead out onto the open deck, and then right forward are the steps leading up to

Constant advances in radio technology has always kept the radio room of the QE2 one of the busiest places on the ship. A radio officer is on duty 24 hours a day so that passengers can place or receive telephone calls and facsimile messages anywhere in the world. (Photo courtesy Robin Ebers.)

The decor in the Queen's Grill Restaurant has been changed on a number of occasions but it has always featured the carved wooden crest of Her Majesty Queen Elizabeth II. (Photo courtesy Robin Ebers.)

The Queen's Grill Restaurant was created for the exclusive use of the passengers accommodated in the Penthouse Suites that were added in 1972. All the meals served in this restaurant are exclusively prepared in an adjoining kitchen by one of the most senior chefs on board.

the forward observation area (under the wings of the bridge).

All the lifeboats are stowed in davits on the Boat Deck. There are twenty lifeboats of various types with a capacity for 2,244 people. In addition, there are inflatable life rafts for 1,400 more. Together, the life rafts and lifeboats provide a lifesaving capacity for 25 percent more passengers than the ship is certified to carry. The four larger lifeboats have twin propellers and are also used as tenders when the ship is at an anchorage port. The two forty-five-foot cruise tenders that were installed on the ship in December 1983 were especially designed for improving the service at anchorage ports. They can carry 118 people, and their 212-horsepower engines give a speed of 10 knots.

The Boat Deck is popular with joggers and walkers—five circuits of the U-shaped track is one mile.

The decor of the Queen's Grill Lounge complements the adjoining restaurant. The small intimate bar and large windows with views out over the ocean provides a peaceful setting throughout the day and evening. (Photo courtesy Robin Ebers.)

The Board Room on the port side of the Boat Deck has full conference facilities and is available during the voyage for passengers' use. There is direct access into the upper level of the Theatre.

The International Shopping Promenade, which stretches down both sides of the upper level of the Grand Lounge, now covers an area that has quadrupled in size since the QE2 came into service. A huge variety of goods can be purchased from small souvenirs to luxury items and the latest fashions in clothing. (Photo courtesy Robin Ebers.)

Upper Deck

A number of changes have taken place on this deck over the years. The first, in 1972, was the demise of the Lookout Bar which was the only public room to have a view looking forward over the bow. The space was converted to a kitchen to serve the Mauretania Restaurant. This restaurant was originally known as the Britannia Restaurant; escalators in the center led to the Columbia kitchen one deck below, which is where the waiters had to go to obtain food orders. Although the removal of the popular Lookout Bar was disappointing, taking out the escalators considerably improved the efficiency of service in the restaurant and increased the seating capacity to 792 people.

Later the Britannia was divided into five different cultural-theme sections: Parisienne, Florentine, Londoner, Flamenco, and Oriental and became known as the Tables of the World Restaurant. In 1977, it was changed yet again. The decor reverted to a central theme throughout and became the Mauretania Restaurant. At the same time the International Food Bazaar was introduced as well as a dance floor under a mirrored ceiling. This restaurant currently seats 486 people.

Immediately aft of the Mauretania Restaurant on the starboard side is the cocktail bar that serves the Princess Grill Starboard Restaurant, which was installed when the ship was in Hamburg for a refitting in 1990. Stairs lead to the restaurant one deck below.

Further astern on the starboard side is the entrance to the lower level of the theater/cinema which has a capacity for 491 people. Gaby Schreiber, who was one of Britain's foremost designers, was responsible for the theater. It is also used as a conference room, and the captain holds an interdenominational

From one of the QE2's launches looking up the top of the funnel towers 169 feet, 1 inch above sea level. The funnel is painted in the traditional Cunard colors used since August 1982.

church service there when the ship is at sea on a Sunday.

Next comes the Theater Bar, also on the starboard side. When crossing to the port side at "D" stairway, three glass-framed royal standards can be seen; and between them is the commemorative plaque presented to the ship by Her Majesty Queen Elizabeth, the Queen Mother, on the occasion of the vessel's safe return from the Falkland Campaign. The silver plaque bears the welcome-home messages exchanged in telegrams between the Queen Mother and the master of the ship, Captain Peter Jackson, as the *Queen Elizabeth 2* sailed up the River Solent. There is also a large carved wooden plaque presented by the First Sea Lord, Sir John Fieldhouse. A more recent addition on display is a silver cup presented to the R.M.S. *Laconia* on the occasion of the first Cunard Line world cruise in 1922. In the foyer of the "D" stairway there is an embossed leather picture depicting old sailing ships. This was originally hung in the first-class smoking room of the German steamer *Kaiser Wilhelm Der Grosse*. At the time of her commissioning in 1898, the vessel was the world's largest passenger ship and the first to gain the blue ribbon for Germany. The picture

One of the two specially constructed forty-five foot tenders with their own hydraulic launching arrangements. Each tender can carry 118 people ashore at a speed of 10 knots. (Photos this page courtesy Robin Ebers.)

Whilst QE2 lies at anchor, one of her tenders heads away from the ship taking passengers to the shore. This tender is also certified as one of the twenty lifeboats each of which can be launched by gravity within a few minutes.

was presented to the *QE2* by the Lloyd Werft shipyard who carried out the re-engining and the major conversions in 1987.

Nearby is the movie projection room and the control center for lighting and sound. Two large 70-millimeter projectors are used to show hundreds of films each year. On the world cruise alone, enough movies are carried to show a different one each day. Facilities also exist to show 16- and 35-millimeter films as well as audio slide presentations.

The Players Club Casino on the port side was totally remodeled during the Hamburg refitting in 1990 and was extended forward to include the area previously used as the Casino Hideaway Lounge. When the ship was first commissioned, most of this area was occupied by the Upper Deck Library. This library, designed by Dennis Lennon, was over twice the size of the existing Quarter Deck Library and was regarded by many as one of the most comfortable and peaceful rooms on the *QE2*. The entrance to the movie theater and the Mauretania Restaurant is at the forward end of the casino.

Amidships are the red-carpeted "E" stairway and a bank of four elevators. These are the only elevators that stop at every floor between the Boat Deck and Five Deck—a total of eight stops in all.

Just across to starboard is the Cruise Staff Center where a member of the staff is on duty to assist with leisure inquiries and the video film lending library. The office and the adjacent band practice room combined were originally the tour office. Outboard on the starboard side is the photographers' gallery, where pictures that have been taken during the cruise are exhibited and sold.

Further astern is the Grand Lounge. It was designed in its original form by Jon Bannenberg and was known as the Double Down Room. An impressive feature of the Double Down Room was a wide, curved staircase at the after

The Mauretania Restaurant stretches the width of the ship. Daylight from the large windows on each side is reflected into the center by the mirrored ceiling. The dining room was originally known as the Britannia Restaurant, and then it became the Tables of the World before being changed again to the present name. (Photo courtesy Robin Ebers.)

The Princess Grill Starboard in the newest dining room on QE2. It can seat 110 people and it is reached by a private stairway leading down from the cocktail lounge on Upper Deck. (Photo courtesy Robin Ebers.)

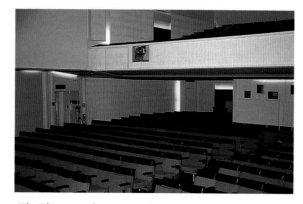

The Theatre, with a capacity for 491 patrons on two levels, is the scene of a variety of events which include movies, plays, concerts and lectures.

The Theatre Bar features live music and dancing and being centrally located on the starboard side of Upper Deck, is a popular meeting place day and night for those going to the cinema, casino or Grand Lounge. (Photo courtesy Robin Ebers.)

end connecting the room to the deck above. In 1987 when the room was remodeled, the curved staircase was removed and a twin staircase was fitted at the forward end with a retractable stage. The starlight paneled ceiling was fitted and a modern sound and lighting control box installed opposite the stage. Seating arranged on three levels makes the room especially suited for the production shows and guest entertainers regularly featured on board. It is one of the largest rooms on the ship, covering 20,000 square feet and seating 800.

Beyond the Grand Lounge on the port side is the Tour/Travel Office. On the starboard side is the Teen and Youth Club with its popular video game machines. This area was formerly the site of the Flower Shop, which has now been relocated on Three Deck aft.

The after end of the Theatre Bar Lounge blends into the photographers' gallery where the hundred of photographs that are taken each day are put on display.

In 1987 the Yacht Club replaced the Double Down Bar which can also be reached from the "G" stairway landing. The nautical decor with the wave-shaped ceiling features pictures and models of yachts that participated in the America's Cup races. The Yacht Club is a popular bar complemented with a glass-enclosed grand piano.

Doors lead out onto an open deck where the paddle-tennis court and golf practice nets are located. This area was substantially altered in 1983, when the Magradome was fitted over the Quarter Deck swimming pool. Steps lead to the roof of the dome and then aft down to the Quarter Deck.

Quarter Deck
The hatch lid of the cargo hold and two associated cranes are on the Quarter Deck forward. Although not accessible to passengers, these can clearly be seen from the observation point on the Sports Deck. Each crane has a safe working load of five tons, and both are used for loading vehicles and stores. The larger of the two cranes is a replacement and was fitted in 1987 at Bremerhaven. There used to be a portable swimming pool that fitted into the top level of the cargo hatch for the use of the crew when the ship was cruising. Toward the end of 1991, a new pool was especially made, and it is lifted on to the port side of the hatch when required.

Astern of this area, the majority of the superstructure above the Quarter Deck level is made of aluminum separated from the steel below by a bimetallic joint. This dual method of construction considerably reduced the weight of the ship and made it possible for her to have a draft much less than the old *Queens*.

From the open deck, a door leads into the Columbia kitchen. The kitchen stretches the total width of the liner. A number of changes have taken place over the years that reflect the modernization of cooking equipment and the improvement of hygiene and service efficiency.

The Princess Grill is on the port side and is serviced by the Columbia kitchen. The grill, maintained in its original design and color scheme of Bordeaux red velvet and leather, creates an intimate and romantic atmosphere with seating for only 110 people. The life-size statues by Janine Janet representing the four elements—fire, earth, air, and water—are striking visible features made entirely of marine items such as shells, coral, and mother-of-pearl. Access to the Princess Grill is either by the "C" elevator or a spiral stairway up from the Princess Grill Bar on One Deck.

On the opposite side of the ship is the new Princess Grill Starboard, which is similar in size, atmosphere, and design to the original Princess Grill. This restaurant was added during the 1990 refitting at Hamburg.

Adjoining the after end of the two Princess Grills is the Columbia Restaurant, which can accommodate 562 passengers. The captain hosts a table just to the left of the center. He and the staff captain alternate tables every other evening in the Columbia and Mauretania Restaurants. The midnight buffet is usually held in the Columbia.

As one leaves the Columbia by the center entrance, a majestic panorama stretches across the opposite wall. Three tapestries by Helena Barynina Hernmarck depict the launching ceremony of the liner by Her Majesty Queen Elizabeth II on September 27, 1967.

To the port side is what could probably be the largest oil painting on canvas afloat. Painted by Tom Hemy in 1908, it measures 99 by 73 inches and depicts the *Mauretania* leaving the Tyne on her maiden voyage.

Opposite the painting is the entrance to the Card Room. This room has recently been remodeled, and the panels of green suede and baize have been re-

The Players Club Casino was extended and re-designed in 1990 by Graham Fayhe and features modern slot machines, blackjack, roulette, craps and poker.

Before the refitting in 1987, the Grand Lounge was known as the Double Up–Double Down Room. During the refit a spiral staircase was removed from the after end and replaced by the twin staircase each side of the stage. For production shows, the sound, light and starlight ceiling, are controlled from a balcony on the upper level opposite the stage.

placed with brighter wall coverings. The design includes a collection of nautical pictures and a fine model of the Cunard ship S.S. *Russia* built in 1867. This room is also available to passengers for private functions.

Nearby can be seen the toteboard, the center of traditional daily activity that takes place when the ship is at sea. Each morning the navigator on the bridge estimates the distance that the ship will have cruised by noon for the previous twenty-four hours. Twenty consecutive figures are then marked on the tote board and passengers are invited to place a bet on the mileage they think the ship will have traveled. Shortly after midday the distance will be announced, and winners can collect their share of the pool.

Past the "E" stairway and just forward of the Queen's Room is the library designed by Michael Inchbald. In addition to the continuously updated selection of magazines, current best-sellers, classics, novels, and reference books, there is a wide selection of foreign-language publications and books in large print. The library is a popular room on the ship, particularly when authors are on board and their books are made available for purchase and signing.

On the starboard side of the ship there is a large jigsaw puzzle on a table convenient to passengers strolling by. Above the jigsaw puzzle is a map of the

Each of the ten giant cauldrons in the Columbia kitchen can be used to prepare 40 gallons of soup at a time. They are also used to boil fresh lobsters which are a regular feature on the QE2's extensive and varied menus. (Photos on these pages courtesy Robin Ebers.)

All the working surfaces and equipment in the kitchens are made of good quality stainless steel. In addition to the captain's weekly inspection, regular visits are made by British and American health authorities to ensure that high standards of hygiene and food handling practices are maintained.

world showing evidence of continual use!

The Midships Bar is a few feet away. The decor of dark green and the gold-leaf ceiling have remained the same since the ship was launched—a credit to the designers, Dennis Lennon and Partners. At the after end of the room is a brass armillary sphere (showing the relationship of planets to the earth and the signs of the zodiac), which was presented to Cunard by the Institute of London Underwriters when the ship was commissioned.

Spanning the width of the ship, the Queen's Room has a warm inviting atmosphere day or night. It is the scene of many activities, from yoga classes in the morning, afternoon tea, and predinner cocktail parties to the evening cabaret. The structural columns are encased in great inverted trumpets of white fiberglass. The trumpet shape in reverse used to be reflected in the design of white chairs upholstered in natural hide but these have now been replaced by cubelike armchairs in brown leather. At the forward end surrounded by the sculptured-appearing wall of walnut blocks and mirrors is the bronze bust of Her Royal Highness Queen Elizabeth II, by Oscar Nemon.

A short passage from the Queen's Room leads to the entrance to the Club Lido. David Hicks designed the original room, then known as the *Q4*. The *QE2* herself was popularly known as the *Q4* before she was christened. A new ship had been designed to follow the *Queen Mary* and the *Queen Elizabeth* and was referred to as the *Q3*. The design was subsequently scrapped, and when the *QE2* first appeared on the drawing board she was nicknamed the *Q4*.

The first stage of major changes made to the *Q4* came during the period it took the government to restore the ship to service after the 1982 Falklands campaign. The bar was removed from the after end and temporarily located on the port side. This enabled the after end to be opened up, thus creating a

The Princess Grill Port has maintained its original design since the Queen Elizabeth 2 *came into service in 1969. Many of the regular passengers whose cabin grade assigns them to the the Queen Grill Restaurant often request a table here to enjoy the small and intimate atmosphere.*

much lighter and therefore more versatile room in the daytime. A small kitchen provides the facilities for the breakfast and lunch buffets.

The second stage was carried out in 1983 in Bremerhaven. The bar was repositioned and the glass floor laid with the adjacent bandstand and control center for music and lighting. The prefabricated Magrodome was lifted into position over the swimming pool within two days of the vessel's arrival at Bremerhaven. The retractable glass roof created a complete indoor/outdoor entertainment and leisure area.

One Deck

One Deck is the longest deck on the ship, having a total length from stem to stern of 963 feet. The forward part is known as the foredeck and, again, it can be seen from the observation point on Sports Deck under the bridge. When the ship is docking, an officer will be seen right forward supervising the mooring operations, which take place from the deck below.

There are two anchors housed in the bow, each weighing 12½ tons. The anchor chain, or cable, as it is known to the seafarer, leads from the anchor up

With seating to accommodate 562 persons, the Columbia Restaurant is the largest dining room on board. The traditional "Captain's Table" is near the center of the room beyond the magnificent silver urn given to Samuel Cunard by the people of Boston in 1840.

the hawse pipe and along the deck, passing around the capstan and then down into the chain locker. The total length of each chain is 1,080 feet and the links are 4 inches in diameter and have a breaking strain of just over 500 tons. The anchor that can be seen on the port side of the foredeck is a spare. This used to be housed in the stem but was repositioned following damage during a North Atlantic storm in 1981. During an earlier storm in 1976, the spare anchor was lost altogether and now lies on the ocean floor somewhere in mid-Atlantic. Between the anchors the forward whistle can be seen mounted on a tripod. It is operated by remote control from the bridge. If the ship is in fog or restricted visibility the whistle can be programmed to sound automatically at one- or two-minute intervals.

Aft and inboard are some of the staff quarters. There is a shop, a hairdresser, a gymnasium, a library, recreation rooms, and a mess room with its own servery and galley.

Just astern and in the passenger area is the photographers' darkroom. The team of four resident photographers can produce about 1,600 pictures a day in addition to making video films of the cruise.

The launching ceremony of the QE2 is depicted in three magnificent tapestries created by Helena Barynina Hernmarck hung in the Quarter Deck lobby of the "D" stairway. Since this photograph was taken, the tapestries have been re-hung in frames for protection. (Photo courtesy Robin Ebers.)

The Quarter Deck landing of the "D" stairway is the main entrance of the Columbia Restaurant. Paintings by world-renown artists are displayed on the stairway which leads up to the Boat Deck and theatre balcony. (Photo courtesy Robin Ebers.)

The library on Quarter Deck is one of the most popular rooms on the ship. It is staffed by a qualified librarian and carries a selection of books unequalled by any other ship at sea. Authors frequently travel on the QE2 and when they do so their books may be purchased here. (Photo courtesy Robin Ebers.)

The Queen's Room, spanning the width of the ship, always has an inviting atmosphere which can be changed with lights and curtains to suit the occasion. The bronze bust of her Royal Highness Queen Elizabeth II adds a subtle dignity to the room.

This photograph of the tall windows on the starboard side of Quarter Deck looking towards the Queen's Room highlights how the designers achieved their desire to open as many rooms as possible to views of the sea. The Midships Bar is on the right of the picture. (Photo courtesy Robin Ebers.)

The Quarter Deck swimming pool was uncovered until the Magrodome was added in 1983. This combined the night club and pool into one enormous space that can be used for buffet meals during the day and disco in the evening regardless of the weather conditions. (Photo courtesy Robin Ebers.)

In good weather, the Magrodome can be opened at the touch of a switch to allow sunshine into the pool area. (Photo courtesy Robin Ebers.)

Near "C" stairway on the port side is the Princess Grill Room Bar, which is a small and intimate room for those dining in the restaurant above that is reached by a spiral stairway.

On One Deck by the "D" stairway is the Harrod's of London shop, installed in 1984, and the only branch of Harrod's at sea. When the ship was commissioned, this was the One Deck Shop and sold very exclusive jewelry. During the 1972 conversion the shop was moved up to Boat Deck, and the area was converted into a bar known as Club Atlantic. When the liner *France* ended her service on the North Atlantic run, staff members from the ship were employed on board the *QE2* to work in this bar, and service was offered in five different

The 963 feet of One Deck make it the longest deck in the ship. Far forward lies the foghorn, which can be heard for a distance of 10 miles. The huge anchor chains (1,080 feet long) and capstans also are here.

There are twenty one different categories of cabins available on the QE2. All cabins have a private shower and this "E" grade room on One Deck will also have a bathtub.

languages. The bar was subsequently closed and the area converted to a shop specializing in china and crystal.

Before the installation of the penthouses, the cabins on One Deck were the highest-grade accommodations available on the ship. Many of them have connecting doors to adjoining cabins. Over 70 percent of the cabins on board the *QE2* are outboard, and all rooms have their own bath and/or shower. Each cabin also has a console for selecting music or radio news broadcasts from a selection of six channels. From time to time announcements will be made from the Purser's Office which will overide the program. As a safety feature, priority announcements from the bridge will be heard in all cabins regardless of whether the channels are switched on or off. A telephone is connected to a central exchange from which calls can be made to anywhere in the world. The telephone system was completely renewed in 1987 to provide automatic wake-up calls, direct dialing throughout the ship, and ship-to-shore worldwide. Cabins were also fitted with televisions and VCR's.

Toward the after end of One Deck by the "G" stairway is the hair and beauty salon, operated by Steiner's of London. Here, highly qualified hair stylists cater to men and women clients. The salon is constructed on the open-plan principle so that shampoo, setting, and drying areas are located in the main body of the room with adjoining private sections for beauty care consultation.

Passing the salon, doors lead to the outside barbecue grill and pool bar. The swimming pool area was totally refurbished in 1987 with the addition of the jacuzzies and the Cunard lion depicted in vivid red mosaic tiles.

Two Deck

In the very foremost part of the vessel on Two Deck are the mooring winches. When the *QE2* is in port, she will normally be made fast to the quay by three synthetic-fiber ropes and three or four flexible-steel wire ropes at each end of the ship. The ropes are set in position first, followed by the wires. The wires have a breaking strain of 103 tons and are attached to self-tensioning winches that keep them tight regardless of tidal conditions. Also in this area are the bosun's stores and paint lockers where enough stock is carried to enable maintenance to be carried out on a continued basis.

The Computer Learning Center is situated in the square near "A" stairway. This facility is available twenty-four hours a day and is equipped with sixteen computers. A little farther astern and out of the public eye is the finance office. Records are stored in a computer of the food, beverages, dry stores, and spare parts kept on board. Personal wage records of over 1,000 crewmembers are also held in the computers. The Finance Office is responsible for administer-

The introduction of the Computer Learning Center in 1983 proved to be very popular with passengers of all ages. Accordingly, the center was enlarged and equipment has been continually updated. Classes are given by a professional instructor throughout the day. (Photo courtesy Robin Ebers.)

Calm seas greet the dawn as QE2 steams along at 29 knots. The jacuzzies were added to the One Deck pool when the area was refurbished in 1987. (Photo courtesy Robin Ebers.)

ing passengers' personal accounts as well.

The Midships Lobby on Two Deck is where most passengers and visitors first come on board via the gangway that can be placed on either the port or the starboard side of the ship. This circular sunken area with white leather seating and a white grand piano makes an ideal meeting place. Glass cases house silver plaques commemorating the visits of Her Majesty Queen Elizabeth II, Her Royal Highness, the Princess of Wales, and His Royal Highness, Prince Edward. The ship's bell is at the after end of the lobby. This large brass bell has traditionally been used for christening babies and for ringing out the old year and ringing in the new.

Centrally placed within the ship, the Safety Control Room (S.C.R.) is, like the bridge and the engine room, manned twenty-four hours a day at sea and in port. Master plans of the ship showing all the safety features are on display.

The ship is divided into compartments, each of which can be made completely watertight by hydraulic doors remotely controlled from the bridge. Indicators set out in a diagram on the bridge and in the S.C.R. show whether the doors are in the open or closed position.

The ship is also divided into eight zones with fire-resistant bulkheads and doors that can be remotely closed from the Safety Control Room to prevent fire from spreading. All the cabins and public rooms on the *QE2* have automatic sprinklers. If one of these is set off, an audible alarm is triggered in the S.C.R., and a visual indicator of the danger area will appear on the master diagrams. The break-glass alarm push buttons situated throughout the ship are similarly indicated. Certain areas are also equipped with smoke and vapor detectors which set off alarms in the S.C.R. if any detection is made. In addition, crew specially trained in shipboard firefighting techniques patrol the ship at regular intervals to supplement the detecting aids. Every crew member joining the ship is required to undergo a *QE2* safety familiarization course, and the certificate obtained upon completion must be revalidated every two years.

Consoles in the Safety Control Room also indicate the amount of fuel, fresh water, and ballast water contained in all the tanks. Depending on the speed, fuel may be consumed at a varying rate up to eighteen tons per hour, so it is necessary constantly to adjust the water-ballast tanks. The control of all pumping and transfer of water ballast and fuel is carried out from the control room. Accumulation of water in the bilges is sensed by electrically operated probes and indicated on another console where valves and pumps can be operated directly from the control room.

The Purser's Office on Two Deck by the "F" stairway is the scene of many passenger-related activities and can be compared with the reception desk at a large hotel. The staff at the front desk deal with the majority of passenger inquiries or channel them in the proper direction. On the opposite side of the square is a branch of the Travelex Bank which offers a full range of banking and financial services including foreign currency conversions, cashing travelers checks and the transferring of funds. All major credit cards are accepted. Passenger accounts are dealt with at the cashier's section of the Purser's Office approached from the square at the "G" stairway. At the adjacent counter travel inquiries can be handled and future arrangements made. The safe-deposit box facility nearby is administered by the security department.

The doctor's consultation room and waiting lounge is located on the port side of "G" square. A doctor is in attendance at regularly posted hours during the day. No appointment is necessary.

During the world cruise an office is set up on the starboard side of "G" square and becomes known as the Manifest Office. With the help of computers, staff at this office handle all passport, visa, and immigration matters.

At the extreme after end of Two Deck are mooring arrangements similar to those described at the forward end of the vessel.

Three Deck
An impressive indication of the length and structure of the ship can be seen on Three Deck. Looking aft from the forward end, the deck head appears to

come into contact with the deck due to the curvature built into the construction of the ship. The synagogue designed by Professor Misha Black is located by the "A" stairway. The room is decorated in a peaceful shade of blue with ash panels.

Further aft there is a TV studio and control center for all the cabin entertainment. Feature films, documentaries, and news bulletins are show continu-

The Midships Lobby on Two Deck is the room most passengers see first when boarding the Queen Elizabeth 2, *since it was designed with the New York and Southampton terminals in mind. Boarding ramps connect directly to the Midships Lobby, where Cunard personnel are available to direct the 2,000 new passengers to their cabins.*

ously on selected channels. One channel is dedicated to navigational information directly linked to the satellite position-finding system on the bridge. Another channel is coupled to a television camera mounted on the top of the bridge. The studio was the site of the old telephone exchange. Staff used to be on duty at the exchange day and night, as all calls made from passenger cabin telephones had to be manually connected by the exchange operators. This was all replaced by the computer-supported automated system installed in 1987.

At the after end of Three Deck, on the starboard side, is a laundromat and ironing area for passengers' personal use. Adjacent is the Flower Shop where all the flower arrangements for the ship are prepared.

Four Deck

Four Deck is almost entirely passenger cabins, with crew quarters at the extreme ends fore and aft. Gangways are sometimes located on Four Deck, and facilities exist for cars to be taken on through the same entrances.

Five Deck

As with Four Deck, there are crew accommodations at the extreme ends of Five Deck with passenger cabins in between.

The Purser's Office on Two Deck can be compared to the reception desk of a large hotel, and it is where all day-to-day inquiries are dealt with. A full range of financial services are offered by the Travelex Bank situated on the opposite side of the square. (Photo courtesy Robin Ebers.)

QE2's TV studio and control center is one of the most sophisticated networks of its kind afloat. It produces a continuous variety of programs for the multi-channel televisions fitted in every passenger cabin. Live interviews can be broadcast direct to each cabin from the studio.

Three Deck, with 186 cabins, is the longest passenger deck on the ship. This picture of the corridor gives an impressive indication of the length of the vessel. (Photo courtesy Robin Ebers.)

Along each side of the ship there are nine shell doors. These doors form part of the hull and are very strongly constructed. When closed, they are secured by steel bolts and are watertight. The doors have various uses such as for

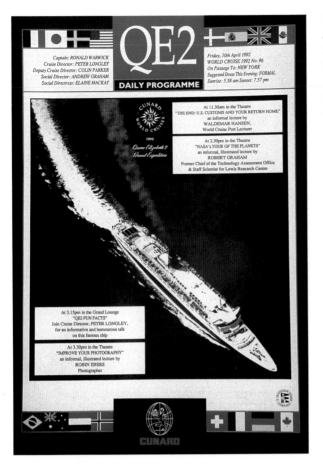

The daily Programme is packed with a choice of activities provided for all moods and tastes. The Programme is delivered to every cabin and it is one of the many items produced each day by the four printers employed on board. (Photo courtesy Robin Ebers.)

gangways and loading and unloading stores and cars. When the ship is at anchor, pontoons are lowered from Boat Deck and are made fast by the opening in use, which provides boarding platforms for the ship's launches. Amidships on each side, the doors give access to the bunkering stations. Oil can be bunkered at a rate of 600 tons per hour on each side. Water can also be taken aboard at this same location.

Watertight doors are fitted at regular intervals along each side of Five Deck and below. The doors divide the ship into fifteen separate watertight compartments and are tested every day the ship is at sea by remote control from the bridge. These doors can also be closed or opened by controls alongside each individual door or from Four Deck.

Six Deck

Six Deck is very much a working area of the ship, and the passageway that runs forward to aft on the starboard side is known as the "working alleyway." Crew quarters stretch from the forward end down the port side to the after end. There is a fully staffed laundromat for crew use near the "A" stairway, and farther aft is an administrative office which deals with the day-to-day affairs of crew members.

The Printer's Shop is also down here. A variety of items are produced including menus, daily programs, newspapers, special invitations, and all the general stationery requirements of the ship.

The hospital is located by the "C" stairway on Six Deck. Being near the waterline and at the center of the ship, it is free from the movement that is some-

The majority of the cabins on QE2 have a window or porthole looking out over the sea. This picture was taken from a crew cabin on Six Deck. Being near the waterline, the porthole has a heavy steel deadlight that can be securely closed in very bad weather. (Photo courtesy Robin Ebers.)

times evident on the upper decks of the vessel. Its location adjacent to working areas also makes it easily accessible to the crew. Consisting of four multibed wards and one single-bed ward, the hospital contains a total of thirteen beds. The single-bed ward is used mostly as either an intensive-care unit or in situations where isolation is required. Serving the wards is a duty room, where indicators show if a patient requires attention. There is an oxygen and nitrous-oxide storage room from which direct lines of each gas lead to every bed in the wards, an operating room, and a dental-care unit. A well-stocked pharmacy caters to a wide variety of medical complaints. To assist with diagnoses there is a small laboratory where pathological tests can be carried out. Should surgery be required, there is a fully equipped operating room. Basic operating instrument packs are kept ready and are resterilized at regular intervals. Specialized instruments can be quickly sterilized in the autoclave.

Separate, but enclosed within the hospital area, are a physiotherapy ward, a lead-lined X-ray room, a fully equipped dental-care unit, and a mortuary.

The hospital is manned by two doctors, three nurses, and three medical attendants. During the annual world cruise this team is sometimes supplemented with a fourth nurse, a physiotherapist, and a dentist. Clinics are held twice daily for both the passengers and the crew. Should a emergency occur outside clinic hours, the whole medical team can be called by a special alert procedure to attend to a patient wherever their location. The team and accompanying emergency equipment can be assembled within a very few minutes.

Moving toward midship, there are the electrical and plumbers' workshops and the technical offices by the entrance to the engine room.

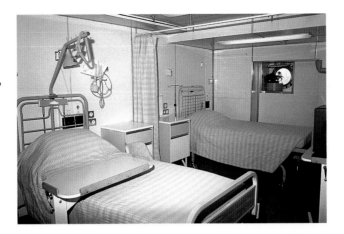

The hospital is situated on Six Deck near the center of the ship where the motion is less evident. Care is provided by highly qualified medical staff consisting of two doctors and three nurses who are all permanently employed by Cunard Line. (Photos this page courtesy Robin Ebers.)

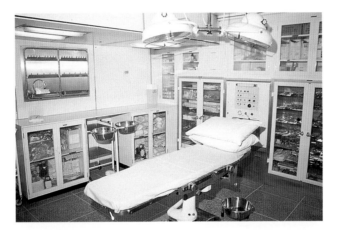

The fully equipped hospital is kept in a constant state of readiness to deal with medical emergencies at sea. The sealed lockers behind the operating table contain sterilised instruments available for immediate use.

Certified personnel from Steiners of London offer exercise classes catering to all ages and fitness levels, as well as one-to-one instruction and lifestyle evaluation.

Aft of the engine room is the Health Spa. Access is from Five Deck via the "F" stairway or elevator. The spa, the first ever at sea, was introduced in 1982 and was directed by the Golden Door of Encino, California. In 1993 it was

Drive on drive off ramps are available in Southampton, Cherbourg and New York for passengers who wish to carry their cars across the Atlantic Ocean. The elevator, on the left in this picture, is mounted on a turn-table to facilitate the stowage and removal of the vehicles. (Photo courtesy Robin Ebers.)

QE2 has two indoor swimming pools. Shortly after this photograph was taken the Seven Deck pool was converted into the most luxurious Spa afloat. Some of the new features include a steam room, hydrotherapy baths and high pressure water massage. (Photo courtesy Robin Ebers.)

modernized and remodeled by Steiners of London. A total fitness and exercise program is run by Steiner personnel to fulfill the needs of individual passengers. Daily activities include yoga, aerobic exercises, jogging, swimming, and lectures on nutrition, stress management, and a variety of other topics relating to health. The spa has a large exercise area, a pool with a teak platform for hydrocalisthenics, and three large jacuzzi whirlpool baths. The latter facilities replaced the Turkish baths.

Seven and Eight Decks

Right forward on Seven and Eight Decks is a bulk beer store capable of holding a total of 13,000 gallons in twenty-seven stainless-steel tanks. The tanks are in an air-conditioned room from where the beer was piped directly to the bars. Draught beer is no longer served on the ship, so the equipment has not been used for some years now.

The domestic storerooms are all situated forward in the ship and provide a total capacity of about 20,000 cubic feet of storage. Additional space is gained by using the holds when the ship is on the annual world cruise. Number Two hold is used exclusively for the storage of wines and liquor. The retail value of the liquor alone at the start of the world cruise is in excess of $2 million. Over 20,000 bottles of wine are carried that vary in price from $12 to $425 a bottle.

The laundry stretches the full width of the ship and is equipped with machines capable of washing and pressing the daily complement of restaurant, bed, and bath linens used by the passengers and crew. The dry-cleaning department provide a full valet service.

Cars driven on board at Four or Five Deck levels are taken below to the holds by the two car lifts. The lifts are of the turret type so they can turn, thus

enabling the cars to be driven off into the holds in any direction. When the *QE2* was first commissioned in 1969, about seventy cars could be carried; but the space has gradually been taken up in order to carry essential stores and spare parts, and now there is only room for twelve. In 1987, Number Six hold was converted into a garbage-processing plant. Garbage from throughout the ship is delivered to this area where it is sorted, shredded, compacted, and stowed in a refrigerated storeroom where it remains until it can be landed ashore. This facility replaces the incinerator equipment that was situated on Six Deck.

On Seven Deck, reached by "C" stairway or via the elevator, is the second indoor swimming pool, saunas, and a gymnasium.

The entrance to the Engine Control Room is on Seven Deck. From here three is access to the various engine compartments and machinery described in chapter 8.

Builders: Upper Clyde Shipbuilders
Keel laid: 5 July, 1965
Launched: 20 September, 1967
Maiden voyage: 2 May 1969
Port of registry: Southampton
Signal letters: GBTT
Official number: 336703

Tonnage
Gross tonnage: 69,053
Net tonnage: 36,038

Dimensions
Length overall: 963 feet (293.52m)
Breadth overall: 105 feet, 2½ inches
  (32.07m)
Bridge height of eye: 95 feet (28.96m)
Bridge to stem: 238 feet, 2 inches
  (72.59m)
Bridge to stern: 724 feet, 10 inches
  (220.93m)
Mast height above keel: 200 feet,
  1½ inches (61.00m)
Funnel height above keel: 204 feet,
  ½ inch, (62.22m)

Draft
Loaded draft: 32 feet, 4½ inches
  (9994mm)
Freeboard: 23 feet, 6¼ inches
  (7169mm)
FWA: 7½ inches (190mm)
TPI/cm: 151.5   60.6

Tanks
Fresh water: 1,852 tons
Laundry water: 532 tons
Boiler feed water: 114 tons
Ballast: 4,849 tons
Fuel oil: 4,578 tons

Lubricating oil: 383 tons
Diesel oil: 231 tons
Oily water: 243 tons
Sewage: 269 tons
Sludge: 13 tons

Anchors
Forward: 2 at 12½ tons, each attached
  to a 4-inch diameter cable of 12 shack
  les, in length equal to 1,080 feet
Aft: 1 at 7¼ tons attached to a 3-inch
  diameter cable of 8 shackles, in length
  equal to 720 feet
Spare: 1 at 12 and ½ tons—stowed
  on deck

Machinery
9 Diesel engines
Makers: MAN B&W of West Germany
Type: 9L 58/64 Nine cylinder medium
  speed
Weight: 217 tons
Capacity: 10,625kW at 400 rpm

9 Alternators
Makers: GEC Turbine Generators Ltd.,
  England
Rated: 10,620kW (14,236hp)
  at 400 rpm
Output: 10kV at a frequency of 60Hz

2 Propulsion motors
Makers: GEC Large Machines, Ltd.,
  England
Rated: 44MW (590,005hp) synchronous
  running at 144 rpm
Weight: 295 tons

2 Propellers
Makers: Lips B.V., Holland
Diameter: 22 feet
Weight: 42 tons

Type: Variable-pitch outward turning

2 Bow thrusters
Makers: Stone Kamewa
Power: 1,000 horsepower each
Type: Variable-pitch propeller

4 Stabilizers
Makers: Brown Brothers
Length: 12 feet
Area: 70 square feet each

Steering gear
Makers: Brown Brothers
Type: 4 ram electro-hydraulic

Rudder
Makers: A/S Strommens Vaerksted,
   Norway
Weight: 75 tons

Passenger and Safety Certification
Passengers: 1,900
Crew: 1,015
Total: 2,915

Lifeboats: 20, Total capacity:
   2,244 persons
Life rafts: 56, Total capacity:
   1,400 persons
Buoyant apparatus: 5, Total capacity:
   100 persons
Life jackets: adult: 3,329 children: 145
Life buoys: 30

22 Mar. 1975 Acapulco, Mexico
10 Dec. 1991 Agadir, Morocco
01 Oct. 1983 Ajaccio, Corsica
28 May 1981 Alesund, Norway
07 Apr. 1976 Alexandria, Egypt
25 July 1974 Andalsnes, Norway
16 Apr. 1982 Arrecife, Lanzarote
20 May 1982 Ascension Island,
        South Atlantic
21 Apr. 1973 Ashdod, Israel
14 Feb. 1978 Auckland, New Zealand
19 Feb. 1985 Adelaide, Australia
24 Mar. 1978 Balboa, Panama
05 May 1985 Baltimore, United States
29 Apr. 1974 Barcelona, Spain
23 July 1981 Bar Harbor, United States
13 Dec. 1982 Basseterre, St. Kitts
13 Feb. 1978 Bay of Islands, New Zealand
29 July 1973 Bergen, Norway
26 Aug. 1983 Block Island, United States
11 Feb. 1975 Bombay, India
01 Oct. 1971 Boston, United States
09 May 1975 Bremerhaven, Germany
22 Nov. 1969 Bridgetown, Barbados
24 Feb. 1983 Brisbane, Australia
20 Oct. 1989 Cadiz, Spain
02 Mar. 1993 Cairns, Australia
25 Jan. 1986 Callao, Peru
30 Apr. 1974 Cannes, France
11 Oct. 1973 Canso Strait, Canada
10 Nov. 1970 Cape Town, South Africa
03 Dec. 1969 Caracas Bay, Curaçao
26 Mar. 1975 Cartagena, Colombia
17 Dec. 1970 Castries, St. Lucia
03 Dec. 1989 Charleston, United States
25 Nov. 1969 Charlotte Amalie,
        St. Thomas
15 Nov. 1969 Cherbourg, France
27 May 1969 Cóbh, Ireland
17 Feb. 1975 Colombo, Sri Lanka

09 Oct. 1973 Come by Chance, Canada
17 Mar. 1980 Constantza, Romania
2 Mar. 1993 Cooktown, Australia
19 July 1972 Copenhagen, Denmark
12 Aug. 1983 Cornerbrook, Canada
19 Jan. 1986 Cozumel, Mexico
25 Mar. 1975 Cristobal, Panama
30 Oct. 1970 Dakar, Senegal
10 Mar. 1979 Darien, China
05 Mar. 1993 Darwin, Australia
05 Mar. 1980 Djibouti,
        Republic of Djibouti
07 Nov. 1970 Durban, South Africa
20 Feb. 1989 Ensenada, Mexico
06 Sept. 1982 Falmouth, England
03 July 1981 Flaam, Norway
24 Nov. 1969 Fort de France, Martinique
10 Feb. 1971 Frederiksted, St. Croix
01 Feb. 1971 Freeport, Bahamas
18 May 1982 Freetown, SierraLeone
22 Feb. 1985 Fremantle, Australia
02 Apr. 1970 Funchal, Madeira
28 July 1973 Geiranger, Norway
21 May 1983 Genoa, Italy
24 Apr. 1970 Gibraltar, Crown Colony
25 July 1990 Greenock, Scotland
27 May 1982 Grytviken, South Georgia
24 Apr. 1973 Haifa, Israel
11 Oct. 1973 Halifax, Canada
21 July 1972 Hamburg, Germany
25 Mar. 1971 Hamilton, Bermuda
25 July 1973 Hammerfest, Norway
28 July 1973 Hellesylt, Norway
20 Feb. 1978 Hobart, Tasmania
27 Feb. 1975 Hong Kong, Crown Colony
15 Mar. 1975 Honolulu, Hawaiian Islands
29 Sept. 1983 Ibiza, Balearic Islands
17 Aug. 1984 Ingonish, Canada
29 Apr. 1970 Istanbul, Turkey
13 Mar. 1979 Kagoshima, Japan

29 Mar. 1983 Kailua Kona,
    Hawaiian Islands
02 Feb. 1990 Kaohsiung, Taiwan
01 Mar. 1986 Karachi, Pakistan
15 Feb. 1984 Keelung, Taiwan
08 Jan. 1970 Kingston, Jamaica
24 Jan. 1971 Kingstown, St. Vincent
05 Mar. 1975 Kobe, Japan
01 Mar. 1977 Kota Kinabalu, Malaysia
25 Dec. 1981 Kralendijk, Bonaire
30 Apr. 1984 La Coruna, Spain
11 Jan. 1971 La Guaira, Venezuela
14 Feb. 1991 Lae, Papua New Guinea
04 Mar. 1992 Laem Chabang, Thailand
20 Mar. 1982 Lahaina, Hawaiian Islands
28 Dec. 1968 Las Palmas,
    Grand Canary Island
02 May 1969 Le Havre, France
28 Apr. 1969 Lisbon, Portugal
24 July 1990 Liverpool, England
19 Mar. 1975 Los Angeles, United States
03 Nov. 1970 Luanda, Angola
11 Feb. 1985 Lyttelton, New Zealand
18 Feb. 1982 Madras, India
02 Feb. 1986 Magellan Straits, Chile
08 Feb. 1975 Mahe, Seychelles
12 Oct. 1982 Malaga, Spain
11 Mar. 1978 Manila, Philippines
4 June 1985 Martha's Vineyard,
    United States
01 Mar. 1990 Masan, South Korea
04 Apr. 1978 Mazatlan, Mexico
22 Feb. 1978 Melbourne, Australia
06 June 1973 Messina, Sicily
18 Feb. 1978 Milford Sound,
    New Zealand
05 Feb. 1975 Mombasa, Kenya
04 Apr. 1992 Monte Carlo, Monaco
04 Feb. 1979 Montevideo, Uruguay
09 Feb. 1983 Moorea, Tahiti
09 Jan. 1971 Mustique, Mustique Island
10 Mar. 1977 Nagasaki, Japan
02 May 1970 Naples, Italy
10 Mar. 1971 Nassau, Bahamas
07 May 1969 New York, United States
11 June 1988 New Haven, United States
02 Oct. 1982 Newport, United States
13 Nov. 1985 Newport News,
    United States
15 Jan. 1972 Norfolk, United States
11 Feb. 1981 Nuku'alofa, Tonga Islands
12 Apr. 1976 Odessa, Russia

08 Feb. 1971 Oranjestad, Aruba
02 Apr. 1988 Osaka, Japan
18 July 1972 Oslo, Norway
22 Feb. 1975 Padang Bay, Java
03 Oct. 1983 Palermo, Sicily
30 Apr. 1972 Palma de Mallorca,
    Balearic Islands
25 Mar. 1975 Panama Canal Transit
05 Feb. 1978 Papeete, Tahiti
28 Feb. 1982 Pattaya, Thailand
01 Mar. 1984 Penang, Malaysia
25 Apr. 1982 Philadelphia, United States
17 Nov. 1971 Phillipsburg, St. Maarten
27 Apr. 1970 Piraeus, Greece
27 Dec. 1985 Pointe-a-Pitre, Guadeloupe
30 Dec. 1970 Port au Prince, Haiti
08 Dec. 1980 Port Canaveral,
    United States
04 Feb. 1992 Port Chalmers, New Zealand
21 Dec. 1971 Port Everglades,
    United States
23 Feb. 1982 Port Kelang, Malaysia
12 Feb. 1982 Port Louis, Mauritius
01 Mar. 1978 Port Moresby,
    Papua New Guinea
20 Mar. 1981 Port Said, Egypt
22 Jan. 1993 Port Stanley,
    Falkland Islands
07 Mar. 1980 Port Suez, Egypt
29 Dec. 1969 Port of Spain, Trinidad
05 Dec. 1988 Porto Grande,
    Cape Verde Island
02 Feb. 1993 Puerto Caldera, Costa Rica
16 Oct. 1984 Praia da Rocha, Portugal
21 Jan. 1986 Puerto Limon, Costa Rica
31 Jan. 1986 Puerto Montt, Chile
17 Feb. 1989 Puerto Vallata, Mexico
10 Mar. 1982 Pusan, South Korea
19 Mar. 1983 Qingdao, China
20 July 1981 Quebec, Canada
11 Feb. 1983 Rarotonga, Cook Islands
29 Mar. 1992 Rhodes, Greece
17 Nov. 1970 Rio de Janeiro, Brazil
10 Nov. 1979 Roadtown, Tortola
04 Dec. 1974 Rotterdam, Holland
20 Nov. 1970 Salvador, Brazil
14 Dec. 1989 San Diego, United States
01 Apr. 1978 San Francisco, United States
02 Apr. 1973 San Juan, Puerto Rico
26 Apr. 1969 Santa Cruz, Tenerife
10 Feb. 1976 Santo Domingo,
    Dominican Republic

04 Apr. 1985 Santos, Brazil
23 Feb. 1990 Shimizu, Japan
20 Feb. 1975 Singapore, Malaysia
25 July 1973 Skarsvaag, Norway
02 Jan. 1969 Southampton, England
23 Nov. 1969 St. George's, Grenada
27 Dec. 1973 St. John's, Antigua
30 May 1980 Stavanger, Norway
23 May 1987 Stratford, United States
07 Mar. 1980 Suez Canal Transit
11 Feb. 1978 Suva, Fiji
24 Feb. 1978 Sydney, Australia
26 June 1979 Sydney, Canada
16 May 1973 Tangier, Morocco
09 Mar. 1988 Tianjin, China
28 Dec. 1989 Tokyo, Japan
28 Aug. 1988 Torquay, England

08 Feb. 1979 Tristian de Cunha,
          South Atlantic
07 July 1981 Tromso, Norway
27 July 1973 Trondheim, Norway
19 Oct. 1989 Valencia, Spain
29 Jan. 1986 Valparaiso, Chile
09 Feb. 1978 Vava'u, Tonga Islands
12 June 1974 Vigo, Spain
03 July 1981 Vik, Norway
31 Aug. 1991 Villefranche, France
22 Mar. 1991 Walvis Bay, Nambia
16 Feb. 1978 Wellington, New Zealand
13 Mar. 1989 Whitsunday Passage,
          Australia
27 Mar. 1988 Xiamen, China
16 Mar. 1980 Yalta, Russia
07 Mar. 1975 Yokohama, Japan

APPENDIX: 3
MASTERS OF THE *QUEEN ELIZABETH 2*

Captains that have sailed in command of the *QE2* and the date of their first appointment as such:

Commodore W. E. Warwick, C.B.E., R.D., R.N.R., 23 Dec. 1968

Captain G. E. Smith, 12 June 1969

Captain F. J. Storey, R.D., R.N.R., 17 Oct. 1969

Captain J. E. Wolfenden, R.D., R.N.R., 8 May 1970

Captain W. J. Law, R.D., R.N.R., 19 June 1970

Captain M. Hehir, 3 June 1971

Captain P. Jackson, 6 Aug. 1973

Captain R. H. Arnott, R.D., R.N.R., 22 May 1976

Captain L. R. W. Portet, R.D., Cdr. R.N.R., 13 Apr. 1977

Commodore T. D. Ridley, R.D., Captain R.N.R., 26 Aug. 1978

Captain A. J. Hutcheson, R.N.R., 13 Mar. 1982

Captain R. Wadsworth, 15 May 1983

Captain K. H. Stanley, 9 Apr. 1984

Captain A. C. Bennell, R.D., R.N.R., 10 July 1987

Captain R. A. Woodall, R.D., R.N.R., 1 Nov. 1987

Captain J. Burton-Hall, R.D., Cdr. R.N.R., 7 Mar. 1990

Captain R. W. Warwick, Lt. Cdr. R.N.R., F.N.I., 26 July 1990

APPENDIX 4:
THE CREW OF THE *QUEEN ELIZABETH 2*

Depending on the nature of the voyage and the number of passengers carried, there can be anywhere from 970 to 1,015 crew members on board at any one time, of which approximately 20 percent are female. It is not unusual to have between 35 and 45 different nationalities represented.

The most senior person on board is the master (captain) who heads up the shipboard management team comprising the staff captain, chief engineer, and hotel manager. They, in turn, have the responsibility for the day-to-day administration of their respective departments. On a typical voyage the following personnel may be carried, and in most cases they will come under the jurisdiction of one of the department heads:

Able seamen 24	Doctors 2	Pianist 1
Accountants 1	Dry cleaners 2	Plumbers 4
Baggage masters 2	Electrical officers 6	Printers 4
Bakers 5	Electronic officers 2	Projectionist 1
Bank staff 3	Engineer officers 15	Purser 1
Bartenders 17	Entertainers 9	Quartermasters 3
Beauty therapist 1	Executive chef 1	Radio officers 3
Bell boys 2	Fitness instructors 6	Receptionists 3
Bosun 1	Florists 2	Restaurant managers 13
Butchers 3	Garbagemen 5	Secretaries 2
Butlers 4	Hairdressers 12	Security staff 5
Cabin stewards 63	Hotel officers 29	Shop assistants 21
Cadet officers 4	Joiner 1	Social director 1
Carpenters 5	Laundry staff 15	Sports directors 2
Carpet layers 2	Librarian 1	Storekeepers 5
Cashiers 1	Linen keeper 1	Tours staff 3
Casino staff 16	Lounge stewards 24	TV station manager 1
Chefs 80	Masseuses 4	Utility staff 98
Chiropodist 1	Mechanics 42	Waiters 184
Cleaners 45	Medical attendants 3	Wine waiters 21
Clerks 6	Musicians 26	
Cooks 18	Navigating officers 8	
Cruise director 1	Night stewards 4	
Cruise staff 16	Nursery nurses 2	
Dancers 12	Nurses 3	
Deck stewards 4	Painters 2	
Dentist 1	Personnel manager 1	
Disc jockey 1	Photographers 4	
Dishwashers 17	Physiotherapist 1	

The Main Control Room (MCR) was the senior watch-keeping station in the machinery spaces and was located on a deck above the main alternator room. It was air-conditioned and soundproofed. Windows looked out over the turbo alternator machinery. On the forward side were the switchboards and group starter panels for main and auxiliary machinery. The main control console housed electrical controls for the main alternator run-up schemes and various electrical circuit switching, main boiler control systems, combustion controls, main engine telegraphs, feed systems and forced draft fan controls, domestic service systems, stabilizer, and bow thruster controls. There was a comprehensive telephone and public-address system, from which, as in the Turbine Control Room, the officer had direct communications with all machinery spaces.

The Turbine Control Room, located in the engine room forward of the main turbines, and had similar features to the MCR. The turbines were remotely controlled from this room, and it replaced the traditional engine maneuvering platform. All remote controls and gauges associated with the complete control of the main power plant were located in this one spot.

The original thinking that went into the machinery design dates back to 1954 when John Brown (Clydebank) were asked to prepare proposals and designs for a new ship, at that time known as the *Q3*, to replace the old *Queens*. When the order was placed for the *QE2*, the machinery was largely based on that proposed for the larger quadruple-screw ship.

Schedule requirements for a weekly transatlantic service called for an average speed of 28.5 knots, which necessitated a service shaft horsepower of between 85,000 and 95,000. In order to give a reserve of power, the main turbines were designed for a maximum output of 110,000 horsepower.

The power was shared equally between the two propellers, each driven by an independent set of turbines. The two sets of double-reduction geared turbines were supplied with steam from three high-pressure water tube boilers. Each unit was composed of a high-pressure and a double-flow low-pressure turbine which transmitted their power through dual-tandem reduction gears.

Designed by Foster Wheeler and manufactured by John Brown Engineering, the boilers were the largest ever to be fitted in a marine installation. Each boiler weighed 278 tons and was fitted with superheaters designed to operate at outlet temperatures of 1,000 degrees Fahrenheit and 850 pounds per square inch of pressure.

The propellers were attached to 250-foot-long shafts by large nuts with an internal diameter of 23 inches, which at the time were the largest ever made. The two six-bladed propellers were supplied by Stone Manganese Marine, Ltd., at a cost of over £500,000. Each weighed 31.75 tons and had a diameter of 19 feet and a pitch of 21.65 feet.

Electricity was supplied by three AEl turbine generators, each of which was capable of producing 5,500 kilowatts of power at 3,300 volts 60 hertz, and at the time they were the largest ever to be built for shipboard use.

BIBLIOGRAPHY

Albion, Robert Greenhaigh,
  Naval and Maritime History,
  Connecticut, 1963.
Anderson, Roy,
  White Star,
  Lancashire, 1964.
Angas, Commander W. Mack,
  Rivalry on the Atlantic 1833–1939,
  New York, 1939.
Appleyard, Rollo,
  Charles Parsons: His Life and Work,
  London, 1933.
Armstrong, Warren,
  Atlantic Highway,
  New York, 1962.
Arnott, Captain Robert H.
  Captain of the Queen,
  Kent, 1982.
Aylmer, Gerald. *R.M.S. Mauretania:
  The Ship and Her Record,*
  London, 1934.
Beaudean, Baron Raoul de.,
  Captain of the Ile,
  New York, 1960.
Beesley, Lawrence,
  The Loss of the S.S. Titanic,
  Boston, 1912.
Bensted, C. R.,
  Atlantic Ferry,
  London, 1936.
Bisset, Sir James,
  Ship Ahoy!
    London, 1932.
  Sail Ho,
    London, 1958.
  Tramps and Ladies,
    London, 1959.
  Commodore,
    New York, 1961.
Bonsor, N.R.P.,

  North Atlantic Seaway,
    Channel Islands, 1980.
  South Atlantic Seaway,
    Channel Islands, 1983.
Bowen, Frank C.,
  A Century of Atlantic Travel 1830–1930,
  Boston, 1930.
Brady, Edward Michael,
  Marine Salvage Operations,
  NewYork, 1960.
Braynard, Frank O.,
  By Their Works Ye Shall Know Them,
  New York, 1968.
Brinnin, John Malcolm,
  The Sway of the Grand Saloon,
  New York, 1971.
Broackes, Nigel,
  A Growing Concern,
  London, 1979.
Buchanan, Gary,
  Dream Voyages,
  Jersey, 1989.
Corson, F. Reid,
  *The Atlantic Ferry in the Twentieth
  Century,* London, 1930.
Cunard Line,
  *The Cunarders 1840–1969, A Transat-
  lantic Story Spanning 129 Years,*
  London, 1969.
Dunn, Laurence,
  North Atlantic Liners: 1899–1913,
  London, 1961.
Dunnett, Alastair M.,
  The Donaldson Line: 1854–1954,
  Glasgow, 1960.
Fry, Henry,
  *The History of North Atlantic Steam
  Navigation,* London, 1896.
Gibbs, C. R. Vernon,
  Passenger Liners of the Western Ocean,

London, 1957.

British Passenger Liners of the Five Oceans, London, 1963.

Grattidge, Harvey,
Captain of the Queens,
NewYork, 1956.

Hoehling, Adolph, and Mary Hoehling,
The Last Voyage of the Lusitania,
New York, 1956.

Hutchings, David F.,
QE2 — A Ship for all Seasons,
Southampton, 1987.

Hyde, Francis E.,
Cunard and the North Atlantic: 1840–1972, London,1975.

Isherwood, J. H.,
Steamers of the Past,
Liverpool, 1966.

Johnson, Howard,
The Cunard Story,
London, 1987.

Kludas, Arnold,
Great Passenger Ships of the World,
Cambridge, 1975.

Lauriat, Charles E.,
The Lusitania's Last Voyage,
New York, 1915.

Lee, Charles E.,
The Blue Riband,
London, 1930.

Lindsay, W. S.,
History of Merchant Shipping,
London, 1876.

Lloyd, Wertf,
Queen Elizabeth 2 — The Story of a Conversion, Bremerhaven, 1976.

Lord, Walter,
A Night to Remember,
New York, 1955.

Lowdnes, Russ,
Samuel Cunard Bicentennial: 1787–1987,
Halifax, Canada. 1987.

Maber, John,
North Star to Southern Cross,
Lancashire, 1967.

McCart, Neil,
Atlantic Liners of the Cunard Line,
London, 1990.

McLennan, R. S.,
Anchor Line: 1856–1956,
Glasgow, 1956.

Maginnis, A. J.,

The Atlantic Ferry,
London, 1900.

Maxtone-Graham, John,
The Only Way to Cross,
New York, 1972.

Cunard — 150 Glorious Years,
Devon, 1989.

Moody, Bert,
Ocean Ships,
London, 1971.

Moxom, Peter, M. Fimister, and A. Burney, *QE2 — Cunard's Flagship*, Surrey, 1990.

Oldham, Wilton J.,
The Ismay Line,
Liverpool, 1961.

Potter, Neil, and Jack Frost,
The Mary,
London, 1961.

The Elizabeth,
London, 1965.

The Queen Elizabeth 2,
London, 1969.

Preble, Rear-Admiral G. H.,
History of Steam Navigation,
Philadelphia, 1883.

Shaum, John H. Jr., and William H. Flayhart III, *Majesty at Sea, The Four Funnel Liners*, New York, 1981.

Smallpeice, Sir Basil,
Of Comets and Queens,
Shrewsbury, 1980.

Smith, Eugene W.,
Passenger Ships of the World — Past and Present, Boston, 1963.

Spedding, Charles T.,
Reminiscences of TransAtlantic Travelers,
Philadelphia, 1926.

Staff, Frank,
The Trans-Atlantic Mail,
London, 1956.

Stevens, Leonard A.,
The Elizabeth: Passage of a Queen,
New York, 1968.

Thomas, David St. John,
The Cunard Book of Cruising,
Devon, 1990.

Winberg, William M.,
QE2 — The Official Pictorial History,
California, 1988.

Bought at the Ocean Bookshop

Queen Elizabeth 2

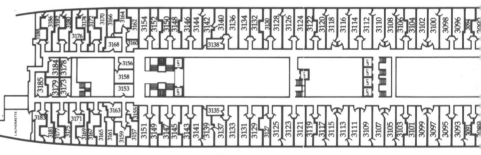

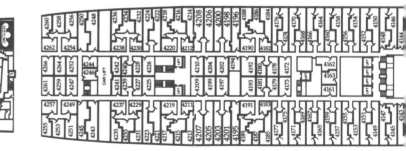

Six Deck

Seven Deck